MAKING MARKS
DISCOVERING THE CERAMIC SURFACE

12/07

Robin Hopper, Canada, "Hummingbird Series Plate," porcelain, masked and sandblasted glaze, brushwork and bone fuming. 1987.

MAKING MARKS

DISCOVERING THE CERAMIC SURFACE

By Robin Hopper

©2004 Robin Hopper

Published by

kp books

An imprint of F+W Publications, Inc.

700 East State Street • Iola, WI 54990-0001
715-445-2214 • 888-457-2873

Our toll-free number to place an order or obtain
a free catalog is (800) 258-0929.

Library of Congress Catalog Number: 2004093872

ISBN: 0-87349-504-7

Edited by Barbara Case and Susan Sliwicki

Designed by Dana Boll

Printed in the United States of America

Front cover: Robin Hopper, "Trifoot Plate – Southwest Series"

Back cover, upper left: Ricky Maldonado, USA, "Turban Vessel," 13" x 11".

Back cover, upper right: Judi Dyelle, Canada, "Pierced Bowl," porcelain,
microcrystalline glaze, gas fired cone 10.

Back cover, lower left: Frank Boyden, USA, "Smoky Fish Vase," wood-fired porcelain.

Back cover, lower right: Ron Myers, USA, "Lidded Jar," red earthenware, white slip,
colored engobes, transparent glaze, fired to cone 04, 16" x 11", 2000.

I dedicate this book to Judi,

without whom it would

never have seen the light of day.

Acknowledgments

Any book is a team effort. I wish to express my gratitude to all of the people who have helped in the development of this book.

To my wife, Judi Dyelle: potter, computer whiz, illustrator, photographer and chief sounding board. Judi particularly wishes to thank James Brown and Vic Cromarty for their generosity with advice on computer graphics and Mac technology.

To my secretarial assistant and stepdaughter, Morgan Saddington, who now has kept me organized for five books in a row.

To Arlene Yarnell, who keeps the studio running while I disappear to write and research.

To the late Tom Marsh and Ginny Marsh, who got me into the writing game in the first place.

To the artists who have helped directly in the genesis of this book: Randy Brodnax, Steven Hill, Steve Irvine, Lorne Loomer, Lily Liu, Martha Naranjo, Bill Porteous, Xane St. Phillips, Heather Spears and Rimas VisGirda, who wrote the chapter on post-firing and cold processes.

To historians, curators and museum assistants: Dr. Edmund Carpenter; Martha Mayberry of the Mint Museum, Charlotte, N.C.; Dr. Dorie Reents-Budet, Dr. Louana Lackey, and Susan Kowalczyk of the Schein Joseph International Museum of Ceramic Art, Alfred, N.Y.; Sue Jefferies of the Gardiner Museum of Ceramic Art; Art Gallery of Greater Victoria; and the Winnipeg Art Gallery.

To the many writers, teachers and artists from whom one learns, sometimes directly, sometimes by example, sometimes by their writings, sometimes by their pots, and sometimes by osmosis and without their awareness, including Hans Coper, Lucie Rie, Arthur Barnett, Michael Cardew, Mick Casson, Harry Horlock-Stringer, Bernard Leach, Glenn Nelson, John Reeve, Jim and Nan McKinnell, Don Reitz, Tom Coleman, Rick Malmgren, John Neely and Daniel Rhodes.

To the many people and companies who have helped with providing both materials and advice: John and Darlene Williams of Trinity Ceramic Supply; Frank Tucker of Tucker's Ceramic Supply; Greenbarn Pottery Supply and Nanaimo Pottery Warehouse, Canada; Hank Murrow Tools; the Dolan family at Dolan Tools; Philip Poburka of Bison Studios; Meira and Logan Mathison; Mason Color Works; and Keith Lebanzon, the brushman.

To Barbara and Justin Kerr, whose "rollout" images of pre-Columbian ceramics grace many chapters.

To the many ceramic artists from around the world who generously have given their support and loaned illustration material to the tune of 20,000 images — 250 of which made it into the final selection. To those who didn't make it in this time, thanks so much for trying, but there was just an overabundance of really fine work.

To the hundreds of thousands of potters of the last 10,000 years, from whom we continue to learn and gain understanding and inspiration for our own further development. May we tread forever softly in your footprints and honor your collective memory.

To my editors, Barbara Case and Susan Sliwicki, whose understanding and encouragement are exemplary, and whose lightness of touch but firmness of vision have kept me striving for perfection, a goal I know I'll never reach, but well worth the effort involved. To the crew at KP Books, who continue to improve on my own visions of my books.

To all, my sincere thanks.

Robin Hopper
Victoria, Canada
April 2004

Contents

In moments of crisis, only imagination is more important than knowledge.

Albert Einstein

PART 4: GLAZE PROCESSES

PART 5: FIRING AND POST-FIRING PROCESSES

Introduction

This book is about options, ideas and the use of tools. It is probably the most personal of my books, since the ceramic surface and its variations and meanings have been a particular passion since I was a mid-teenager some 50 years ago. It is largely the approach to the ceramic surface that determines the ultimate personality of the work that is done. A visit to any museum or art gallery that has a collection of historical ceramics can't fail to impress the viewer with the incredible variety of decorative processes used and the diverse personalities of the works shown. Through the pages of this book, I hope to stimulate an awareness of these processes and offer directions for further meaningful development of the decorated or enriched ceramic surface. Almost every chapter could have been expanded into a book of its own, but space was limited and the subject matter inexhaustible. In many cases, this can be looked at as a pointer toward further reference and study. The bibliography suggests a few of the books I have found helpful in the development of this one. Beyond the books, there is the incredible resource of the Internet, where you can find out just about anything for further in-depth study.

Throughout the last few decades of the 20th century and into the first decade of this one, there seems to have been a slow decline in exploring personal identity. "Movements" that seem to remove the individual from much of the work by overuse of faddish or fashionable ceramic processes seem to have overtaken sizable segments of the studio ceramic world. It's a little like "flavor of the month"! Much sameness abounds: the excesses of "flash" raku as seen at ubiquitous art shows; the current phenomena of wood-firing variations; the incipient wave of crystalline glazed wares; and the multisprayed glaze coatings represent comparatively simple solutions to the finishing of ceramic surfaces. Not all wood-fired work is wonderful, raku ravishing, crystallines captivating, or spray glazing splendid — too often the forms let the overused surfaces down. The artist often becomes subservient to the process, and individuality often is quashed as a result. This is not to say that all who work with these processes produce mindless work. Far from it. There are always leaders who do the research and make a major commitment to a segment of the field, expanding it for others to follow. And there are always followers, many of whom blindly work without knowing the original research. Copying is an important and well-recognized stage in the learning process. It should be seen as a steppingstone to further personal development, however, and not an end in itself, which leads to plagiarism instead of preparing the way for new visions. To develop your own identity using an age-old process, you must be diligent about resisting imitation and exploring your own direction. When simple processes are too omnipresent, the leaders often move on. Surfacing processes that demand more manipulative skill, technical understanding, thought and experience beyond the vagaries of the firing process seem to be at the far end of the pendulum at this point in time. By carefully learning controlled processes, the enjoyment, understanding and acceptance of "uncontrol" or serendipity becomes more meaningful. Uncontrol doesn't mean out of control. Most of the very best ceramists of today have learned tight control, and, if it seems to reflect their personalities, have chosen to move to looser practices with the background of knowledge and skill. Fortunately, a pendulum always reverses its direction, and now appears to be the time that more control is beginning to be in evidence. More challenging and complex surfacing processes now are increasingly being seen as artists strive for a personal identity that comes with developing an awareness of the incredible breadth of potential of the ceramic surface. Work that stands out from the crowd because of its differences is far more likely to be noticed. On a world scale, the best of ceramics today are probably more exciting and varied than ever through history.

When I was in the teaching profession in the 1960s and early '70s, I used to look for books with specific ceramic subject matter for my students. At that time there were few books that said what, from my personal studio experience, I felt the student needed to know. Ten years after resigning my teaching position in favor of full-time studio work and glaze research, those books still weren't around. I felt that I had enough experience and had done enough personal research in glaze and color work to put a book together. My first book, published in 1984, was "The Ceramic Spectrum." Its subject matter was a simplified approach to glaze and color development. This book is designed to explain and facilitate palette development at all temperature ranges and in differing atmospheric conditions. My second book, "Functional Pottery," first was published in 1986. This book is primarily about form and aesthetics, particularly related to the functional object. By this time, I had some 30 years experience in producing functional work and felt that observations from my experiences might help others treading the same road.

As a former student painter and printmaker, I became a potter who has always had a love affair with the ceramic surface, a natural extension of the surfacing and content concerns of painting and printmaking. Since I have, at some time, explored most historical decoration processes and ceramic surface enrichment and done much research for my own personal understanding and development of this art form, I felt that a third book could be useful to other clay workers. I feel that "Making Marks" completes a trilogy and forms a circle of ceramic experiences that has taken me on an exciting personal journey for nearly half a century and that might be of assistance to others looking for ideas and new directions. It also allows me the opportunity to give back to the ceramic community much of what I have learned working on four continents during this time.

This book is about ceramic surface enrichment, the processes used for achieving it, and the thought concepts, idea development and personal research behind it. "Making Marks" is a generalized term used throughout the visual arts when referring to the alteration of any surface by any of the tools that artists employ. In using this term for the title of this book, I am referring to the huge variety of marks that may be achieved through ceramic decoration processes, at any or all of the varied and various stages that the clay object goes through in its transformation from soft, wet, malleable clay to heat-hardened, impermeable ceramic. The text

of this book is organized into five parts: Fundamentals, Plastic and Liquid Clay Processes, Pigment Processes, Glaze Processes, and Firing and Post-Firing Processes. Throughout this book I use the word "process" to indicate the method of doing something. The word "technique" properly refers to the degree of skill with which a process or method is done. The more often a process is employed, the better the technique is likely to become, giving greater fluency to the work at hand through compounded experience.

Part I — Fundamentals

Throughout a lifetime spent making pots, teaching, giving workshops and jurying exhibitions in different parts of the world, I often have noticed that people learning to make pottery and ceramic objects spend a great deal of time unconsciously excluding or just not thinking about how the object is to be finished once the form is made. Considerations of form and surface should go hand in hand to develop well-integrated and fully resolved completed objects, whether that object is functional or nonfunctional in intent.

The processes of surface enrichment in ceramics are many and varied. Before decoration is done, the stages at which the specific process might be done also have to be considered. Will it be done on wet, leather-hard, bone-dry or bisque-fired clay, or as an underglaze or even in or after the glaze firing? There are decorative processes for any stage in the cycle. The surface of a ceramic object can be altered at any time, even hundreds or thousands of years after the object was originally made.

Through our many surfacing options we can visually enhance or destroy form by what is done to the surface. Managing this surface and marrying it to its form is an art. It is the great divide where the true artist and the artisan often take different paths. Where you find yourself in this dichotomy usually depends on your background training in art and design. Good basic art training manipulates the eye and brain to observe, visualize, conceptualize and create based on learned skills. These skills include drawing, color and design and are the foundation of any visual art discipline. Without them, the art discipline in question will fall flat, amorphous and lifeless. For those who have a good basic training in art and design principles, the first section of this book may be redundant. For those who don't, the first five chapters are designed to give a short, basic, art school primer by encouraging exploration, experimentation and development in the world of visual art by applying the knowledge and skills to the world of clay, minerals and fire. With expanded visual and manipulative skills, the processes of surface enrichment should develop in a more coherent way, leading to more exciting and personally satisfying work. Unlike the painter who squeezes paint from tubes and mixes them together visually in a "what you see is what you get" approach, the ceramic artist not only creates the "canvas," but usually also creates the palette of color from combinations of minerals. These minerals interact in a range of temperatures and atmospheric conditions inside the kiln, almost totally changing in appearance after firing. The ceramist has to learn how to work with the invisible through vigilant testing and acute observation of results.

Starting with Chapter 6, each subsequent chapter looks at different processes or different groupings of processes in surface enrichment that have a similar methodology or are done at the same stage in the making cycle. The potential richness of the ceramic surface often is increased exponentially by combining processes at different stages, somewhat like the process of layering paint in different ways in painting, or with the translucency of inks in printmaking.

CHAPTER 1: DRAWING IN TWO AND THREE DIMENSIONS

Drawing is the basic tool of communication in any art form. Ceramic forms can be thought of as three-dimensional drawings in space. The marks that make up the ceramic surface require some basic drawing and observational skills in order to explore surface and linear pattern making. This chapter looks at some basic approaches to drawing with particular reference to the ceramic artist. Drawing on a circular or three-dimensional form is, in a sense, always abstract because of the role that perspective plays in viewing. By using drawing tools, you easily can make comparisons to tools used to mark or decorate the ceramic surface, tools with which you might have a special individual affinity.

CHAPTER 2: SIGN AND SYMBOL

Hidden meanings have been incorporated into the decorated ceramic surface since pottery was first made. This chapter looks at many of these motifs and their meanings.

CHAPTER 3: PATTERN AND SPACE

This chapter is a natural progression from the drawing exercises in Chapter 1 and the symbolism and signs of Chapter 2 and a lead-in to the color theory of Chapter 4. Pattern is all around us, and its development and use have been one of the major preoccupations of clay workers since the first impressions, scratches or daubs of color were put on the earliest of man's clay creations. Patterns of nature, as well as man-made objects, are illustrated. Methods of pattern development and spatial placement also are explained.

CHAPTER 4: COLOR THEORY

Color is part of the ceramic artist's means of expression. For the most part, the ceramic artist is at a disadvantage in his use of color since almost all colors change dramatically in the process of firing and look little like the original work. Chapter 4 is concerned with the basic understanding of color theory and considers principles common to all visual arts. The ways artists use color — and the public's reaction to it — often influence the success artists gain in the marketplace. This chapter is aimed at developing an understanding of color, how the human eye perceives it and how the brain reacts to it.

CHAPTER 5: COLOR AND THE CERAMIC SURFACE – ART, ALCHEMY, OR SCIENCE?

Color in ceramics generally is not achieved by squeezing from a tube. It is a complex science that often baffles the majority of clay workers, making them accept compromise rather than developing exactly what they want and previously have visualized. Glaze making, however, can be as simple or as complex as you want to make it. This chapter includes an overview of what makes glazes behave the way they do and what makes them so variable. It also explains how glaze surfaces and color are affected by the variables, such as material use, temperature, atmosphere, colorants and opacifiers.

Part 2 — Plastic and Liquid Clay Processes

CHAPTER 6: MARKS OF SLASH, SCRATCH, CARVE AND CUT

This chapter is concerned with the process of decoration using graphic tools such as knives, sticks, scalpels, fluting, modeling, sgraffito, expanded spring wires and twisted cutting wires.

CHAPTER 7: MARKS OF ADDITION AND REMOVAL

This chapter looks at additive and subtractive approaches to surface enrichment, including texture, sprigs, modeling, hand-building, slip-soaked fibers and washed wax or shellac resist.

CHAPTER 8: MARKS OF IMPRESSION

The concerns of this chapter are with the impressed pattern or mark, those made with stamps or recessed in some way, including linocuts, woodcuts, routed wood, electrical and electronic circuitry diagrams or carved fiber printing blocks.

CHAPTER 9: MARKS OF LIQUID CLAYS

This chapter looks at the use of liquefied clays, from terra sigillata to traditional European slipware methods of trailing, combing, marbling, feathering, dotting, mocha diffusions, and the Oriental methods of Mishima, Hakeme or Onda style.

CHAPTER 10: MARKS OF COLORED CLAYS

This chapter explores the varied uses of colored clays — Egyptian paste, agateware, neriage, nerikomi or millefiori.

Part 3 — Pigment Processes

CHAPTER 11: THE CERAMIC SPECTRUM AND ELECTRIC PALETTE

This is an extension of Chapter 5, particularly relating to the variables of ceramic colorants and basic suggestions for their use and development, mixing, and application. The chapter is divided into three parts of the spectrum: "Hot to Trot" (red, yellow, orange); "Play It Cool" (green/blue); and "Mood Indigo" (darker aspects).

CHAPTER 12: THE MARK OF THE BRUSH AND SOFT STAMP

This chapter looks at brushes as expressive graphic tools, their various types, the marks they make and their use with pigments. The use of the sponge stamp also is examined here.

CHAPTER 13: MARKS OF RESISTANCE

Resist processes using hot wax, latex, rubber, petroleum jelly, wax crayons, candles, floor wax, paper, Tyvek® and masking tape are explored in this chapter.

CHAPTER 14: MARKS OF PENCILS, CRAYONS, PENS AND TRAILERS

The uses of underglaze pencils, pastels and ceramic crayons are looked at here, together with the uses of pens and trailers of different types.

CHAPTER 15: THE MARK OF THE SPRAY

This chapter explores the use of the spray, from the simplest spattering of the toothbrush to the complexity of the airbrush.

Part 4 — Glaze Processes

CHAPTER 16: MARKS OF THE GLAZE AND ITS APPLICATION

The various processes of glaze application are shown in this extensive chapter, including brushing, dipping, double dipping, pouring, spraying, trailing, multiple glaze application and glaze intaglio.

Part 5 — Firing and Post-Firing Processes

CHAPTER 17: MARKS OF HEAT, FLAME AND SMOKE

The effect that various types of firing have on both body and glaze are looked at in this chapter. From the inert atmosphere of the electric kiln through primitive firing, general reduction and post-firing reduction to the flame markings and fluid glaze of wood firing, a surface can be altered in a variety of ways, either as a special quality in itself, or in conjunction with other surface development methods already mentioned. Reduced or Arabian style lusters also are discussed in this chapter.

CHAPTER 18: MARKS OF VAPOR AND FUME

Salt and soda vapor glazing are discussed here, together with the effects that various forms of fuming can have on the fired surface.

CHAPTER 19: MARKS OF FIRED SURFACE REMOVAL

Alteration of the fired surface in the bisque or glazed state can create interesting and beautiful surfaces impossible to achieve in other ways. Sandblasting, grit-blasting, carborundum cutting and acid etching are discussed here.

CHAPTER 20: MARKS OF MULTIPLE FIRING, BY RIMAS VISGIRDA

Post-glaze firing (usually third and subsequent firings) allows a great variety of further surface development by the use of on-glaze processes such as china painting or overglaze enamels, lusters, decals and photographic applications. Processes more identified with the ceramic industry than the studio potter also are discussed here, including ground laying and printing techniques.

CHAPTER 21: MARKS OF THE MAKER

This chapter analyzes examples of how the path from conception to reality has been followed. Using examples from different periods of my own work, I trace its development with the integration of form and development of imagery, discussing necessary technical research and processes of final surface enrichment.

Photo montages illustrate journeys from the inspiration source to the reality of completion.

CHAPTER 22: MARKS OF EXCELLENCE

The key to achieving excellence in ceramic artwork lies in the strength of vision of the maker and the technical ability to carry it through from concept to reality. This final chapter looks at a small portfolio of work by artists from around the world for whom the ceramic surface is both a challenge and an inspiration. The artists were chosen for their special abilities in different variations of process that convey the breadth of possibilities the ceramic medium offers. It takes a great deal of tenacity to work through the many technical problems inherent in this medium. However, when enough attention and understanding are given to these important aspects, the doors open to limitless potential and variation. Each variation of surface enrichment adds to the artist's vocabulary and increases the ability to create poetry from mundane, earthy materials.

Maya, Late Classic, 600-950 C.E. Cylindrical form — clay covered with polychrome paints, low fired and burnished.
A group of individuals drinking alcoholic beverages and smoking. Rollout photograph © Justin Kerr.

Part 1
FUNDAMENTALS

Mahmoud Baghaeian, Canada, "Tile," porcelain, reduction fired in a gas kiln.

Maya. Late Classic 600 to 950 C.E. Clay covered with stucco and incised. A ruler emulating the maize god contemplates his namesake's severed head, hanging in an abstract tree. Rollout photograph © Justin Kerr.

Chapter 1

Drawing in Two and Three Dimensions

Some subjects learned in formal or foundation art training are invaluable to a lifetime of personal artistic growth, regardless of the medium in which we later work. Drawing and color theory are two such academic studies. Even if your ceramic work never directly utilizes them, it will improve because of your greater awareness and understanding of these two fundamentals. I always recommend the study of art fundamentals to the many people who come into ceramics without formal training and who often find themselves at a considerable disadvantage in the creation of their work. It is somewhat like learning a language — you always learn more vocabulary, grammar, syntax and punctuation than strictly necessary to communicate. However, the more you know of any language, the better you can communicate, and the more subtle the meanings can be. Art is a universal form of language and sharing of ideas that transcends all other languages. It can be interpreted and appreciated worldwide regardless of verbal or written language. The small investment in time spent learning to draw will pay handsome dividends in being able to see, visualize, and communicate.

At one time everybody drew. It was the foundation of written communication between people in the form of sand drawings, petroglyphs, and pictograms (see

Chapter 2). Drawing is the basic tool of communication in any visual art form.

Ceramic forms themselves can be thought of as three-dimensional drawings in space — a line surrounding a volume of air. The marks that make up the ceramic surface are improved greatly by some

Photo: Judi Dyelle

Drawing tools.

16

basic drawing and observational skills in order to explore ideas and facilitate surface and linear pattern making. This chapter looks at some basic approaches to creative drawing adaptable to the ceramic artist, be it representational, narrative, interpretive or abstract. The basic concepts of drawing and the use of drawing tools can be taught and learned in a short space of time. Thereafter, it is a matter of practice to expand on the basic skills and visual understanding.

Drawing is comprised of two essential varieties: 1) Visual expressions of the human mind, ideas and inspirations; 2) Representations of life or objects directly in front of the viewer, searching for rhythms, movements and relationships. Drawing is invaluable for honing observation and visualization skills and also gives the artist a form of shorthand for developing ideas. Drawing on a circular or three-dimensional form is, in a sense, always abstract because of the role perspective plays in viewing. By using drawing tools, you easily can make comparisons to tools used in the marking or decoration of the ceramic surface, tools with which you might have a special individual affinity. Drawing tools can be referred to as either dry or wet media.

Dry Media

The tools used for drawing on paper and on clay range from sharp and scratchy to soft and smudgy. Each drawing tool leaves its own individual mark, and most graphic tools for work on paper have a similar equivalent in tools used on clay.

Hard graphite pencils, ranging from 6H to HB, pens and scribers leave marks, lines and texture similar to pin tools, scalpels and knives used on clay. The pressure of the knife mark and the twisting of a blade cutting through the clay surface easily equates to the thin-to-expanding-width pen line that develops through increasing pressure on a pen nib. Whether on paper or clay, these tools usually leave a sharp clean line.

Drawing tools of medium softness for working on paper include conté (usually with various earth tones), charcoal, crayon, pastel, soft 4B to 6B pencils and brushes of many types. For drawing on dry or bisque-fired clay, there are ceramic pencils with "leads" made from compressed clays and colorants that usually have been fired to low heat to harden them. There also are pens with ceramic ink, ceramic pastels and brushes. See Chapter 14 for further information on drawing tools for

ceramic surfaces. Conté also can be drawn on clay or bisque and fired, since it is made from compressed clay or clay shale and mostly leaves marks in a range of tan to dark brown, often similar to sepia inks used by the great masters of painting for their preparatory drawings. Soft drawing tools are very suitable for smudge drawings, where the thumb or a finger is used as the direct drawing implement on paper or clay.

Familiarity with various types of drawing tools leads to freedom of expression in selecting the implement that does the best job. Some people prefer the tight, sharp quality of the scratchy tool, while others gravitate toward the lyrical responsiveness of a brush. With the exception of drawings made with wax or oil-based materials such as crayons or oil pastels, drawings made on paper with dry media usually need to be sprayed with a fixative to protect them from smudging.

Wet Media

Wet media are mainly inks, watercolor paints, gouache, poster paints and dyes that may or may not be permanent, depending on how they are manufactured. They may need fixing for permanency. Although wet media normally are applied with either a brush or pen, you also can experiment with all manner of unusual tools from fingers to sticks, split grasses, quills, sponges, toothbrushes or anything that seems to offer interesting marks. Although any paper is fine for exploring general mark making and trying out available tools, the type and quality of paper should be considered if you want to elevate the drawings beyond the disposable exercise stage. The surface used also is important, because it allows for the character of the drawing medium to have full play.

Wet materials, such as watercolor, ink, or oil pastel, require paper with a rag content, which is made to be used for water media. Rag or linen fibers keep the paper from buckling, which can cause craters that distort the flow of paint and ink. For wet use, paper can be stretched by soaking it in water, attaching it to a drawing board with 2" wide brown glue tape, and letting it dry before use. The paper will flatten out when more water is applied.

Dry media require a surface with some tooth or hills and valleys that catch the dry materials and keep them from falling off as dust. For "finished" drawings in dry media, a fixative spray is a must.

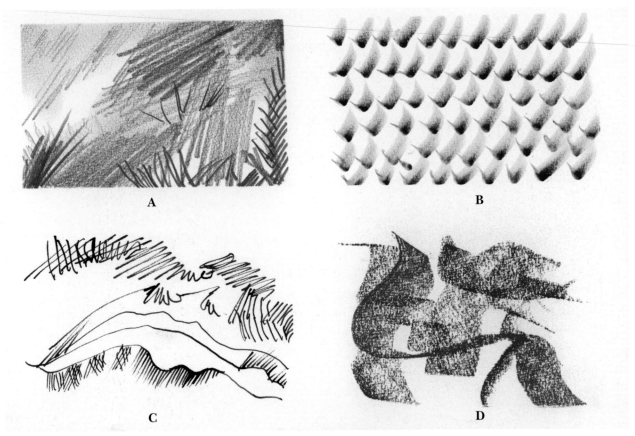

Drawing tool marks – A) 2B pencil; B) Oriental brush pen; C) Pen and ink: D) Conté.

Although there may be artists who have a natural flair for drawing, it is a skill that can be taught to almost anyone. It is a combination of learning to work with the tools and training the observation, analytical and visualization skills at the same time. Like riding a bike, once learned it is unlikely to be forgotten and allows the artist a form of "visual shorthand" for depicting things seen by the eyes or developed in the realm of the mind.

The first exercise in drawing is to play with all the available tools on the cheapest paper (newspaper or newsprint), then selecting one or two that you feel most comfortable with and that produce the sort of marks you enjoy. Then try every conceivable variant of mark making using the selected tools. Use the tip, edge and flat surface to explore the range of possibilities. Try all of the tools available to you and do exhaustive explorations of their potential. This will help you gain fluency with many tools and give a good understanding of their differences.

For almost every drawing tool used for working on paper there is an equivalent for working on clay. Eventually you will develop an affinity for certain types of tools and marks based on your comfort level and the type of work you plan to do. Most people born and educated in Western countries are accustomed to scratchy tools, such as pens and pencils, whereas those from Eastern countries have early experiences in brush usage. Westerners often feel acutely uncomfortable using a brush, and Easterners often feel the same about pens. If you have a preference, explore its possibilities and limitations. Gaining familiarity and confidence with the tools encourages freedom of movement of your arm, wrist and finger grip. The larger the working surface, the more expansive the movement and physical gesture can be.

Most drawing media produce lines that are relatively narrow and clearly defined, although brushes can be used with side or flat strokes, and conté, chalk, pastel and charcoal laid on their sides will produce broad marks.

In the process of exploring the making of lines and other marks with various tools, you've started the first

Courtesy of Lorne Loomer

Brush marks from a pounded cedar bark brush.

exercises in drawing — learning how the line moves and how to use pressure or movement to gain expression. Six main factors give the expressive power of drawing: line and dot; enclosure; tone and texture; volume; conceptual and visual space; and rhythm.

Line has no limits in its potential for variation. All lines belong to one or more of four basic types: *straight*, *equal curve* (such as a part of a circle), *angular* and *modulating curve* (opens or closes in progress). Longer lines get their expressive qualities from variations in length, width and rhythms that are embodied in them. There is immense potential for exploring linear expression with lines that give direction, rise and fall, droop, energize or crawl. Lines can play with other lines — crisscrossing, intertwining, colliding and mimicking movement.

One of the principal functions of lines is that of **enclosure**. Enclosure can be fluid organic shapes; static geometric shapes such as circles, semicircles, squares, rectangles, and triangles; or their three-dimensional equivalents of sphere, hemisphere, cube, cylinder, parallelepiped (shoebox shaped), pyramid or cone. These two- and three-dimensional shapes are at the basis of visual analysis of underlying structures.

We are all familiar with stick figure drawings where different-length articulated lines are topped with a circle and sometimes with larger body sections such as the chest and pelvis delineated as polygons. You can make complete figure compositions by assembling groups of simple enclosures. Learning simple perspective also can give drawings a three-dimensional aspect and help to develop a greater understanding of visual interpretation.

Learning to simplify complex forms into groups of easy to grasp and draw shapes is one of the ways drawing has been taught for generations. There always is an underlying structure. Having established the basic structure, you can then work down from the structural mass to the finest detail. The drawing of a shoe (at right) by Bill Porteous shows this process in action.

Tone and texture are normally flat layers done by crosshatching, flooding or brushing an area to rim, stripe or fill it. Tonal shapes can be overlaid with vivid linear action through small, repeated, graphic marks, like raindrops or snowflakes against a gray sky. Tone can be used to emphasize volumes of three-dimensional depictions with darkened volumes and cast shadows.

Volume and three-dimensionality in drawings tend to occur as you isolate parts of a drawing, dividing positive volume from negative space. A ball thrown in the air becomes positive volume, while the space around it becomes negative space. When the ball is placed on a table, the ball and table visually join to become a positive form surrounded by negative space. As you develop drawn symbols or two-dimensional images for solid bodies, you also imply the space in which they exist, and the drawing surface becomes either conceptual or visual space.

Conceptual space shows the relationship and placement of objects on the drawing surface — above, below, to one side, to the other side, outside, inside, smaller or larger. Not much actual depth or visual field is shown.

Visual space is developed through three techniques: overlapping, shading and altering the volume of forms. As you place objects behind each other on a flat plane, their visual solidity is established by shading to give a sense of three-dimensionality.

Rhythm is where linear markings establish the dynamism of a drawing, capturing the essence of the subject. The visual comprehension of the subject, combined with speed, movement and assurance of graphic markings, is what makes a few lines on a sheet of paper an invaluable reference for future exploitation. It becomes the source for ideas and continual growth and development.

Washed Chinese ink drawing.

Playing with lines — brush and ink.

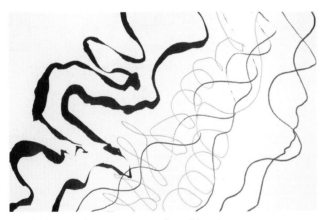

Simple line marks — pen, pencil, and brush.

Organic enclosures.

Geometric enclosures.

Stick figures with geometrics.

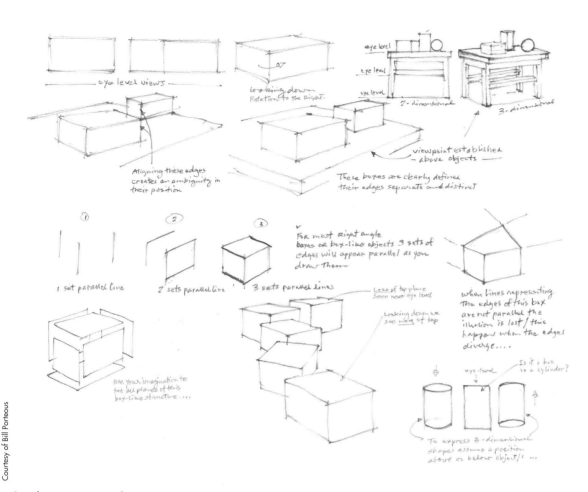

Simple perspective — boxes.

You might learn to draw by scrutinizing objects of a geometric nature and experiencing them through graphic marks with drawing tools and paper. Sometimes the simplest objects seem the hardest to depict graphically, but continual practice and analysis of what you are doing quickly leads to great improvement. It is mainly the process of learning the tools and rhythms that breaks down the mental barriers that so often cause people to say, "I can't draw a straight line." A boring straight line is usually harder to make than an exciting rhythmic one!

Perhaps the most exciting drawing tool to become available to artists since the brush and pen is the personal computer, particularly the Apple Macintosh group of computers. These tools, along with a bewildering and ever-changing range of software applications, allow and encourage a degree of manipulative graphic freedom never before available to the artist. Although it helps greatly to have basic drawing and design skills already developed through traditional hand methods, computer programs generally have the electronic equivalent of all artists' materials and tools, and then some, to explore and manipulate the graphic image. Ideas rapidly developed via computer graphics can be used or reinterpreted using the traditional tools of the artist. The next page shows digital photographic images manipulated and translated into drawings that could easily be further developed on the clay form through traditional drawing methods. Such images easily could be made into silkscreen images for tile work or flat ware. There is no end to the potential for development.

Learning to draw can be intense, often tiring, and it drains energy quickly because the process requires acute concentration, observation and critical visual

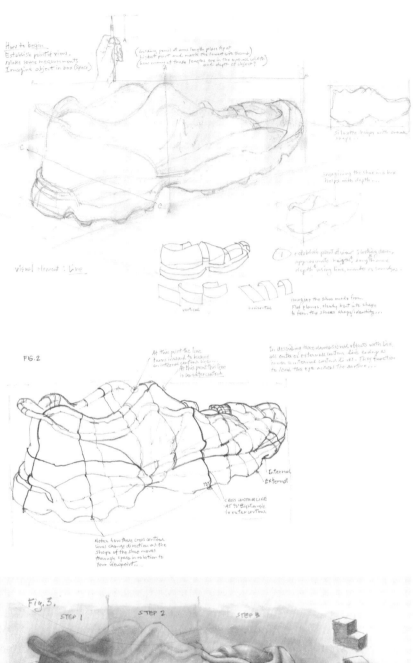

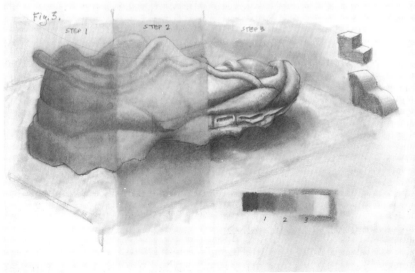

Study of a shoe.

Sphere and shadow.

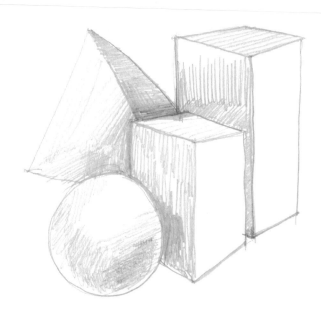
Three-dimensional rendering.

analysis — things that most of us don't usually do in our everyday lives. We tend to look rather than see. We don't normally scrutinize intensely and analytically.

It's not a good idea to do observation drawing when you are tired. Pushing yourself generally will achieve little or no further development. Try to draw only when you are fresh and your eyes are rested. This will lead to greater improvement in your skill development and alleviate frustration.

The great benefits of learning to draw lie in training yourself to see, encouraging visual awareness and giving yourself one of the major tools of visual thinking and interpretation of ideas. It is mainly a process of learning by doing, whether it is a sustained graphic study of something or merely scribbles or doodles while the creative mind searches for direction. Practicing drawing as much and as often as possible will increase your skills exponentially.

A good drawing teacher who continually challenges

your visual skills often is hard to find. If you take classes, make sure the instructor realizes that the skill you are working to achieve also is geared toward working with clay. The approach often is quite different.

For a different view from someone who is continually drawing and teaching drawing, I asked a very experienced drawing teacher and colleague, Heather Spears of Canada and Denmark, to share her thoughts on drawing. Her essay is at the end of this chapter.

Making marks on clay tablets was one of mankind's earliest forms of written or graphic communication. Using pointed and wedge-shaped impressions, it was developed from pictographs, signs, symbols or abstracted drawings by the Sumerians and Assyrians. It continued in use for more than 3,000 years. The next chapter identifies some of these and other signs, symbols and concepts that have been used, reused, stolen and expropriated by artists and craftsmen from time immemorial.

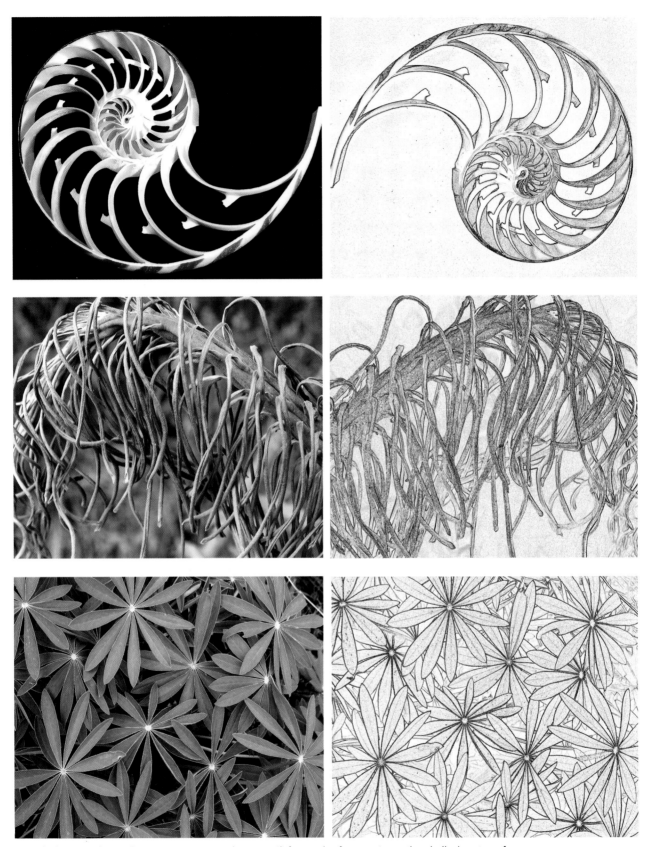

Digital photography and computer generated images (left to right, from top) nautilus shell, drawing of a shell, shaggy plant, drawing of shaggy plant, leaves and drawing of leaves.

DRAWING

By Heather Spears

Drawing concerns itself primarily with line.

It would be a good idea to start, then, by defining what line (drawn line) *is*. You easily can recognize a line. A young child, given a crayon, takes to it with ease. Line can be simply defined as an "extended mark made on a surface." *Extended* to differentiate it from the smudge or point, *mark* for its visibility against a ground, and *surface* for that (always necessary) ground. And *made* — perhaps the most important attribute — to remind us that line is created. It does not occur naturally; it is not waiting out there to be copied by the artist.

Line is an abstraction, and drawing is thus the most abstract of the visual arts (in painting, color can be copied directly; in sculpture, shape). The abstract nature of drawing too often is overlooked, yet to accept it allows you to respect line as a tool, a gift, an instrument to which you can become more sensitive and increasingly can exploit. Line remains essentially personal and human.

Having established what line is, you can go on to investigate what line *can* do — and here the possibilities are almost open-ended — in its capacity to express and explain and to represent the visible and conceptual (or imagined) world.

How can line be used? First and foremost, to represent edges or boundaries. This statement seems self-evident, but it opens huge questions about the nature of visual perception. We do not see line, yet for some reason we believe we do. Neurologists have isolated distinct areas of the visual cortex devoted to responding specifically to the visual array: clusters of neurons that will fire off only when certain directions are perceived. The brain, in a sense, loves line, loves to make the translation from visible chaos to ordered line. No wonder we are attracted to beautiful drawings, and to making them as well as we can: In the beautiful drawing, the hard work of abstracting and explaining has been done for us, and we bask in its presence.

In representative drawing, we are attempting to explain some portion of the visual field in line, usually by separating a shape or shapes from a ground according to its boundaries.

Some drawing manuals direct you to see monocularly (as if with one eye) in order to organize the array, which is to be seen flat, as if through a sheet of glass (painting on glass was a method used during the Renaissance to record the information beyond it). This kind of drawing can attain a degree of accuracy to which many aspire. Grids and other ocular aids, and a whole theory of (monocular) perspective also were developed, with innumerable aids to proportion, all of which served to assist the artist in choosing and representing edges and boundaries precisely. More recently, artists like Giacometti have explored and questioned what the eye actually sees, a far more profound and difficult quest, striving to understand the mystery of how we perceive the visual world.

This leads us to concepts. Lines that demarcate edges are chosen according to gestalts or concepts, not just according to what is out there. To name is human, and from early childhood our human task is to name the world, essentially to separate it into its recognizable pieces, each with a boundary. Our drawings reflect this uncannily: Children and untrained adults draw according to the named concept, even when the object they are drawing is in front of their eyes. In most student life drawings, for example, the contour line "skips" from named part to named part, literally leaving a gap on the page, a cognitive jump, where there is no name to interest and involve the eye. The great drawing is the one in which more profound combinations, unities and truths previously overlooked are discovered.

These visual concepts (or gestalts) are shortcuts, enabling us to make our way, to understand and to function faced with the violent chaos of the unsorted visual field. The shapes of things important or interesting to us are learned — recognition means, after all, *knowing again*. Physiologically, we trace their path with rapid eye movements called *saccades*. The repeated pattern is learned; certain neurons in the visual cortex become devoted to it, responding whenever we see (or even imagine) the object. Neurologists have dubbed these neurons "grandmother neurons," claiming that they are so specific in function that a certain cluster will respond only to your grandmother's face.

Representative drawing, of course, makes use of saccades. It is easier for us to draw what we have learned and incorporated than to actually look. Indeed, the difficulty in looking at something already conceptualized, a face for example, is almost insurpassable. Though we did not consciously choose them, these scan paths are personal to each one of us and are laid down irrevocably. Once you have "learned to see" (to recognize) in early childhood, there is far more information pouring outward along the ocular pathway than inward. Drawing could be likened to swimming upstream against a very strong current. As drawing students in this culture we are highly skilled to start with, and having learned to write, we can make marks exactly where we choose. The difficulty in drawing accurately is conceptual. In a sense, we "know" too much, and we need to find ways to eliminate that knowledge.

It amounts to this: To see clearly, the scan paths have to be jammed in some way. Drawing upside-down is a famous example. Another method that gives very good results is to bypass the names (names and concepts seem to be pretty much one and the same) and regard the object as nameless or — with a complex object like the human figure — give it a new name for new combinations, which alters the way we tend to see it. In life drawing, you can learn to draw "between the names." *Attention*, a physiological opening of the visual system, can occur, as anyone who has drawn with this kind of wordless receptivity can attest.

Line can do much more than represent edges and boundaries. To most of us, an idea of *movement* turns up in any consideration of line. Line does not in itself move, yet it has a brief temporal existence in its creation — as the hand moves across the surface. Here, too, the brain plays a main role, not only responses to edges but also to movement — even to the specific direction of a movement — are precisely located in the cortex.

We know that even to look at the static line seems to call forth a sense of motion — the eye "follows" it with ease and pleasure and is also able to choose between several lines where the artist has worked (David Hockney terms it "groping") toward the truest solution. The several attempts echo the eye's overlapping perceptions of a moving form, and the observer senses "life" in such a drawing, as opposed to a more perfected drawing where all the *pentimento* have been erased or traced away.

Another eye movement also is involved in drawing — that of *drift.* As you look at an object, your gaze falls naturally and corrects itself. As with the eye tremors called saccades, you are not consciously aware that your eyes are moving; it seems that you are gazing quietly. Yet when your eyes are not permitted to move, after three seconds everything goes black. Drawing in tune with the drift, allowing the line to fall slowly as you watch a vertical boundary, can give pleasure that is reflected in the quality of the line. Drawing with the drift to record the long contours of a standing figure, for example, produces beautiful

results, particularly if combined with keeping your eye on the model while you draw — a precept of Rodin's (who said he didn't have time to look at the paper) now used commonly as a drawing exercise.

Line can, of course, be used decoratively; you need only consider Celtic designs to be reminded of how appealing complex lineal design is to the observer. Using line can be purely playful.

The texture of some drawings — thick, wooly hatching, or the patient thousandfold overlaying of intricate strokes — is their strongest attraction. It is not just our admiration for the time spent, but also our brain's delight in responding to the depth and intricacy of detail. Whoever has watched fractals unfolding on a screen knows this kind of physiological delight.

And finally, line can express a great range of emotions — for example agitation, fury, tenderness. Line is a divine gift. It is up to the artist to extend his or her oeuvre — just as a violinist given a Stradivarius can, with attention, desire, and respect for the instrument, deepen and extend range, repertoire and sensitivity.

As for personal style, we can leave that to take care of itself, because we each are immersed in our personal style or "handwriting," and our efforts should rather be toward what Giacometti called "the impossible task" — that of coming a little nearer to the accuracy of perceived truth.

Heather Spears is a Canadian artist and award-winning poet who lives in Denmark and works in both Denmark and Canada. Primarily a medical artist, she also is a dynamic educator in figurative drawing and sculpture. She is the author of many books of drawings and anthologies of poetry and, most recently a historical novel.

Fifteen mixed symbols: astrological, chemical, religious and philosophical.

CHAPTER 2

Sign and Symbol

The transition from a simple drawn or impressed tool mark to a mark that implies meaning begins with human graphic communication. The distance from the simple pencil mark on paper or the scratch mark on clay or rock to images with meaning is short indeed. Imagine the world without the simple directional arrow.

The arrow sign has been used since prehistoric times to direct others to follow a particular path. It is just one of many basic signs of early man. Signs were around long before writing was developed. Signs — in the form of petroglyphs made by prehistoric man and found scratched or painted on boulders, rock walls and in caves the world over — probably symbolize many things that had powerful significance, from graphic representations

of, and directions to, water, good hunting, food and shelter, to more ritualistic or magical connections.

In early history, man expressed his activities and needs, such as hunting, food gathering, fertility rain and the continuation of life after death, by symbols. Much of the so-called decoration of archaic and primitive or tribal pottery is abstract symbolism full of meaning to the peoples who created and used it. Abstract and stylized symbols of animals, plants, human figures and objects were, and still are, carriers of meanings and are used by agreement, custom and tradition for messages. These symbols express an invisible meaning by a visible form. According to historians and anthropologists, the stroke, point, zigzag, wavy line, check and spiral patterns are a sign language

Rock art: Hunting Scene – Gila Petroglyph, style, picture rocks, Tucson Mountains, Arizona.

and not just decorative patterns. These same symbols are found throughout the pottery surface enrichment of almost all early cultures with great similarity of use. Much of mankind, particularly tribal groups and native peoples, still believe in the magic power of symbols, with which they may fulfill wishes and hopes, make the gods gracious and gain protection against evil and demons. Even many contemporary, highly educated human beings have a tendency to believe in messages emanating from the signs of the zodiac through astrology!

The earliest written languages were official or religious scripts made on clay tablets by Assyrians or Sumerians between 3500 and 2500 B.C. in the region around Babylon, in what is now Iraq. Based on pictographs and pictograms (pictures representing ideas or ideograms), the simple impressions made with wedge-shaped pointed tools were the foundation for other writing systems that followed. Egyptian hieroglyphics, Chinese characters, Arabic letter forms and Japanese Kanji scripts all are based on simplified pictures of objects.

					Bull
					Corn
					Men
					Woman
					Birth
					Birth Slave
					Head

Assyrian/Sumerian cuneiform letters/pictograms.

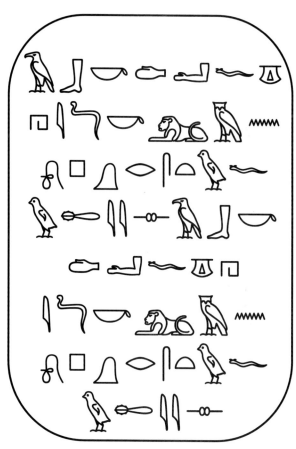

Egyptian hieroglyphic script.

Assyrian/Sumerian cuneiform clay tablet.

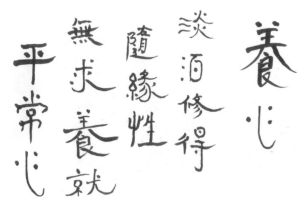

Chinese characters.

Arabic script, six variations.

Courtesy of Lorne Loomer

Noncharacter calligraphy.

A dictionary definition of *ideogram* is as follows: 1) A symbol used in some writing systems, for example, those of China and Japan, that directly but abstractedly represents the thing or concept itself rather than the word for it; 2) A graphic character or symbol used to represent a word such as +, =, 4, &, $, %. These signs commonly are used and universally understood as representing a specific idea.

It is important to differentiate between *sign* and *symbol*. A pointing hand, like the directional arrow, when used as a sign means to follow a specific path or go in a particular direction. If used in a painting or piece of ceramic art, the pointing hand will have a much greater meaning as a symbol that touches our inner understanding and subconscious knowledge. Instant world trade, communications and the availability of almost anything from almost anywhere have made us superficially familiar with symbolic art and design from many exotic cultures. Much, if not most, of this exotic

worldwide art contains hidden symbolic references or meanings of which the average Westerner is unaware. Anthropologists and art historians who have made exhaustive studies of different cultures often are able to inform us of the cultural meanings hidden in the exotic works we collect and use as starting points for the development of new directions in our own work. To know the meaning of the symbolic imagery of different cultural objects can only enrich our senses toward them, and when we borrow from other cultures, as artists always have done, we should do it with utmost sensitivity and, if possible, with full knowledge of the original content and meaning. Many artists expropriate symbols from other cultures and use them in their own work, often having little or no understanding of the original meaning, which may well have explicit sexual, religious or demonic meanings. We need to be careful in what messages we may be inadvertently putting into our work!

Mankind always has had the urge to decorate or ornament his creations and surroundings, sometimes as depictions of objects or sometimes in the form of signs and symbols. A symbol can be defined as a thing that means more than it is. We mostly use symbols to convey meanings too complex or subtle for verbal language. When we design with symbols or read someone else's symbols, we must rely on our intuition and spend time when feeling our way into their meanings. Symbols of this kind don't have simple right or wrong meanings. In using the symbolic language of art you can't stop at the convention that a white rose or lotus stands for purity. Purity in this sense is only an abstraction, and a white rose or lotus may actually symbolize a host of different things to different people in different places.

Each mark, stroke, cut, surface, shape or color we produce by design is a symbol, meaning something different from and more than what it actually is. A drawn line might mean the sinuous tracery of a tree branch, a hint of a shadow, the contour of a chair, a wrinkle in a face, the curve of a breast, a leaf or the movements of clouds. The meaning of any of these may lie beyond words, being sensuous, intuitive and optical. It is through the context of other symbols into which the mark or symbol is integrated that the viewer can interpret it. This narrows down its possible meanings to those that are relevant to the total image. Learning to use and read these kinds of symbolic language is the basis of art education. Works of art and design convey their meanings through shapes similar in form and color to other elements of our visual and tactile experiences.

Words usually do not sound like the things they mean, but visual symbols often look like what they mean.

In early history, man expressed his activities and needs with symbols. Much of the graphic mark making on the surfaces of archaic and primitive or tribal pottery is abstract symbolism, full of meaning to the people who created it. Abstract and neutral signs — animals, plants, human figures, objects — were, and still are, carriers of meanings and are used by agreement, custom and tradition for messages. These symbols express an invisible meaning by a visible form.

Man made for himself clay images of gods, idols and fetishes with human features that symbolized power and sometimes fear. These were deifications and personifications of the powers of nature that were, and are, thought of as being present in the images. The source of these ideas is animism, the belief that a living soul can be in inanimate objects and natural phenomena. By the magic of analogy, what happens in front of the object also happens to the gods. Many ceramic objects, such as utilitarian objects of daily life and cult objects, have

Cycladic Greek jug (Oinochoe), 675 B.C.

Lekythos, Greek, 500 to 550 B.C.

been found in tombs of archaic times and were believed to accompany the dead person to the next life. In some cultures, a tomb ceramic tradition was developed, which must have occupied a whole industry (in the Old Kingdom of Egypt, in China, and with the indigenous peoples of South and Central America, to mention just three regions). Not only were tomb vases and urns found, but also a host of clay figures — servants, craftsmen, musicians, dancers, sportsmen, soldiers, house models, boats, animals, and gods — that would serve the departed in the next world to give him pleasure and protection as they had in his life. In China these figurative tomb offerings were sometimes larger than life size and were put on show before the burial, so that the number, size and beauty of the ceramics were a symbol for the deceased person as well as his mourners.

The magic ritual cult turned into a mythological one, with Greek pots becoming the pictorial carriers of gods and legends. Mixed beings — half man and half animal, such as centaurs, sirens, minotaurs, chimera, sphinx and beings with wings — and fabulous animals were created as personifications of qualities such as virtues and vices, etc.

In contrast to the Greek paintings on pots, for some 200 years the Islamic religion forbade any representation of the human image, and decorative surface development concentrated on floral, geometric and calligraphic motifs. The rich innovation of Islamic ceramists was not limited to pottery, but found a huge field in architectural creations on facades, domes and mihrabs of mosques. Several forms of Arabic script were used in an effective asymmetrical way not only on architecture, but also for religious inscriptions from the Quran, the Islamic religious text, on plates and jugs as prayers or wishes for happiness.

In Asia, even today, the dragon is the symbol of happiness and wealth. In its original meaning it symbolized the powers of nature and is shown as a creature of fantasy composed of the head of a camel, the eyes of a rabbit, the horns of a deer, the ears of a water buffalo, the pads of a tiger, the talons of an eagle, the neck of a snake and the belly of a frog covered with scales. In Christianity, by way of contrast, the dragon of European mythology is seen as representing the forces of evil. Christian symbols are common in many European countries such as Italy, Germany, Spain, France, Holland and Hungary where scenes of the crucifixion, sacred

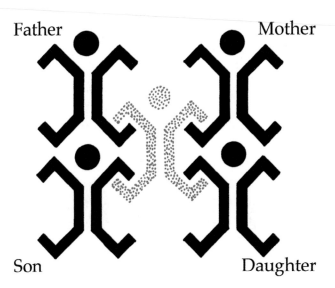

Genealogical development, family grouping, "Patterns that Connect," Carl Schuster and Edmund Carpenter.

Islamic Roundel (Mandala), 11th century A.D.

signs of Christ, Mary and the martyrs were used.

Geometric signs, hexagrams, pentagrams and mystical numbers both real and symbolic have been used in cult art and customs in connection with symbolic colors. Even now, symbols play a great role in our lives,

Six basic figurative forms, "Patterns that Connect," Carl Schuster and Edmund Carpenter.

Extending lineage. "Patterns that Connect," Carl Schuster and Edmund Carpenter.

although we may not be conscious of it. Our alphabet consists of abstract signs; flags and heraldic arms symbolize nations; religion uses sacred symbols and liturgical colors; political groups define themselves by signs and colors; and traffic signs show traffic regulations.

Many old pagan signs still are used but have different meanings. Now when we see a cockerel or snake as an ornament, we no longer think of it as a fertility symbol. It is a form of decoration for decoration's sake with no deeper meaning.

If you are interested in exploring signs and symbols from other cultures, or those that have universal meanings, fertile areas to research include: plants; animals; reptiles; insects; alchemy and chemistry; astrology and astronomy; Coptic, Celtic, Egyptian, Demotic (everyday Egyptian) and Greek art; erotic symbolism; heraldry; monsters and imaginary figures; Japanese family crests; cattle brands; hobo signs; symbols of birth and regeneration; signs of the zodiac; and genealogy.

For much of the 1920s through 1950s, Dr. Carl Schuster, a well-known American anthropologist and art historian, traveled many parts of the world, collected artifacts and photographed tribal patterning on objects such as ceramics, wood, metal, stone and fiber, as well as body markings, such as scarification and ritual tattooing, to develop theories on how and why pattern developed, and the similarities in arts from diverse cultures in many areas. But in 1969, after more than three decades of collecting, Schuster died before he was able to write the book he had planned about his discoveries and theories. With more than 40,000 photographic images, he felt he hadn't enough evidence for his study. Subsequent to Schuster's death, his colleague, Dr. Edmund Carpenter, condensed the research to a series of 12 large volumes with the title "Social Symbolism in Ancient and Tribal Art" published by The Rock Foundation, New York, in 1986. The 12 volumes were further distilled by Dr. Carpenter and published as "Patterns that Connect" in 1996 by Harry N. Abrams Inc. of New York. Material from this book is used with permission from Dr. Carpenter. Schuster's research on symbolism and pattern led him to the theory that a significant amount of the patterning and designs of mankind in general was in fact based on genealogy.

Dr. Schuster's studies concluded that genealogical images developed through six basic figurative images in the form of stick figures or solid shape figures. The figures show outstretched limbs, curved limbs, stepped limbs, hanging limbs, the hourglass, and the hocker, or squatting figure. These basic "bricks" are conventionalized human figures. Each figure is designed to be joined limb to limb with adjacent figures, with the intention of illustrating descent or relationship. To depict descent, figures generally are linked arm and leg with diagonally adjacent figures. Patterns of the figures are so constructed that arms and legs are indistinguishably fused, and the observer is lost in an anatomical puzzle. However, the confusion is deliberate: This is a graphic representation of the puzzle of procreation itself, in which there is neither beginning nor end. In the making of extended pattern, the head is usually left out and the spine often reduced to a zigzag or double lines with protuberances like vertebrae.

As the six basic figurative building blocks get further stacked together, they achieve an infinite variety of complex pattern including herringbone, honeycomb, undulating rhythmic lines, zigzag, hexagon with triangles, spiral and all manner of stepped designs from angular arm and leg references. The further you look into this in-depth study, the more you'll realize that there is unlimited potential for further exploration in the field of genealogical symbolism and the development of these complex patterns from ethnography and anthropology.

Turned sideways, with arms and legs thrust forward, the further potential of the simplified stick figure for rhythmic design increases exponentially, as shown in the diagram at right. Symbolic meanings, if there were any other than obscure genealogical references, are lost in the mists of time. Patterns based on genealogical symbolism are infinite and global in extent.

A study of signs, symbols and the potential for their use on contemporary ceramic surfaces leads to greatly enriched decorative processes. The opportunities are boundless. There is little that is totally new in art, most being revisions and extensions based on earlier examples, or transformations of an existing image to an extent that its origins become unrecognizable.

Side view variation. "Patterns that Connect," Carl Schuster and Edmund Carpenter.

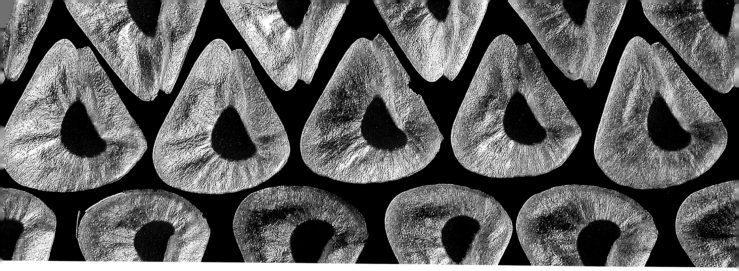

Cardiocrinum giganteum seeds. Photo: Judi Dyelle

CHAPTER 3

Pattern and Space

Proportion is the power that brings out the smile on the face of things.

Le Corbusier

The famous and highly influential 20th century Swiss architect Le Corbusier could equally well have said the same thing about pattern as he said about proportion. Like many other highly influential architects such as Frank Lloyd Wright, Louis Sullivan, Antonio Gaudi, Buckminster Fuller, Moshe Safdie, Philip Johnson, Arthur Erickson, Raymond Moriyama, Michael Graves, Frank Gehry and a host of others, Le Corbusier was obsessed with and excited about all facets of his architecture, from the massive to the minute. For an architect, the preoccupation often is with the placement and design of windows, doors, flooring and even furnishings and landscaping — the details that humanize the edifice. Much of the ceramic medium is akin to creating miniature architecture, where form is basic structure, and lids, handles, spouts, feet and necks provide the ceramist with an endless variety of architectural detail with which to play. Add to that the incredible potential for enriching and coloring the surface, and the simple pottery form becomes a microcosm of world architecture.

This chapter is a natural progression from the drawing exercises in Chapter 1 and the signs and symbols in Chapter 2, and it is a steppingstone to the color theory of Chapter 4.

We become aware of pattern early in life. As a person born on an island, the patterns I most remember from early childhood are the rhythms and counter-rhythms of moving concentric circles seen on a pond after throwing in a stone, or the patterns of beach sand after the tide goes out. For a city-raised child it might be the patterns of bricks, cracks in the sidewalk or stains on ceilings. No matter where our earliest memories were formed, they most likely include pattern in some form. Pattern and our personal experience of it is one of the most positive and visually stimulating aspects of the world around us, whether the patterns are of nature, are derived from our view of nature, are man-made (such as weaving), or arrive through the process of mechanical production, like expanded metal sheet or saw cuts on wood. Pattern is found throughout nature in such incredible detail as butterfly wings, bird feathers, seed shapes, fern fronds, lichens, shells, the scales and colors of fish and the forms and colors of flowers, to name but a few eye-catching images that might intrigue us and invoke design concepts to enrich the surface of our works.

Pattern

The photographs on page 37 show images of plants and details of plants. The variety of plant forms, colors and details in the photos taken in a couple of hours could be enough to keep a fertile mind working for weeks. Both the processes of photographing and

Photos: Franc D'Ambrosio and Terry Kopeck, courtesy of D'Ambrosio Architecture and Urbanism

The Chapel of Notre Dame du Haut, Ronchamp, France by Le Corbusier, 1956.

Euphorbia myrsinites.   Euphorbia characias.   Hellerbore hybrid.   Hellerbore hybrid.

Japanese painted fern.   Crested fern.   Gunnera chilensis.   Gunnera.

Cardiochrinum.   Trachystemon orientale.   Tulipa saxatilis.   Magnolia soulangiana.

Photos: Judi Dyelle

Organic natural pattern sequence.

drawing force the eye to look intensively at the subject, a major method of training the eye to see things that might be glossed over. The type of pattern becomes much more obvious with close scrutiny. A magnifying glass or 3-D microscope offers further depth of study in looking at an object. Whether plants have a particular pattern form, such as spiral, axial or radial symmetry, have patterns that move outward from the center or inward toward the center, or are found in the form of whorls all are details that become like small worlds when subjected to close scrutiny. The infinite variety of natural patterns can be a continual and expanding source of visual stimulus, whether it is in the form of line, repeating pattern or color.

Pattern is all around us on a daily basis. Its

development and use have been one of the major preoccupations of clay workers since the first impressions, scratches or daubs of color were put on the earliest of man's clay creations. Continually looking at the environment, whether rural or urban, is a rich and endless source of inspiration. Many artists in all media keep a file of images, slides, photographs or clippings from magazines to stimulate the brain into the forming of pattern or design.

Nature, combined with the patterns from man's ingenuity, surrounds us with beautiful images ranging from the simple to the highly complex.

Surfaces of inorganic natural objects, such as rocks and wood, as well as man-made objects from our working or living environments contribute much that

Sardine cans.   *Auto hubcap.*   *Enamel grinder.*   *Sandstone rock.*

Floor mat.   *Drain cover.*   *Road marking.*   *Worm-eaten wood.*

Objects.

can be interpreted as designs for potential ceramic surface development. Decoration or ornament usually is designed to adorn, beautify, embellish or enrich in an aesthetically pleasing and considered way. It can be as simple as a line or impression or as complex as a patterned grid of tightly defined strokes, or it can be a loosely broken line or color study. Just about anything that excites visual stimulation can be used for ideas to develop. Singular motifs or repeating patterns can develop visual stimulus.

Pattern is any decorative device, design or figure, and it can refer to either an individual motif or a combination of motifs. Pattern is also often mathematical or geometrical. The amazingly complex patterns of Islamic tile work show images of nature, such as twining vine tendrils engaged in a rhythmic interaction, based in geometry. These beautiful designs are referred to as *arabesques*. How you interpret any form of pattern into the reality of the ceramic surface depends on how you visualize. It could be anything from direct drawings on paper to direct drawings on ceramic, to glaze interpretation developed from color and texture, depending on skills and knowledge. For an artist whose particular bent is drawing and painting, linear decoration

might be most suitable. For a glaze specialist, visual interpretation in the form of color and texture might be preferable. It is quite possible to learn enough about the behavior of ceramic materials and their interaction under heat and kiln atmosphere to develop glazes of just about any color and texture. Chapters 5 and 11 discuss this aspect of the ceramic medium in some depth, as does "The Ceramic Spectrum," my first book. For many people the concept of making glazes to look like some other material, organic or inorganic, is beyond their experience. With a focused study of material behavior, almost anything is possible. Ceramic surfaces are some of the most chameleon-like in the world of art.

Throughout history mankind always has decorated things. In some time periods, some cultures have preoccupied themselves with advanced pattern making or surface design on ceramic surfaces. A few such patterns are shown in the eight-image grouping on page 40. Those of most interest might be Archaic Greek, Roman, Medieval European, Central and South American, Islamic, Chinese, Korean, Japanese and others where a decorative arts tradition was particularly important to the culture. Patterns and designs taken from natural phenomena and abstracted into a few strokes of a

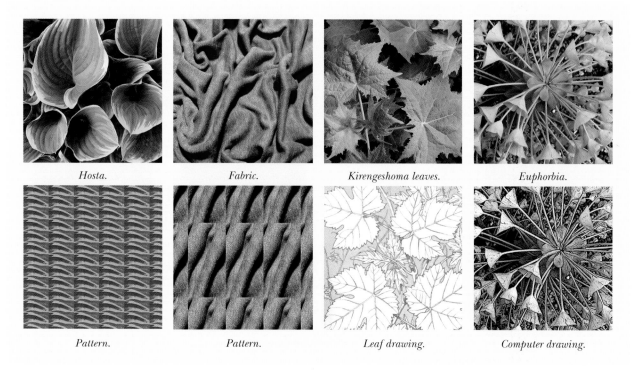

Hosta.   *Fabric.*   *Kirengeshoma leaves.*   *Euphorbia.*

Pattern.   *Pattern.*   *Leaf drawing.*   *Computer drawing.*

Photos: Judi Dyelle

Designs from nature.

brush, scratches from pointed tools or gouges made with cutting or fluting tools often are based on simple repeating formats to cover larger surfaces. Natural shapes often are abstracted or given geometrical variations. The commonly found spiral design is changed to the squared spiral, as shown on page 40.

Circles often turn into squares, pentagons, hexagons or octagons with smaller geometric forms placed between the main units of design. Just how the image is used on the form easily can give the optical illusion of pattern on ground. Playing with variations of positive and negative images, such as that shown on page 41, where the ewer image is drawn first as white on black, then reversed to black on white, gives a different character to the visual quality of the object. It is here where concern for the overall decorated surface becomes integrated with spatial concerns of placement on a surface. Besides positive and negative variations, you might consider individual or group motifs, rhythmic movements, or variations that explore large and small, tall and wide, or light and dark possibilities.

Grids of various shapes and sizes provide a framework for individual patterns or design motifs. The use of grids is a great way to both explore pattern and

its potential placement on an object. Here's a simple exercise that will help you visualize and develop pattern repeats. Duct tape together two small rectangular mirrors (6" x 8" or larger) down one side at the back forming a hinge so they can be opened book-fashion to a 90-degree angle. Place the mirrors on top of a drawing or design. They will reflect the image in four directions, showing how repeat patterns may be developed. This is a cheap and particularly useful tool for designing tile or any quatrefoil patterns. The hinged mirror can be opened further than 90 degrees to form trefoil patterns, or gradually closed to develop many variations of radial images. Looking at the way the reflected image changes through movement in the axes of the mirrors can spark many pattern and design concepts.

Space

When working with the ceramic surface, it is helpful to develop ideas of how a design might be placed on a form. There is virtually no limit to shape variation, and it would be impossible to categorize all shapes and variations. The diagrams on pages 42 and 43 show a variety of ways a form might be partitioned or broken up. Imagine the rectangles as tall, vertical, cylindrical

"Owl," Christopher Dressler.   *William Morris wallpaper.*   *Greek pattern.*   *"Paper," Christopher Dressler.*

William Morris wallpaper.   *Crystalline glaze.*   *Greek design.*   *Encaustic tile.*

Designs from historical sources.

forms, and you can appreciate a few of the possibilities. Turned on their sides, the same rectangles form short, wide cylinders, giving further ideas. Similar graphic variations can be made for any forms to explore options in the division of forms and placement of major and minor aspects of design.

Surface design can be either symmetrical or asymmetrical. European and Western hemisphere surface design tends to be more symmetrical, often fitting into a geometrical structure. Oriental surface design, particularly Japanese, is more likely to be asymmetrical, tending to favor the naturalistic pattern, or abstractions of naturalism. Much Central and South American pre-Columbian surface imagery also tends toward abstracted naturalism.

Single divisions of a form can create interesting and dynamic balances between the parts. Diagrams on page 42 show such divisions of a tall cylinder (or short cylinder when turned on its side). The relationships show aesthetically pleasing uses of proportion. Various proportionate systems such as Golden Mean, Golden Rectangle, Fibonacci or Summation Series, the Japanese Tatami module and Le Corbusier's Modular series give

From top: Axial symmetry, radial symmetry, and whorls — drawings.

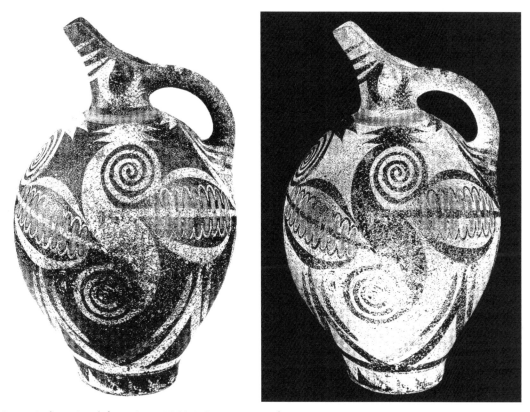

Ewer, Archaic Greek from Crete 1900 B.C., positive and negative views.

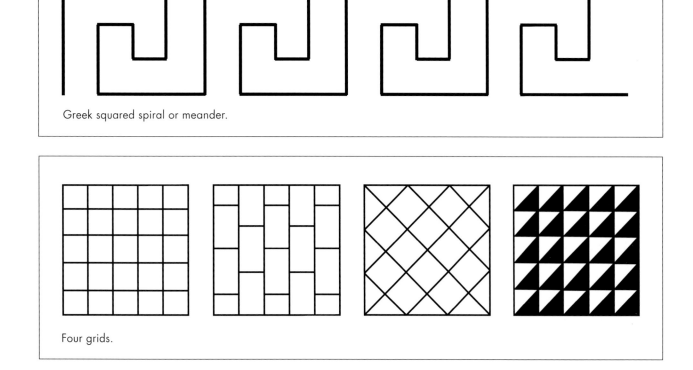

Greek squared spiral or meander.

Four grids.

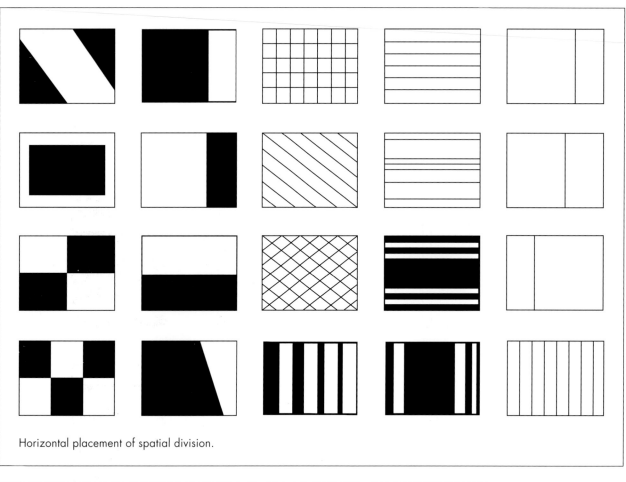

Horizontal placement of spatial division.

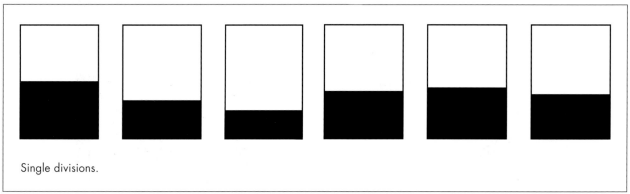

Single divisions.

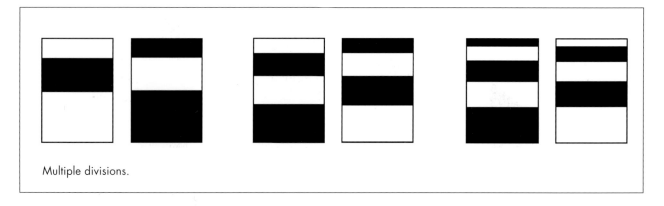

Multiple divisions.

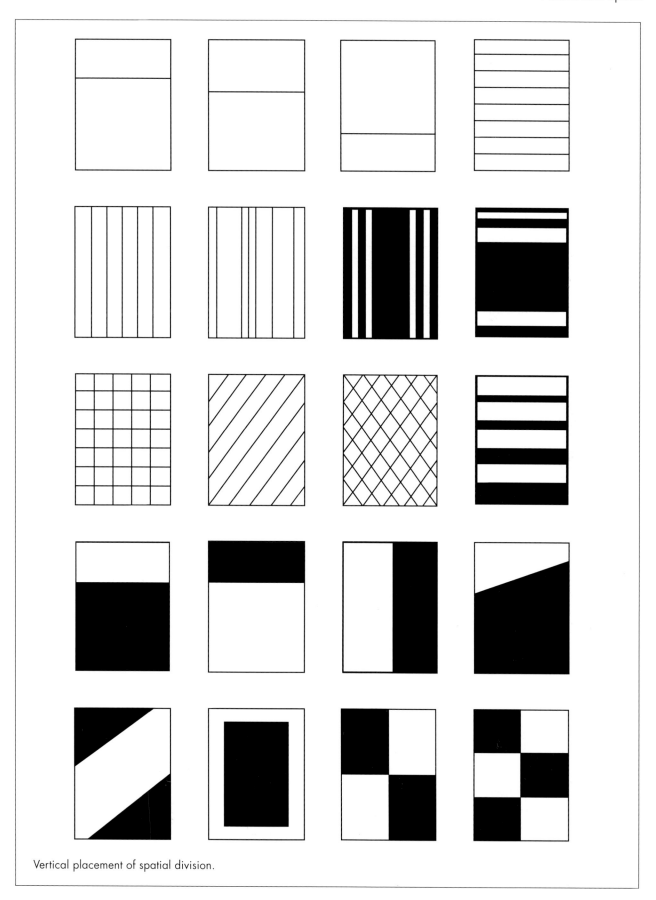

Vertical placement of spatial division.

slight variations on pleasing proportions. In my book, "Functional Pottery," Chapter 6 is devoted entirely to proportion and ratio. There isn't space to repeat the information here. However, concerns of how parts of an object relate to other parts in terms of proportions can easily make the difference between aesthetically

pleasing form or surface and discordant ones. According to psychologists, 95 percent of Western people relate positively to the Golden Mean proportions. All proportionate systems are mathematical.

The grouping of diagrams at the bottom of page 42 shows a series of rectangles with multiple divisions. On cylindrical forms, all divisions could be made by banding on a decorating wheel. In learning about formal division, it is worth working with models that easily can be made by wrapping paper tubes around tin cans and sticking them down to paint on. A small amount of time spent working with divisions will lead to greater intuition of where best to place horizontal lines when working on ceramic forms. Paper is expendable, whereas ceramic forms represent quite a lot of work.

The figure at left shows similar formal divisions in the form of concentric circles of progressively increasing size. These variations would be useful in considering areas of decoration on a plate, for example. Combinations of banding and patterned sections in pleasing variations of proportion can be worked out in this way.

The illustration below shows how forms can seem to change depending on how the divisions are made, whether vertical, horizontal, or diagonal. Horizontally placed stripes make the object look wider, and vertical stripes make the object look taller.

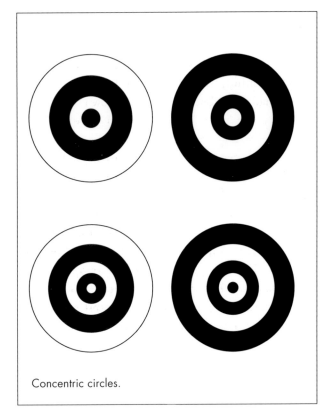

Concentric circles.

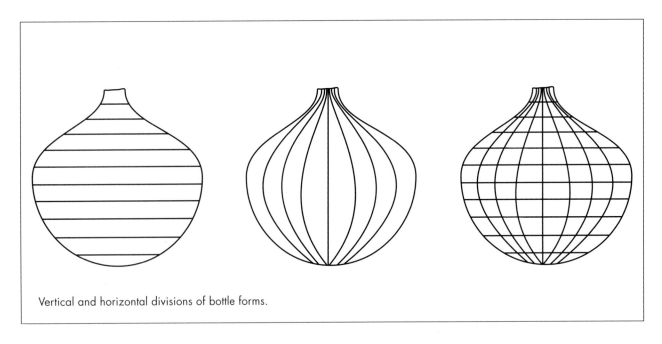

Vertical and horizontal divisions of bottle forms.

Marking Divisions

Marking divisions on bisque-fired ware for decorating ceramic surface can be done with regular graphite pencils. If the decoration is to be done on top of a glaze, majolica fashion, it is better to make preparation marks with a fine brush and vermilion watercolor paint. Both pencils and watercolor will burn out during subsequent firing. There are various graph-like tools available to help the ceramics painter accurately divide forms if simply marking the surface of the decorating wheel is inadequate.

How you use pattern and spatial variations depends completely on the type of work you are doing. Since the field of studio ceramics comprises every variable from dinnerware to sculpture, and from egg cups to architectural installations, any discussion on pattern and space can only touch and be useful to part of the ceramic community. From a point of view that is purely inspirational, creating or finding awareness of how you can use surface design variations to individualize your work is a lifelong pursuit. Keeping your eyes and mind open to the smallest and most unlikely visual stimuli is part of what being any kind of artist is all about. Because of visual training or retraining, artists often see things that others don't, and they are able to interpret ideas or concepts into whatever medium in which they are working. It is a simple but special skill that comes from acute observation of the world around you. Ideas and concepts are transformed into reality through the use of processes.

The processes you use to make the marks and the placement of the marks on the form can make or break the integration of the elements that creates a totality. Be on the continual lookout for and receptive to whatever form of inspiration comes your way. Ideas often come like a sudden flash of light; other times they are painfully worked through. It is wise to always keep a small sketchbook handy to jot down thoughts or drawings that might be useful later. It is so easy to forget things that visually caught your attention or jumped into mind. Your sketchbook provides a quick record whenever the opportunity arises or is needed. My own sketch/idea book is at least two years ahead of where I am in working through new concepts. My own ideas tend to come through interests in plants, gardens, landscape, human cultures, architecture and music. Whatever interests inform the type of work or surfacing processes you might want to do, a ready reference or sourcebook for ideas always is handy for when the mind is less active and when latent or elusive ideas stay dormant.

18th Centruy Delft tiles.

Color is a property of light.

CHAPTER 4

Color Theory

Along with the basic skill of drawing, understanding color is one of the most important foundations for work in any of the visual arts. Unless you are going to work only in black, white and shades of gray, you will have to deal with color in some manifestation. For the potter or ceramic artist, color is achieved in a convoluted way that includes chemical change and the physics of heat and kiln atmosphere. But the finished object is viewed with the same set of visual responses as that of a painting, print or other art form where chemical transformation is not part of the process. The painter or printmaker usually squeezes paint from tubes and mixes colors by eye. Other than a possible lightening or darkening of the pigment as it dries, what you see is what you get. If it turns out to be unsatisfactory, it is usually relatively easy to repaint or reprint another color over the original. With ceramics it is just not that easy. If an object is refired with another glaze or altered glaze over an offending color, it will almost certainly be affected by what is beneath, and often other changes occur in the good areas due to further chemical reaction and atmospheric change. Unless you paint your ceramics with acrylics, oil paint or egg tempera, what you see before firing is certainly not what you get afterward.

All color is pigment or chemical combination on a surface. These pigments or chemical compounds reflect a certain wavelength of light. Watercolor is a compound where the bits of pigment are suspended in gum arabic on a sheet of paper. A ceramic object uses the same principle; particles are suspended in a glaze on a surface where they reflect a certain wavelength of light, which we see as color. The making of ceramic art has two distinct parts: making the form and applying a surface to that form or parts of the form. The making of the form has endless variations. The surface treatment has many possibilities: transparent or opaque, smooth or textured, shiny or flat, dull colors or bright colors, earth colors or atmospheric colors, to name only a few. Then, with the addition of color, a whole realm of expressive and formal qualities can be introduced. But color always is seen in relation to the color that surrounds or neighbors it (simultaneous contrast).

The ability to use color is based on understanding basic characteristics of color, then using them in combination. Many color choices are made by intuition. In ceramics it is often a given what color the untouched and fired clay will be. It is the awareness of color theory that allows the artist to make informed use of the later-applied colored layer that becomes the neighboring color.

Color has such strong psychological and even physiological effects on us that any formula about its use would be doomed to fail. The best advice is to keep it simple. Keep in mind what you are trying to communicate, and make it look right to you. Look carefully and critically at how nature and other artists

The 12-part color wheel is derived from the primary colors of yellow, red and blue, with the secondary colors of orange, green and violet.

use color. Learn first by observation and then by using color in your own work.

Although color is a major part of the ceramic artist's means of expression, for the most part, we are at a disadvantage, since almost all colors and surface textures change dramatically in the process of firing. When the firing is completed, the result generally looks little like the prefired work. Building a variety of color changes and layered surfaces may require several firings.

Unless you are quite experienced in the technical aspects of ceramics, you often are working with certain unknown or little-known reactions. Where you can easily work with paints or inks through visual understanding and immediate observation, it is impossible to be inside of a kiln watching exactly what happens as mixtures of powdered rocks, clays and coloration minerals fuse, melt and interact. For the ceramic artist, there is a definite difference of approach to color development.

Since the art of the ceramist is judged by the same set of conventions as that of the painter in terms of their visual acceptance, it follows that some knowledge of color theory is as important for the ceramist as for any other visual artist. It isn't necessary for you to have as thorough a grounding of color theory as the painter because you are not working with a direct "what-you-see-is-what-you-get" situation. The concern here is with a basic understanding of pigmentary color theory and principles common to all visual arts.

Color, in all of its forms, has been at the center of research for scientists, artists, paint manufacturers and psychologists for several centuries. The subject of countless books and academic theories, color is a fascinating and complex field of study that touches all avenues of society. Since this book only has space for a short introduction to color theory, I have chosen to concentrate on the teachings of Johannes Itten, master of color at the Bauhaus in Germany and one of the most prominent color theorists of the 20th century. There are many other color theories that could have been used.

Science tells us that color depends on light and the ability of the human eye to discern variations in light waves. Color is what is seen when differing wavelengths of light bounce off different surfaces. The human eye can only see light of wavelengths between 400 and

Hues, tints, and shades from red.

700 nanometers. Human vision is the result of three interlocking processes:

- Physical — the action of the light waves;
- Physiological — what happens in the eye; and
- Physiological — what happens in the brain when the message from the eye is received and decoded.

Although we see color in our brain, the receptors in the eye tell your brain at what you are looking. There are two sets of receptors in the retina in the back of the eye: rods and cones. There are about 125 million rods (named for their shape). They are very sensitive to light but mostly are colorblind. We use them in dim light, and so the saying, "all cats are gray in the dark" came to be. We use our rods to detect the *quantity* of light reflected from a surface.

The color detectors in the eye are the cones.

Hues, tints, and shades from yellow.

Hues, tints, and shades from blue.

There are about seven million of these in three forms concentrated in the center of vision. Individual cones can only sense one of three narrowly defined frequencies of light: red, green and blue. The response from these three primary colors is sorted in our brain to give us the perception of color. In a colorblind person, one or more of these color receptors malfunctions. Our cones detect the *quality* of light. The sensitivity of the human eye is awesome, registering light values varying from the glowing tip of a cigarette in the dark to white paper in the noonday sun, a surface one million times brighter. The average human eye can also detect 17,000 color variations.

Color Physics

Color is a property of light. Our eyes see only a small part of the electromagnetic spectrum. Visible light is made up of the wavelengths of light between infrared and ultraviolet radiation (between 400 and 700 nanometers). These frequencies, taken together, make up white (sun) light. White light can be divided into its component parts by passing it through a prism where the light is separated by wavelength and a spectrum is formed. Sir Isaac Newton was the first to discover this phenomenon in the 17th century, and he named the colors of the spectrum.

Colored surfaces behave almost the opposite of light. A black surface absorbs most of the light, making it look black. A white surface reflects most of the light, making it look white. A green colored surface, for instance, absorbs most of the frequencies of light that are not green, reflecting only the green light frequency, because all colors other than the pigment or surface colors are absorbed. This is called the *subtractive* color theory. When you combine all colors in a glaze, they would reflect no light and look black.

The other system of color is called *additive*, like on your computer screen, television or a stage light, where

Analogous colors.

all colors give white light when combined.

Pigments display color by absorbing wavelengths selectively, reflecting back to the eye only those wavelengths that are not absorbed. Mixing pigments is called *subtractive mixing,* because the more pigment colors are mixed, the more light is absorbed, eventually ending up with dark gray, brown or black. With pigments there are three primary colors — red, yellow and blue — from which all other colors can be made.

Understanding color can be achieved most readily by understanding the color wheel, shown on page __. The wheel is simple in its design but can yield countless new opportunities for expression and creativity. Artists often are afraid they won't understand it, so they read quickly through a textbook without applying the principles. They mostly stop at a picture of a color wheel, which, in fact, is only the beginning.

In the center of the 12-part color wheel is a triangle showing the three primaries: yellow at the top, red at lower right and blue at lower left. Between the wheel and the central equilateral triangle are three isosceles triangles, each with a secondary color. Secondary colors are produced by mixing equal parts of two primaries: yellow + red = orange, yellow + blue = green, and red + blue = violet. In the ring beyond the colored hexagon (all the triangles together in a six-sided unit), where the points of the hexagon touch, are the primary and secondary colors. Starting at the top is yellow, and going clockwise are orange, red, violet, blue, and green. Between each of these colors on the wheel are the tertiary colors, each made from the mix of primary and secondary colors.

Colors that are directly opposite each other on the wheel are called *complementaries* — red/green, blue/orange, yellow/violet. Simply stated, this means that if you are working in red, the juxtaposition of green will vibrantly affect the two colors. The same will hold true of any diametrically opposed colors. Many painters have used complementaries as their main method of working out color schemes for painting, including the French Impressionists, Van Gogh, Cézanne, Signac, Seurat and others.

Any three colors next to each other on the wheel are referred to as *analogous.* Any use of analogous colors in a painting or any other art will produce harmonious relationships. Analogous colors put with

the complementary of the central of the three-color group are called *split complementaries.* They will form harmonious relationships. For example, if you put red-violet with green, yellow-green with yellow, orange with blue-green, or blue with blue-violet, these would produce harmony. For the ceramic artist, these rules may seem difficult to consider because we seldom work with exact pigmentation, although we can get very close. In the ceramic medium, we seldom have exact hues of primary, secondary or tertiary pigment colors, because the colorant needs a glaze to be the vehicle for delivery. Glazes may be transparent, translucent or opaque, which immediately modifies pure color to some extent.

The sequence of colors that make up the color wheel is that of a rainbow, or natural spectrum. At full spectrum strength these colors are called *hues.* Hues can be modified by the addition of white or black. A color mixed with white is referred to as a *tint;* a color mixed with black is referred to as a *shade.* Between white and black are a series of gray tones.

When separated by 10 percent intervals, we get what is referred to as a *gray scale.* An 11-point gray scale with nine stages between white and black is more than adequate for most purposes in painting.

In colored ceramic glazes, the use of an opacifier or whitener, such as tin oxide, will produce tints of the color. The use of a black ceramic pigment usually will produce shades. Black ceramic pigments are made from combinations of a number of mineral colorants. Many contain cobalt. Under different firing conditions, and with different glazes, they may take on predominantly dark blue or dark brown tones rather than pure black. Opacifiers and black pigment can be added to glazes in increments. It is not usually necessary to do an 11-point gray scale. Increments of 2.5 percent, 5 percent, 7.5 percent, and 10 percent will probably be fine. If the required subtlety is not forthcoming at these volumes, add more. Since you have to fire the glazes, they won't be exactly like using painting pigments, but you can get very close.

You may have seen a painter squinting while looking at his painting. By shutting out much of the light coming into the eye, only the rods work, so as color disappears the lightness or darkness of an area is more easily seen. In practice, if you want to make something appear lighter, put something darker around it and vice versa.

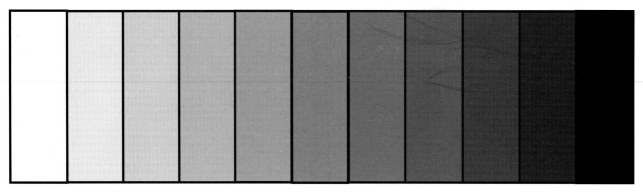

An 11-point gray scale.

Although the average person can see about 17,000 different colors, there are only about 130 different artist's colors sold, so even if you had a tube of every color manufactured, you still couldn't duplicate the range of colors you see in nature. The darkest dark you can see in nature is very much darker than the darkest pigment you can buy. The darkest black paint is about equivalent to a mid-tone in nature, and the most brilliant white you can make is darker than most of the light values in nature. Since it is impossible to duplicate the range of hues in nature, the artist uses their color to *represent* colors in nature.

Color Schemes

Color schemes are based on the traditional color wheel shown earlier in this chapter. Here are the most common, starting with the simplest.

Monochromatic Colors

Monochromatic means using one hue, and changing it by adding white, black or a combination of the two. Change the yellow hue to create a monochromatic burnt sienna or umber, neutralizing the yellow. A monochromatic contrast is set up when you use a single color, then increase or decrease its lightness.

Analogous Colors

These are related colors from a pie-shaped slice of the color wheel. They all have one hue in common, so things can't get too wild. Starting with this scheme, more hue contrasts are possible. This means more freedom and expressive potential, but it is increasingly difficult to make good color combinations. These are any colors directly next to a given color. If you start with orange and want its two analogous colors, select red and yellow. A color scheme that uses analogous colors provides a harmony and blending of the colors similar to what might be found in nature.

Split Complementary Colors

Using a split complement system — the color and two colors on either side of its complement — results in a variation that produces less contrast.

Complementary Colors

Also known as contrasting colors, complementary colors are directly opposite each other on the color wheel. Selecting contrasting colors is useful when you want to make the colors stand out more vibrantly. These colors are as far apart (hue wise) as colors can be, so there is ample potential for conflict. Oddly, though, they actually can complement each other if used in appropriate proportions and with control over saturation.

Triad Colors

These are any three colors that are equidistant on the color wheel, like green, violet and orange. When triad colors are used in a color scheme, they present a tension to the viewer, because all three colors contrast. The primary and secondary color sets are both triads.

Tetrad Colors

These are any four colors that are equidistant on the color wheel, like yellow, red-orange, violet and blue-green.

Warm Colors

Warm colors are made up of the red hues, such as

red, orange and yellow. They lend a sense of warmth, comfort and energy to the color selection. They also produce a visual result that causes these colors to appear to move toward the viewer and to stand out from the page.

Cool Colors

Cool colors come from the blue hues, such as blue, cyan and green. These colors will stabilize and cool the color scheme. They appear to recede from the viewer.

It is important to note that you might find these color groups called different things in different books, but if you understand the basic principles, they will all make sense to you.

One final thing to remember about color is that its use changes. Colors and color combinations popular 10 years ago are not popular today, not because they were bad, but they were right and appropriate for the time. Time changes everything, and we view color differently today than we did a decade ago. This suggests strongly that color has a subjective quality, that it can express a feeling appropriate for this time but not five years from now. It then follows that a color combination can be used as a reference to another time. Don't light blue and green remind you of the 1970s while gray and burgundy remind you of the late '80s? Color also has many objective qualities that, when recognized, allow us to make decisions about our time and the place where color is used. If this doesn't seem possible to you — watch.

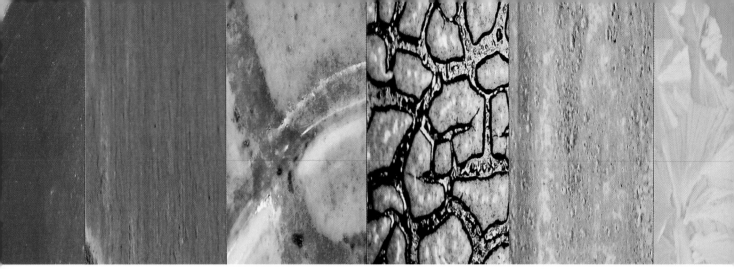

The ceramic surface is probably the most chameleon-like of all surfaces used in the visual arts. Photo: Judi Dyelle

CHAPTER 5

Color and the Ceramic Surface

The most beautiful experience we can have is the mysterious. It is the fundamental emotion which stands at the cradle of true art and true science.

Albert Einstein

ALCHEMY: 1) The empirical, speculative and unscientific form of chemistry, seeking to transform base metals into gold; 2) Any preternatural power or process of enchantment, transmutation and transformation.

SCIENCE: 1) Any branch of knowledge in which the results of investigation have been logically arranged and systematized in the form of hypotheses and general laws subject to verification; 2) Accurate, precise, exact and reliable.

The ceramic surface is probably the most chameleon-like of all surfaces used in the visual arts. Not only does it invariably change color in response to heat, it can be transformed to resemble any texture, from as smooth as silk to as chunky as stone, or as clear as glass to as lustrous as gold. Since its visual and tactile possibilities are virtually limitless, the ceramic surface can be made to look and feel like just about anything. In the process of layering and intermixing mineral coatings of clays, slips, underglazes, sigillatas, engobes, glazes, colorants, salts, ashes, overglazes and lusters, we can create the most incredible and diverse range of surface texture and color. The main difference in approach to using a ceramic/painterly method is that in painting there is no firing process. In ceramics it is nearly impossible to get a full spectrum of color without multiple firings. You can, however, achieve a wider range of surface than painting generally offers.

The Ceramic Color Wheel (at right) shows a color wheel made using glazes from differing temperature ranges and atmospheres.

Gray scales in ceramic glazes can be developed by using opacifiers or modifiers. There are several from which to choose, but tin oxide is usually the most reliable whitener and has the least effect on other coloring oxides. They typically are used in additions of up to 10 percent to the base glaze. Black stains can be used for darkening or modifying glazes, but since they are made from a variety of different colorants they will almost certainly affect the color as well as its shade. Additions of up to 4 percent of any black stain usually will darken a glaze considerably and cause some glazes to become an opaque black.

Analogous color often can be developed by the juxtaposition of different intensities of the same colorant, as shown in the analogous color examples on

THE CERAMIC COLOR WHEEL

The main difference in approach to using a ceramic/painterly method is that in painting there is no firing process, and in ceramics it is nearly impossible to get a full spectrum of color without multiple firings under different atmospheric conditions. With the selection of raw materials, the range of firing temperatures and the variety of kilns, one can achieve a wider range of surface than painting generally offers. This color wheel is but a small example of the potential of color development in ceramic glazes.

The ceramic glaze color wheel.

page 56 and the color progression examples on page 57. A few examples of ceramic glaze interpretations of other surfaces are shown in comparisons on page 59 to give an idea of the approach of developing ceramic surfaces to emulate other materials. You can capture the evanescent qualities of snowflakes and the diaphanous silk-like surface of cardiocrinum seeds with micro and macro crystalline glazes, while you can use reticulation glazes for encrusted surfaces. It takes a combination of imagination and experience to develop surfaces that resemble other materials, from what is shown here to realistic interpretations of precious metals, like silver and gold.

Developing an almost play-like approach to learning about and understanding ceramic materials opens the door to creative surface making. People tend to make things far more difficult than necessary. If you think of it as alchemy, mineralogy and magic, it becomes much

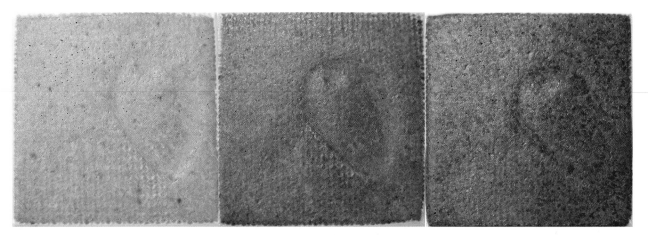

Analogous colors — base glaze colored with differing intensities of nickel oxide.

more creative and fun. Glaze making can be as simple or as complex as you want to make it. Most people prefer simple!

When you think of ceramics in terms of its graphic possibilities of marks on a surface, it has an equivalent methodology of all the processes used in painting, drawing and printmaking combined. Through a minimum of 10,000 years of ceramic historical development that incorporates almost all human cultures and all regions of the world (except arctic or dense jungle conditions), the ceramic medium has been explored and utilized to fill functional, contemplative and spiritual needs. It also has been a major source of communication, as shown in Chapter 2: Sign and Symbol. The development of ceramics became mankind's earliest technical discovery when it was observed that clay could be fired to change its soft, malleable state to a hardened ceramic state so it could be used for storage of both solid and liquid materials and as a container for cooking food. In the course of all this development, clay has been used for the creation of pottery and sculpture in a huge variety of technical variations. It is the ultimate technical art form. With its roots in explosive volcanic action, it is a compelling and seductive combination of art and science, one where the results are dependent on a symbiotic relationship between idea and alchemy.

Clay is an extremely complex mineral, the culmination of volcano-born feldspathic rocks, such as granite, being broken down by erosion and decomposition over eons of time. It also is one of the most abundant and easily recognizable minerals. Often found far from its original mother rock source, washed down rivers and into lake beds, clay particles become finely ground through constant abrasion and tumbling. At the same time, clay picks up all manner of impurities that give it its highly variable color and control its firing ranges. The fine particle size gives clay the plasticity to easily be worked with and formed by diverse methods.

A dry food storage vessel was probably the first vessel put into use, after which probably came liquid storage. Most clays remain porous until high firing, and early kilns couldn't be heated enough to tighten the body. Since mankind's most precious natural commodity is water, liquid retention was a prime concern. Resinous vegetation was rubbed on heated pots to deposit a thin, waterproof film. Later, thin, liquefied clays were used for coating the vessels to improve water storage. They also became part of the decorative vocabulary. Highly refined, watery, clay slip, usually referred to by the Roman name "terra sigillata," was developed independently in various parts of the world, and, until the discovery of glaze-making minerals in the Middle East about 4,500 years ago, remained the most consistently used surface coating for both practical and decorative objects. Liquid clays in various formats provide great possibilities for decorative exploration.

Glazes first were made in the Middle East, probably in Syria, where abundant sodium created easy fusion with the silica in the clay to form a glass. In a fire pit, high sodium-bearing rocks can receive enough heat to fuse together. Lead, in the form of galena or lead sulfide, also was abundant and fused easily onto the ceramic surface, creating glass. As greater understanding of material interaction and fusion developed, so did the great range

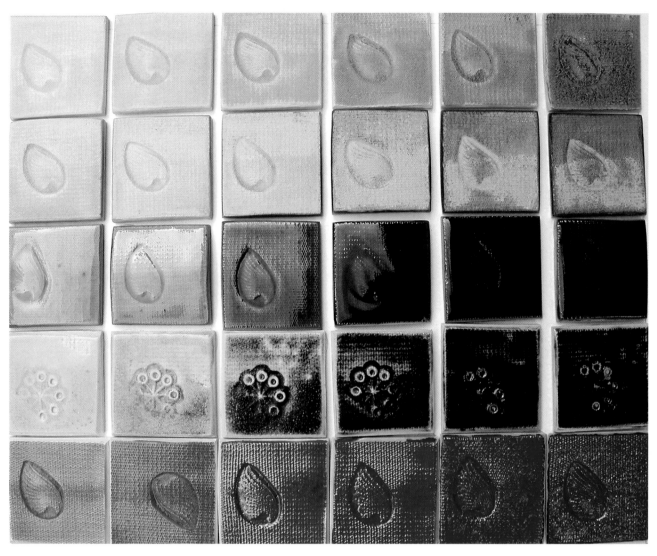

Color progressions on five different glaze bases from 0.5 percent to 10 percent.

of processes for making and decorating low-fired wares. By about 1500 B.C., the Chinese potters had developed kilns capable of higher firing temperatures as well as high-temperature stoneware clays and, eventually, porcelain. With the greater fusion possibilities of higher firing kilns, opportunities for decorative surfacing processes developed exponentially. By the end of the Ming Dynasty in 1644 A.D., Chinese potters had learned to control their materials to the point where anything that could be done in ceramic glaze making already was being done, with the exception of colors and processes that required materials they didn't yet know about, like zinc, titanium, uranium, vanadium and other rare earth materials. Glaze making was done entirely by trial and error methods until an extremely sophisticated empirical knowledge of materials was developed. In the late 19th century, the method of calculating glazes from the molecular weights of constituent glaze-making oxides was developed in Germany. For approximately 97 percent of the time that glazes have been around, they have been made empirically through knowledge of materials gained by experience over time. To efficiently use calculation methods for glaze development, the glaze maker also needs an extensive understanding of materials, something that usually takes a considerable time to amass.

Construction of a Ceramic Glaze

Ceramic glaze is basically just a thin skin of mixed,

powdered rocks and minerals, clays or ashes melted onto a clay surface at a variety of temperatures, depending on the mixture of material and the desired result. Regardless of the temperature at which it's fired, any ceramic glaze is composed of three types of material: bases or fluxes; neutrals or amphoterics; and acids. In a very simplistic view, the acid is the glass-former — usually silica — and it is made to melt at a variety of temperatures by the addition of a flux or mixture of fluxes, many of which are alkaline, and made to satisfactorily adhere to the surface of the clay object by the neutral — usually alumina or clay. The relative acidity or alkalinity of the raw material is what primarily controls color development.

For convenience in calculation, materials are put into three columns with the **Base** (flux, also known as RO or R_2O, sometimes referred to as the blood of a glaze) on the left, **Amphoteric** (usually clay, also known as R_2O_3, sometimes referred to as the muscle) in the center, and the **Acid** (glass-former, usually silica, also known as RO_2, sometimes referred to as the bones of a glaze) on the right. It is the ratio among the three material types that determines the firing range, but primarily the fluxes that control color development.

Additions to the basic glaze include a selection of colorants, granulation materials and opacifiers, if used. For color, those basic raw materials *not* in a glaze are often as important as the ones that are in it, since some materials greatly inhibit the development of some colors. Most colorants vary considerably in their capabilities. Because ceramic color development is a very complex field of research, most books tell you about color in very generalized terms — that iron compounds will produce brown or green and copper compounds red or green, for instance. Iron certainly can give brown and green, but it also can yield yellow, red, gold, gray, pink, black, orange, blue or purple. Similarly, copper can give green and red, but it also can produce turquoise, purple, orange, blue, gray, pink, black and occasionally yellow.

Color and surface in any glaze at any temperature are dependent on three variables: 1) the raw materials that make up the glaze; 2) the temperature to which the glaze is fired; 3) the atmosphere (oxidation or reduction) in which it is fired.

Iron and copper are the most versatile colorants, but all have multiple possibilities. Since underglaze colors and glaze stains are made from premixed and sometimes prefired colorants and opacifiers mixed with fillers, they,

too, are dependent on the three variables for the color responses suggested by the shade cards. Under ideal circumstances with the correct type of glaze, firing and atmosphere, they will behave as expected and produce the colors shown on the shade card. The wrong choice of materials, temperature or atmosphere all can radically change the colors that will be achieved.

To an artist working in ceramics, the most important aspect of the work after developing the form is usually color or surface quality. The preconceived idea of the work usually combines form, surface, and color as an integrated whole. When a clay worker is technically able to make the forms visualized, the development of an individual palette of color and surface is next in importance. It makes little difference whether you are producing functional work, one-of-a-kind ware, or sculpture — the technical end of ceramic development is basically the same. It requires testing and observation, and, through what is essentially a process of elimination, narrowing the field until you achieve the required result. It often is helpful to remember that you are working with combinations of powdered and decomposed rocks you are subjecting to heat similar to or slightly hotter than the surface end of a volcano, and these rocks potentially are able to create any of the colors and textures of natural rocks and minerals in the process. By combining minerals that were not originally together, a whole range of new possibilities can be achieved. Even though the commonly used materials in ceramic glazes number fewer than two dozen, their combined potential for glaze development is limitless. Unfortunately, the process often is erroneously seen as being too technical, and comparatively few ceramists develop totally new glazes. Perhaps the most commonly used alternative is to find a glaze recipe in a book or magazine that sounds more or less suitable, make a small batch, and test fire it. In the long term, this is probably the least satisfactory method. Unless you either compromise your ideas to suit the glaze at hand, or make many adjustments to that glaze, it is usually second best to coming up with your own original recipes or formulas.

Developing a solid understanding of the behavior of materials under heat is the foundation of glaze making. It is an exciting educational and creative journey that opens new worlds of possibilities.

Original glazes are produced either by glaze calculation or by empirical methods (trial and error,

Glaze comparisons — a weathered door painted with bituminous paint and a low-temperature reticulated glaze surface.

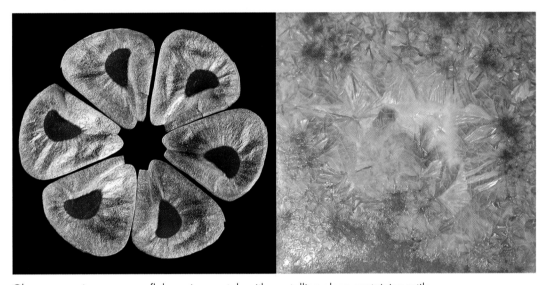

Glaze comparisons — snowflake or ice crystals with crystalline glaze containing rutile.

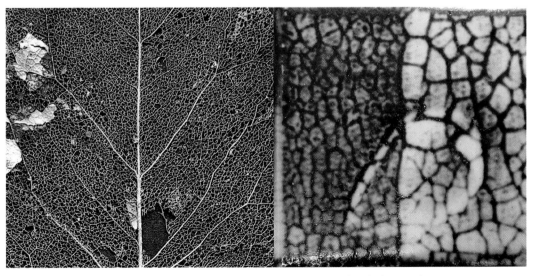

Glaze comparisons — skeleton leaf detail with high-temperature reticulated glaze surface.

understanding the behavior of materials and making educated guesses). The former is a somewhat abstract concept, foreign to most artistic minds. Glaze calculation makes glaze making possible through mathematical formulas achieved by developing and understanding the ratios of different materials that are likely to be incorporated into glazes. Since the original development of the system, limit formulas have been established that show the high and low extents to which any chemical normally can be used in developing a glaze for a given temperature. The limit formula sets up a basic structure from which you can work. The formula is mathematically converted to produce a glaze from available ceramic materials. To be used efficiently, calculation is dependent on direct prior experience with the behavior of ceramic materials. You need this to make an educated guess at the suitability of raw materials. There are various methods of calculation, the most recent of which use computer software programs. They essentially remove the drudgery of doing the math involved in longhand calculation of the formula and conversions to batch recipes, and vice versa.

Calculation has some very useful attributes, but, for the artist, it also has some great deficiencies. Have you ever realized that glaze calculation can't tell you the things you most want to know about glazes? Have you ever wondered why specific color development and control seems to be such an elusive activity? Or why commercially prepared colors and stains often don't look like the manufacturer's shade card? Have you ever wondered why we learn how to calculate glaze formulas by mathematical means? Or why, for the studio potter or individual ceramic artist, this process is largely redundant? Are you prepared to accept what happens with a glaze or color rather than exert control to gain exactly what you want?

Downplaying glaze calculation might appear regressive and seems to be going against long-standing scientific principles. But my reasons for both using and teaching the empirical approach are that the majority of people are inhibited from doing much individual glaze exploration by an imposed imperfect scientific system with its own built-in deficiencies. As students or self-taught clay workers, we usually are not made aware of those deficiencies, and often we struggle in the misguided belief that a scientific approach will open the door to marvels.

Prior to the development of mathematical calculation, all glaze development was done empirically, and information was passed down through family tradition, more often than not with great secrecy, for such knowledge represented livelihood. Glaze making throughout the great and innovative ceramic-producing cultures of China, Islam, Korea and Japan evolved in this way. With the exception of the German salt-glazing process, all glaze development in Europe and later in the colonized Western Hemisphere was based on earlier Middle Eastern or Oriental examples. Very often this was "stolen" information, and it was among the first occurrences of industrial espionage. When the European ceramic industry really accelerated with the likes of Wedgwood, Spode and the many court-based European centers such as Sèvres, Limoges, Meissen and Vienna, it was obvious that something more than alchemy was needed to standardize fine quality wares. Hundreds of years of trial and error finally gave way to calculation, a scientific approach based on the individual weights of molecules composing compounds of materials used in a glaze.

Glaze calculation eventually was developed in the last quarter of the 19th century by the renowned German ceramic chemist Hermann Seger as a means of developing and comparing glaze formulas for the ceramic industry. This industry is understandably concerned with product regularity and quality control, characteristics that calculation of formulas from mineral analysis can achieve quite efficiently. From an industrial standpoint, a properly calculated and formulated glaze is one that usually is clear, fully melted and attached to the clay body in a fault-free coating. It is interesting to note that if calculation had preceded the empirical methods of glaze making, most of the glaze types potters hold in high esteem would have been outside these acceptable parameters. It is difficult to imagine ceramic history without ash glazes, or glazes that flow, crackle, crawl, crystallize or crater — all unacceptable flaws by industrial standards. It also is interesting to note that much current European and Japanese industrial pottery incorporates impurities, such as granular iron, rutile, ilmenite or manganese, into the glazes to emulate the reduction-fired qualities that have been admired by potters and connoisseurs for centuries. Some factories work extremely hard at trying to industrially reproduce the special qualities that can only come from hand making with contaminated materials.

So why do today's clay workers use glaze calculation? There are several benefits: 1) Through its mathematical process it can offer a basic understanding of mineral fusion principles; 2) It establishes the ratios of chemical molecules required to develop a glaze at a given temperature; 3) The use of limit formulas establishes the normal extents of volume in chemical use for a given temperature range; 4) It makes possible easy comparison between formulas; 5) It affords understanding of information in technical ceramic books and journals; and 6) It can be useful in pinpointing what may be causing glaze problems.

But calculation fails to tell us: 1) What the quality of the surface will be: glassy, glossy, satin, vellum, matte, crystalline or dry; 2) Which raw materials should be used in a glaze to obtain a specific color or color range; 3) How colorants or opacifiers or their combinations will behave in a given glaze; and 4) How the glaze will vary in different kilns and firing conditions.

It seems to me that the qualities and colors of ceramic surfaces are what we find most appealing, and therefore a calculation method, though undeniably valid in certain areas, falls far short in those very places that are our greatest concern. What should your concerns be in selecting materials for glazes? This depends on a number of factors: desired firing temperature; type of firing (electric, gas, raku, etc.); surface wanted; colors or color ranges; and finally, materials available.

In theory then, glaze calculation sounds convenient, but it leaves a lot to be desired in practice, as it cannot indicate surface or color potential, the tactile and visual qualities most desired. If, for example, you were looking for a glaze that would be satin-surfaced and crimson in color, the only way you could find it would be through a published recipe, or by trial and error, which is what invariably has to be done in the long term anyway. Unless you are a ceramic chemist continually making and comparing glazes, you probably won't use calculation often, and consequently you will need to relearn the process at each use. From my observations, most ceramists learn it and forget it. There is no doubt that the system works and has some benefits and is even more or less understandable, but what do we lose by using it?

Other than hygienic glazes made for the commercial dinnerware and sanitary-ware industries, I personally feel that glazes developed since the advent of calculation are no improvement upon those achieved by the great ceramic-producing cultures of the past, where purely empirical methods were used. Unfortunately, we generally have lost the intuitive sense of our materials that was so strong in potters of the past. Intuition derives from an innate understanding coming from experience and observation. It is the direct learning or knowledge of something without conscious reasoning. In its place we've largely gained dependence either on published recipes or on questionable scientific principles, which neither tell us the whole story nor give us real comprehension on which to base our work. Why do I say questionable scientific principles? Because the analyses of ceramic minerals supplied by mining companies are averages of the compounds that form the basic raw materials supplied by their mines. Those certainly change from one part of a mine to another. Such is the nature of Nature. Not every bag will be identical, and the same raw material purchased over an extensive period of time is likely to alter considerably. So our science is based on a changeable generality and not on established fact.

The simplest way to understand the nature of ceramic materials and their interaction is to test fire every material you use on small bisque-fired tiles. Mix the material with a little water and brush it onto the tile. To get some idea of how color might be affected, paint a thin stripe of colorant or stain mixed with water on the surface of the raw material. Iron, copper, cobalt and manganese commonly are used, but if you prefer brightly colored stains, try them too. Depending on the firing temperature, you'll find that some of the raw materials melt, others sinter but don't melt, and still others remain completely unmelted. As a generality, you can say that those that melt most have the highest fluxing power, and those that are unmelted, usually silica and the purer clays, need to be fluxed to make usable mixtures.

The second stage of testing is usually to mix a line blend of those materials that melt with those that don't. This is simply the blending together of one material with another in a controlled ratio (usually by weight) — e.g. 90:10, 80:20, 70:30, 60:40, 50:50, 40:60, 30:70, 20:80, 10:90. Thin color stripes can be very informative. As evidenced by many early Chinese glazes, quite beautiful glazes can be made with just two materials.

The third stage of development involves the intermixture of three or more materials in various ratios in a triaxial blend. The fourth would be mixtures of four or more materials in a quadraxial blend.

There are many different approaches to empirical glaze development and understanding, and the more you constructively play with it, the more familiar the reactions of the materials become. Within a fairly short time you really can begin to understand the behavior of the materials and produce your own personal palette of glaze surface and color.

A State of Flux

When developing color in a glaze, the most important ingredient is the flux or mixture of fluxes. By changing the fluxes in any glaze, complete changes in color range and surface quality are both possible and probable. From a learning point of view, it is quite instructive to take any glaze — one that you have developed or one you have picked up in a book or magazine — and exchange one or more fluxes for others.

The materials called fluxes are lead, calcium, alkalines or alkaline earths, borax, boron, potassium, sodium, lithium, magnesia, zinc, barium and strontium. Calcium, which is a vigorous flux at temperature ranges beyond cone 4, has the least effect on color variation. The others may have a profound effect on both surface and color, depending on the other materials that make up the glaze, the firing temperature and atmosphere.

The alkaline fluxes (sodium, lithium, and potassium) have particularly strong effects on glazes containing copper, manganese and nickel compounds. They are found in the following materials: nepheline syenite, soda feldspar, alkaline frits, borax, soda ash, cryolite, sodium nitrate, sodium chloride, sodium silicate, lithium carbonate, spodumene, lepidolite, petalite, potassium feldspar, pearl ash, niter and most wood ashes.

Lead. Because of the often incorrect compounding of lead-fluxed glazes and the possibility of litigation over lead glaze use, lead has unfortunately been more or less banned from the ceramics studio. Lead has a strong and pleasant effect on most colorants, allowing pure colors to be developed; however, it is highly toxic, both in studio use and, if improperly compounded, sometimes in the fired glaze. Therefore, it must be handled with great care. Lead is the only flux that can be used to achieve some colors, particularly bright yellow, orange and red from chromium or uranium, bright grassy greens from

copper, and the sparkling, low-temperature aventurine or goldstone glazes employing iron. *Because of their potential toxicity, lead glazes should be for decorative use only, never applied to functional objects, even on the outside — with special emphasis on avoiding lead glazes on those objects made for storing acidic liquids.* Still, for purely decorative purposes and vibrant color at low temperatures, lead glazes are unsurpassed.

Boron usually is supplied to a glaze by the inclusion of colemanite, Gerstley borate, Cadycal 100, calcium borate frits, boron frits, boric acid or borax. It can be the main flux in a glaze and is similar to lead and the alkalines in its power. It is likely to cause a streaked or cloudy effect, which often is mottled with colorants.

Magnesia has a strong effect on surface texture, particularly in giving smooth, buttery or sugary matte surfaces. It also has a profound effect on color and can cause mauve, lilac and purple to develop from cobalt; salmon pink to gray from copper; and acid greens from nickel. In glaze batches, magnesia is provided by talc, dolomite or magnesium carbonate.

Zinc oxide always is used with other fluxes in a glaze, and it usually causes opaque and sometimes matte surfaces. It is a major performer in the development of crystalline glazes along with titanium or rutile. Its effect on colorants is quite strong, giving pastels from most colorants.

Barium is a strong flux, usually producing soft, silky or frosty mattes. When mixed with boron in a glaze, it usually turns to a more fluid, glassy state. It has a profound effect on most colorants, producing vibrant turquoise and blue from copper; red to purple from nickel; brilliant blue from cobalt; and mellow yellow from iron. The possibility of barium leaching from a glaze makes it a potentially hazardous material for functional ware. But for sculpture or nonutilitarian ware it can produce magnificently rich colors, particularly in electric firing.

Strontium is similar to barium in fluxing and color development effect. It is nontoxic, however, and can be used in place of barium when functional concerns have to be met. It should be used at the rate of 75 percent of the barium volume.

Familiarization with these materials, or even a few of them, and how they perform in a glaze or affect color development will pay dividends in expanding the potential of your work. Glazes really are not that complicated. When you start to work with materials in a logical way to learn about their behavior, practical experience and a healthy curiosity soon lead to good empirical understanding.

The ceramist's basic glaze materials number only about a dozen in common use, six to eight in limited use, and four to six in unusual use. Add to that the colorants and opacifiers, and you have the basic raw material to develop glazes for any clay body to be fired at any temperature in any type of kiln.

Glaze making can be as simple as cooking, only with different ingredients and a hotter oven. The basic concept is the same — mixing a number of ingredients together and cooking them. In cooking, a few ingredients do many things, like flour, butter, sugar, eggs, rice, vegetables, fruits and milk, the basic workhorses of the kitchen. Flavors are enhanced with small amounts of garlic, herbs, vinegar and spices. In ceramic glazes, the workhorses are feldspars, frits, clays and silica. The ceramic equivalent of garlic, herbs and spices are the fluxes, particularly those that are highly active and normally used in relatively small amounts, like lithium, fluorspar, cryolite, bone ash, wood ash, barium, zinc, magnesium and many colorants that do more than just color. An electric kiln is not much different from an electric oven; a gas kiln is not much different from a gas oven; and raku, salt, wood and sagger firings are closely aligned to a barbecue! Some forms of cooking are really easy; the heat is controlled by a number of switches and the cooking temperature is set for a specified amount of time. Others are a challenge and unpredictable, needing constant care and attention, or they will turn the ingredients to charcoal or slag. As with cooking, becoming familiar with the ingredients and the idiosyncrasies of the cooking method is the name of the ceramics game.

Ceramic glaze and color making is too vast a subject for anybody to know completely. However, if not having knowledge hampers your ability to realize what you visualize, you owe it to yourself to get the relevant knowledge! If you have a hunch or idea about how materials might work, try it and see! It is the best and most lasting way of learning, and it leads to a solid foundation of practical experience.

Specific color development is expanded on in Chapter 11. Parts of this chapter and Chapter 11 have been excerpted from my first book, "The Ceramic Spectrum," and from a series of six articles I wrote for "Ceramics Monthly" magazine in 1989 titled, "Color and the Ceramic Surface: Alchemy or Science." They currently are included in the "Ceramics Monthly Handbook 'Glazes: Materials, Recipes and Techniques,'" published in 2003 by The American Ceramic Society (http://www.ceramics.org). The articles are used by permission of The American Ceramic Society.

Color test bowls of crystalline glazes. Photo: Judi Dyelle.

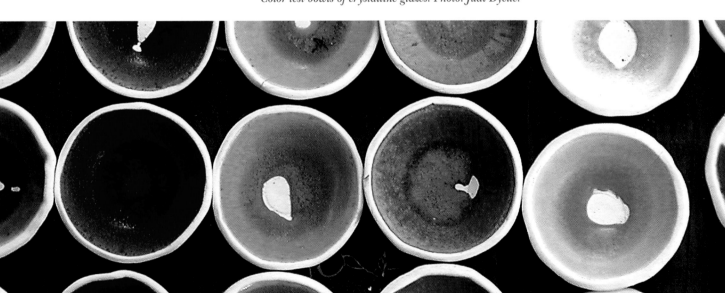

Part 2
PLASTIC AND LIQUID CLAY PROCESSES

Georges Jeanclos, France, "Untitled," sculpture, terra cotta, 1991.

The ceramic medium is a particularly interesting blend of art and science, painting and sculpture, function and nonfunction. With skillful manipulation, clay can be made to look like almost any material from flesh, bone, wood and stone to metal and beyond. It can be worked in many different stages and can be altered at any time, even hundreds of years after seeming to be completed. The qualities of clay sometimes are obvious and grounded, sometimes ethereal, but always challenging.

Before it gets to the firing stage of its development, any clay goes through a number of different states between wet and dry that suit different approaches to surface manipulation or mark making. These states would be described as fluid, liquid or slip; super-soft, wet or mushy; soft but not mushy; soft-malleable (bendable without cracking and impressionable); soft leather-hard (the texture of cheddar cheese, likely to crack in bending and easily cut), stiff leather-hard (would definitely crack when bent but can still be cut with sharp tools); surface dry (stiff leather-hard core); and bone dry. Finding the right tool and the right state are important discoveries that are part of the clay worker's learning curve.

Surfacing processes done before bisque firing, in what generally is referred to as the greenware state, often must occur within a short time frame to achieve the required result. This is when a super-thin plastic sheet, like that used in the dry cleaning industry, is invaluable to maintain the object at the most suitable state for any specific process. Damp boxes fulfill the same role. After bisque firing there is a far greater tolerance, and timing is nowhere as critical because bisque ware doesn't undergo constant change like greenware does in its drying stages. At the point of bisque firing, clay goes through a chemical change by the heat removal of chemically combined water; physical changes in the clay are arrested, continuing to change further only when the clay undergoes additional firing. Descriptions of post-bisque-firing processes start in Part 3.

Over time, you will gain comfort and confidence at many or all stages in the ceramic process and eventually select the clay state to use as part of the concept of the work itself. Although the ceramic surface almost certainly has more potential for development than any other visual art, with its huge variety of available decorative processes, chemical changes and transformations, there is always a point at which the clay and the tool are at their most compatible. The preferred sharpness or dullness of a tool for any specific job is, of course, a personal decision.

Part 2 explores the range of possibilities of working with clay at the pre-bisque-fired stages and shows images of work by artists who have chosen to do most or all of their surface enrichment processes at these stages, manipulating the clay in a variety of ways. There is always some overlap when trying to set parameters on manipulation processes. Artists often use a series of similar processes on a single object, making it difficult to focus on how the object was made and forcing the viewer or user to evaluate the object as a total entity. Chapters 6, 7 and 8 explore surface alteration by physical means. Chapter 9 explores liquid clays on the ceramic surface, and Chapter 10 deals with color variations integrated into the clay rather than just on the surface.

Invariably there are layers in the making of any ceramic object, and the final surface quality of an object is the result of the combination and interaction of these layers. Typical layers are:

- The clay;
- What's on top of the clay before the glaze (slips, sigillatas, engobes, underglazes);
- What goes on top of the glaze or glazes;
- How the object is fired; and
- Any post-glaze-firing processes to further enrich the object.

How simple or complex the process becomes is largely a matter of what the artist knows and wants to say with his work. The options are inexhaustible, restricted only by lack of vision, knowledge or experience.

Maya. Middle Classic 400 to 600 C.E. Clay, burnished and incised, rubbed with red pigment.
A priest contemplates the heavens. Rollout photograph © Justin Kerr.

CHAPTER 6

Marks of Slash, Scratch, Carve and Cut

An infinite variety of graphic marks can be made in soft clay through the use of a wide assortment of knives, forks, scalpels, welding rods, wire-ended or wooden modeling tools, sticks, bones, awls, needles, saws, wires, kitchen utensils and just about anything that can be creatively employed to produce an image, mark or sign. The nature of working with tools is such that artists usually develop favorites that seem to become extensions of their hands. Most potters and ceramic artists I know seem to have boxes of tools selected or made for specific processes of surface enrichment. They invariably are seeking the one tool that will out-perform all others, feel better in the hand or just be more pleasurable in use. Tools either can be purchased or found objects. In sensitive hands, sometimes the most unlikely looking implements give the greatest results. Almost any tool takes time to give out its secrets for best use, so continued play or exploration of potential is a given if you want to use tools to their optimum level. Slight variations of pressure, twist or movement can produce or reveal the most amazing complexity of marks from even the simplest of tools.

Tools and Methods

The tools that seem to perform best with either soft or leather-hard clay — the states where most slashing, scratching, carving and cutting is done — primarily are tools with sharp points or edges. Clays generally are abrasive, finely granular materials that quickly will take the edge off of softer metal tools. Most cutting tools perform best when kept sharp. The types of material used for ceramic tool making varies from fairly soft alloy metals to knife-quality steel and beyond, into tungsten carbide, a fine, very hard crystalline material.

The price of the tool often will indicate the quality. The better the quality, the more efficiently it will do the jobs required of it. Inexperienced clay workers often blame themselves for problems caused by tools that are inadequate for the job. Potters' tools that are packaged as beginner sets often make an already difficult process more so with unsatisfactory tools that quickly become dull from abrasion, causing unwanted "chattering," or bouncing, of the tool on the clay because it is too dull to cut properly.

The best tools usually are individually handmade

Photo: Eva Heyd

Marc Leuthold, USA, "Wheel," Anagama Series, 20" diameter, 2" thick, wood-fired stoneware, 2002.

by small companies that understand exactly what the potter needs from personal experience and discussion with the people who use them. Tools made from high-quality knife steel, such as those made by Dolan Tools, will outperform soft metal tools and keep an edge against the abrasive qualities of clay for a long time. Knife steel easily can be sharpened with a file to maintain a sharp cutting edge.

The best and most long-lasting edge on pottery cutting tools is provided by tungsten carbide, a material considerably harder than steel. Even though it is very hard, crystalline tungsten carbide is extremely brittle, and tools made from it should be used carefully. Avoid dropping these tools on hard surfaces, as they may break. Tungsten carbide tools usually are individually handmade by small companies, such as Bison Tools.

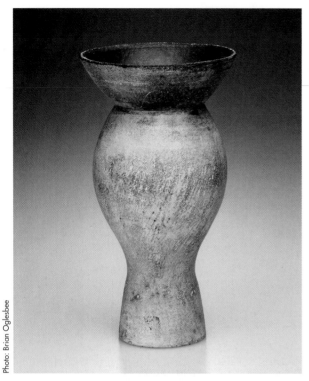

Photo: Brian Oglesbee

Hans Coper, UK, "Vase," stoneware, glazed, 17.8cm x 9.9cm, 20th century. David and Ann Shaner Collection, gift of David and Ann Shaner, Schein-Joseph International Museum of Ceramic Art, Alfred University, 1997.

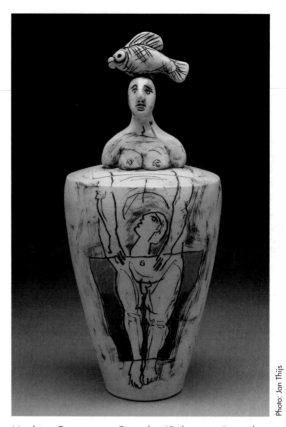

Photo: Jan Thijs

Matthias Ostermann, Canada, "Fisherman," jar, thrown and altered light earthenware, added hand-molded sculpture, clay sgraffito with wiped-down copper wash, added color vitreous engobes, 26cm high, 2002. Courtesy of Prime Gallery, Toronto.

Photo by the artist

Brad Schwieger, USA, "Cut Vase," wheel-thrown and altered stoneware, soda fired, glaze applied by spraying, 24" x 15" x 7", 2003.

Photo by the artist

Rick Malmgren, USA, "Vase," white stoneware fired in cone 6 reduction, Tenmoku and crawl glaze, ballpoint pen spring fastened in cheese slicer, faceted when wet during throwing, 9" x 8", 2000.

Photo: Richard Sargent

Catharine Hiersoux, USA, "Transitions," wood-fired rock vessel, thrown, altered, carved hand-built rock from a mix of clays, 20" tall.

Although more expensive than metal tools, the cutting quality of tungsten carbide tools is much better. They even are capable of trimming and cutting through bisque ware! Should they require sharpening, they can be returned to the company.

For the serious potter, tungsten carbide tools are probably the most satisfactory tools, turning what was often mundane work into sheer pleasure.

Buy the best tools you can afford, or make your own using the best materials you can afford.

Cutting

The way clay cuts depends on both the state of the material and the cutting tool. As a general rule when using knives and scalpels, the stiffer the clay, the more easily controlled the cut, and the softer the clay, the more resistance there will be to the cutting tool. Clay tends to cause the knife blade to drag by sticking to its surface.

Wire Cutting

The potter's wire is much more than a tool for separating a thrown pot from the wheelhead or throwing bat. It can be simply a flexible wire with a handle at each end, or it can be fitted into a handle similar to a small woodworker's bow saw and tightened to form a rigid cutting edge. Such a tool can have numerous interchangeable plain or twisted cutting wires to give a wide variation of possible cuts.

The twist wire shows multiple cuts that pick up on the features of the glaze, emphasizing the thick and thin qualities. Twisted wires with a much greater textural emphasis can be made from sprung wire curtain rod, which often is used for stringing kitchen curtains and usually is covered with a plastic coating. This can be found in old-fashioned hardware stores. After removing the plastic coating, the wire can be gripped with needle-nosed pliers and stretched to create a variety of wavelike patterns of

Photo: Sandi Pierantozzi

Neil Patterson, USA, "Bottle Form," wood-fired stoneware, 9" x 5" x 3", 2001.

Jim Connell, USA, "Red Sandblasted Carved Bottle," stoneware, cone 10, 17" x 6" x 6".

Photo: Peter Lee

Marta Matray Gloviczki, USA, "Yellow Flask" wall piece, gas fired in reduction, cone 10, 12" x 9" x 3".

grooves. Pulling this type of wire through soft clay and moving it from side to side will give a surface evocative of sandy beaches after the tide has receded. Using the process of slab making by throwing a block of clay on a hard surface, wire cutting it into slabs and pulling and stretching the sheets of soft textured clay on a hard surface allows for a great variety of expanded patterns.

Carving

Surface carving usually is done best with a variety of tools — from knives and gouges to wire-ended modeling tools — when the clay is leather-hard. The thickness of the objects to be carved should be considered carefully early in the process.

Surface Expansion

Creating linear images in soft slabs of clay or in soft thrown clay cylindrical forms and then pushing from beneath or inside the thrown form allows expansion of the image and textural development at the same time. Spraying or brushing the surface with a solution of sodium silicate and quick drying it with a blowtorch or heat gun while leaving the underside or inside of the form quite soft will produce remarkable surface textures when the clay expands from beneath or inside. Often resembling aged, tooled leather, these textured surfaces react well with thinly sprayed colorants or glazes or when fired in wood, salt or soda firing kilns.

Tearing

Ripping clay is best done when the clay is soft leather-hard. At this state it is easier to grip without sliding and to either gently tease apart or vigorously tear, depending on how you want it to look or feel. Clay often has a will of its own when being ripped, and sometimes a few guiding pinpricks along the tear line makes control somewhat easier.

Fluting

Fluting is the process of cutting decorative grooves into a clay surface. It is best done on leather-hard clay with wire-ended modeling tools of various shapes, bamboo tools with sharpened edges or metal tools with cutout sections and/or sharpened edges. If the

Photo by the artist

Jim Estes, USA, "Dusk," cone 9-10 oxidation reduction with dry ash glaze, glaze trailing, 15-½" x 15" x 15".

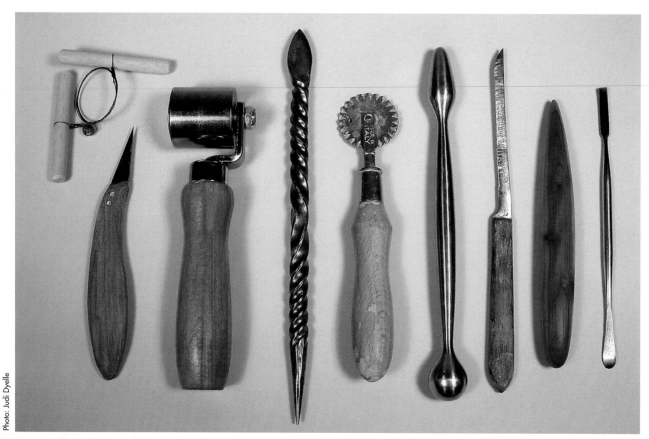

Photo: Judi Dyelle

Cutting and scratching tools.

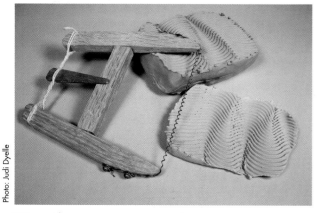

Photo: Judi Dyelle

Wire cut harp.

and time-consuming process.

On a round form, some people mark out exactly how many strokes are needed so the last and first strokes will be equally spaced. Others do it by eye, allowing the spacing to expand or contract as the last few cuts are made.

Fluting often leaves a burr at the edge of the cut mark. If this is undesirable, it can be removed in the leather-hard state with a damp sponge, or in the dry state with a soft, abrasive pad, such as a softened kitchen scouring pad.

Fluting doesn't necessarily have to be deep to be effective. The final quality of this type of mark usually lies with the glaze used over the top. If high-temperature fluted porcelain is covered with a transparent or translucent glaze such as a celadon, the fluting can be very shallow yet still visible because the glaze pools in the slight depressions, giving a variety of tones. Deep fluting is perhaps most effective with high contrast glazes, where there is a strong variation in color from thick to thin and the thinning glaze emphasizes edges dramatically. High iron content Tenmoku glazes that are dark brown to black when thick and almost orange when thin are a

clay is too soft, it may deform the object being fluted; if it is too hard, it may crack the surface or edges of the object. Fluting generally is done in a dragging motion, pulling down toward you in a clean, sweeping motion. The clay will cut cleanly and evenly at this stage if your tools are sharp. If the clay has started to change color or the surface is starting to dry, the tool is more likely to slide uncontrollably than cut easily. Unless you want loose grooving of the surface, fluting is a meticulous

Ron Meyers, USA, "Covered Jar," red earthenware, black glaze, gas fired at cone 04, appliqué drawing, 24" x 15", 1994.

Photo: Walker Montgomery

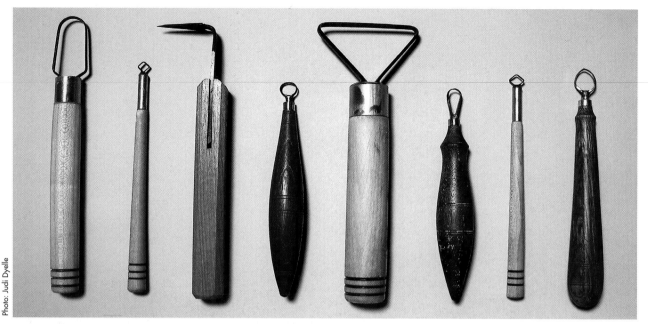

Photo: Judi Dyelle

Fluting tools.

Photo: Judi Dyelle

Fluted pitchers, bisque fired.

good example of high-contrast glazes.

Fluted surfaces often are enhanced greatly by wood, salt or soda firing. With suitable glazes, fluted surfaces can be further altered by sandblasting (see Chapter 19).

Pineapple or Crosscut Fluting

Another traditional form of fluting uses cuts in opposite directions, either diagonally, or vertically and horizontally. This generally is known as pineapple, or crosscut, fluting in reference to the diamond- or square-shaped protrusions left from the original surface. As described above, all fluted objects play beautifully with glazes across their surfaces, emphasizing edges and depths by various color or texture changes.

Faceting

Faceting is done by cutting the clay surface into a series of wide, flat planes. Cutting wires, large knives or carpenter's blades often are used for faceting, and the process is best done on clay between the soft and leather-hard states. Since faceting emphasizes flat planes and edges, it will be enhanced by glazes and the firing processes described for fluting.

Sgraffito

Sgraffito comes from the Italian word for scratch, and it describes the process of making marks by scratching designs into surfaces. The tools used for sgraffito are basically anything with a sharp point. A personal favorite of mine is a 9" length of welder's brazing rod ground to a point or chisel shape, then sanded smooth. The rod has a good heft in my hand, and it has a short length of rubber tubing to enhance the grip.

Sgraffito can be done directly into the clay, through a layer of slip or pigment or even through glazes. For artists who enjoy the drawing process, sgraffito is

Photo: Anne Rybak

Frank Boyden, USA, "Speaking with Herons," wood-fired porcelain, 11-½" x 8-¼", 2002.

Photo by the artist

Biliana Popova, USA, "Black Figures I & II," coil built black stoneware with inlaid white engobe, 21" x 18" x 9" and 16" x 9" x 9", 2003.

Photo by the artist

John H. Stephenson, USA, "Connect Six," terra cotta, thick white slip with inscribed lines, 14-½" x 14-¼" x 15-¼".

similar to drawing on paper with pen and ink or hard pencil. Sgraffito drawings made directly into the clay can be further enhanced by filling the lines with ceramic colorants. The colorants can be applied as a solution with water, then cleaned of the excess with a fine scouring pad. Or they can be applied with a ball of cotton wool and powdered color.

Since sgraffito processes often cause considerable dust, it is recommended that you wear a dust mask. Sgraffito through slips, engobes or underglazes into the body is best done at leather-hard through dry states. Sgraffito through the glaze and down to the bisque usually produces the best results when the glaze is still damp. A colored slip coating on the object before bisque firing often gives greater emphasis to the drawn design, particularly when it contrasts with the glaze color. Glazes for use with sgraffito processes should have at least 10 percent clay content to prevent possible crawling problems caused by glaze loosening from the bisque surface in the scratching process.

Ruthanne Tudball, England, "Two Bottles on Three Feet," wheel-thrown stoneware, flattened, faceted, dipped into black slip with ash glaze trailed on the front of the bottle, 14cm high, 2003.

Saw Blades, Cut Kidneys and Texture Tools

Saw blades; sections of saw blades; flat, metal kidneys with toothed edges; or notched tile installation tools all make great tools for producing sweeping multilinear marks, particularly on soft clay. As with the fluted surface, the marks made by toothed tools are greatly enhanced by many glazes and firing processes. Broken hacksaw and band saw blades can be recessed into wooden handles to make them easier to use. To increase the variation in the linear markings, some teeth can easily be removed with a file or carborundum grinder. The marks can be thought of as miniature fluting, done in a single sweep or movement.

Piercing

Piercing, or perforation, can be done with fine knives; metal tubes, usually brass; drill bits for wood or metal; or small, shaped brass tubes with retractable springs that push the cut pieces out of the tube. Timing is

Harris Deller, USA, "Cup, Volume Series with Concentric Arcs and Ovals," porcelain, 5-¼" x 5" x 4", 1998.

Photo: Bill Bachhuber

Jan Edwards, USA, "West Saanich Birdbrains," dyptich drawing on anagama fired porcelain, incised, stains, and sgraffito, 11-½" x 16-½" x 2", 2000.

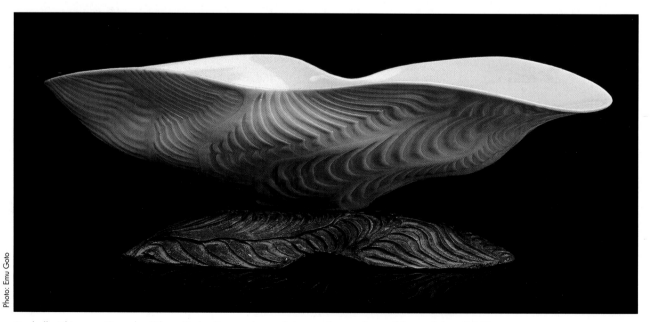

Photo: Emu Goto

Rachelle Chinnery, Canada, "Flores Series," carved porcelain, cast bronze base, 35cm x 24cm, 2003.

of the utmost importance when doing this type of work. It the clay is too soft, the object will deform or warp in subsequent firing. If it is too stiff, it likely will crack under the pressure of the piercing tool.

Fine filigree piercing also can be done after bisque firing when there is less likelihood of risk from breakage. Fine tungsten-tipped drill bits can be used in small Dremel or Foredom type drills. There likely will be a considerable amount of dust, so it's a good idea to wear a safety dust mask and glasses.

Cleaning

Any of the previously mentioned processes that create dust should prompt you to carefully clean the piece before firing or before glazing to prevent glaze application problems caused by dust or loose particle buildup. Crawling is the most serious of these problems. Small, stiff, coconut fiber brushes are available in multiple sizes in ceramic supply stores and are invaluable for cleaning such surfaces.

Jan McKeachie-Johnston, USA, "Vase," stoneware, kaolin slip, 8-½" x 6-½" x 4".

Laurie Rolland, Canada, "Circinate Series No. 2," hand-built using wooden push through mold, electric fired to cone 6, 49cm x 17cm x 29cm, 2003.

Late Classic 700 to 1000 C.E. Clay, paint, carved. A three-dimensional figure of a monkey is attached to the vase. A ruler holding a god K staff is surrounded with other world symbols. Rollout photograph © Justin Kerr.

CHAPTER 7

Marks of Addition and Removal

Adding or subtracting clay from the surface of a form produces what is termed low-relief decoration. Clay can be added to the background object by modeling, sprigging or other additive processes. Or it can be removed from the form by subtractive processes, such as fluting, faceting and carving described in the Chapter 6, as well as those methods given here. In either case, you end up with low relief, or a surface that has variation but is seldom higher than a half inch above or below the base level.

Low-relief surfacing can be a very good form of surface enrichment for trompe l'oeil, or deceiving the eye of the viewer by creating illusions of full-round modeling or elaborate perspective. Further enhancement of low-relief surfaces can be made by dusting on powdered colorants to fill crevices, cuts and corners in the deeper parts and by dry brushing white or colored slips on the more raised sections.

Glazes that emphasize edges and depth through color or texture change can enhance these surfacing variations. An obvious example of this is the lidded form by Elaine Coleman on page 92, where the blue celadon subtly emphasizes all of the slight depth variations in the carved porcelain. Low-relief or textured surfaces

also can be enhanced by side spraying the object (see Chapter 15) and angling the spray to hit the object from the side rather than the front. Side spraying the object on a turntable automatically will produce heavier glaze or color application on one side, increasing the illusion of depth.

Modeling

Modeling is either the direct manipulation of clay being applied to the surface of an object or the formation of an object that is totally produced as a modeled or sculptured work. Since clay is one of the most responsive natural materials, it has been used for form and decoration since man discovered its potential uses some 30,000 years ago. Small modeled, votive, ritualistic or symbolic religious or secular figures made of clay predate by some 20,000 years what archaeologists recognize as the first making of domestic pottery.

Modeling is best done with soft clay being attached to soft or leather-hard clay objects, often using scoring and liquid slip to ensure satisfactory adhesion. With most clays except porcelain, it is too late to attach modeled additions as soon as the clay has started to change color and exhibit a dryness, although it might still be

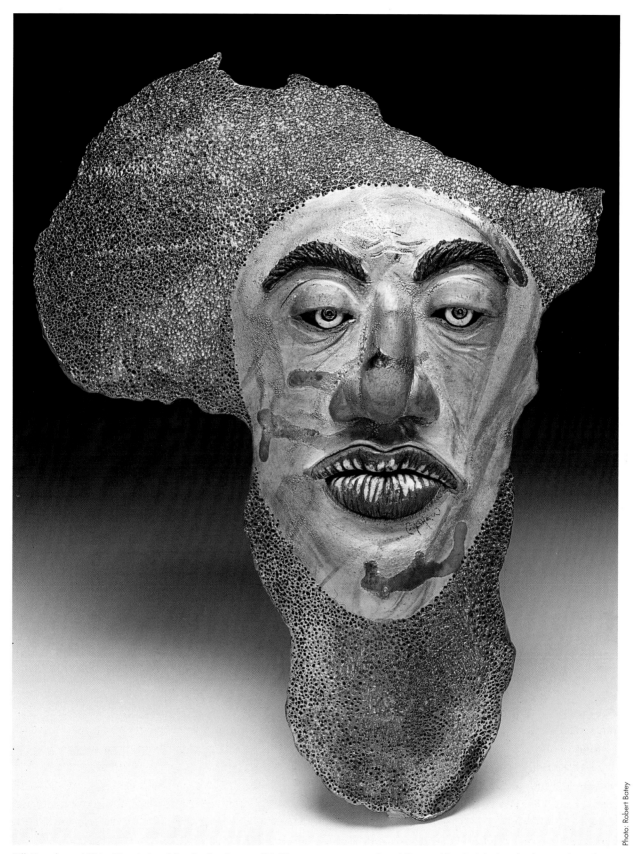

Photo: Robert Batey

Bill Capshaw, USA, "Say it Loud," raku fired cone 07, Hines patina poured and Tomats blue lightly brushed, pencil used for stipple texture, smoked in pine needles and newspaper lining inside trash can, 24" x 16", 2002.

possible to make subtractions, but with more difficulty. Some porcelain clays, certainly not all, can be joined together even in the bone-dry state by wetting the contact surfaces with either water or vinegar. Thorough testing of the working properties of a clay soon will determine what you can or cannot do with it. Dry joining is one of those tests.

Sprigging

A sprig is a small, decorative element made from soft clay pressed into a small mold, lifted out on a spatula and applied to the surface of a leather-hard form to create a low-relief decoration. Sprigs are made of individual modeled pieces or found objects from which plaster casts are taken. The casts allow the easy creation of multiples.

The most historically famous and recognizable use of sprigged decoration is that of Wedgwood Jasperware from England, which has different colored sprigs applied to a variety of colored clay bodies. The most famous variation is that of cream to white sprigs on a blue background. Although it is still being made, the origins of this ware go back to the mid to late 1700s, a period of great interest in classical Greece and Rome, when Josiah Wedgwood made ceramic replicas of a famous Roman cameo glass amphora called the "Portland Vase." The glass original is deep purple with white glass cameo and is in the British Museum in London. Achieving the complexity of design used on these ceramic pieces often takes a large number of small, individual units that together create the full patterns. The outside of these pieces usually is unglazed but high fired.

Sprigged decoration also is found on a great deal of salt-glazed stoneware pottery from England, France and Germany, and it became part of the North American tradition through the products of itinerant immigrant potters from Europe.

Dipping and Draping

The process of dipping or soaking textiles, lace, ribbon, crochet, net, burlap, wool fiber, soft cotton ropes, newspaper or organic materials in liquid clay and applying the slip-soaked material to leather-hard forms to produce interesting textures often is referred to as *dip and drape*. The organic matter burns out during the bisque firing, leaving an imprint of itself. At this stage it is quite fragile. Once fired to a high temperature, it can be quite strong,

Photo: Mark Mamawal

James C. Watkins, USA, "Tea Pot," raku fired, 15″ x 12″, 1996.

Photo by the artist

Halldor Hjalmarson, USA, "Cholla & Hummingbirds," covered jar with sprigs of hummingbirds, insects and cholla cactus, neutral adhering slip oversprayed with several semi-transparent glazes, stoneware, cone 10 reduction, 15″ tall.

Diane Sullivan, Canada, "Covered Jar: Smilacina Racemosa," stoneware, cone 6 reduction, wheel-thrown lid, neck and foot, press-molded and carved body at leather-hard stage, sprigged berries, 24" x 9", 1994.

Richey Bellinger, USA, "Oval Vase," porcelain, liquid clay relief, cone 10 reduction, 11" x 7", 2003.

Silvie Granatelli, USA, "Pitcher," carved leather-hard clay, fired cone 10 in gas kiln, 8" x 5" x 3", 2003.

Ah Leon, Taiwan, "Annual Rings," teapot, stoneware, 2000.

Ah Leon, Taiwan, "Bonsai," stoneware.

even in the form of ceramic lace. This process has been used for at least 200 years to create decorative lacy effects on costumed figurines from many of the court potteries and porcelain companies of Europe.

Only materials with natural fibers should be employed in dipping and draping because synthetic fibers will not absorb the slip in a satisfactory way, causing extreme fragility in the bisque state. Colored slips can be used for added interest or emphasis. The use of deflocculated or casting slips (see Chapter 9), which have approximately a third less water-to-clay ratio to make them fluid, may improve the amount of clay in the draped material. This will give a slightly more substantial coating and consequently greater strength. Casting slips also can be colored.

Washed Wax

Another interesting method of surface removal, particularly for those adept with brushes, is to paint resist on dry greenware. When the resist has hardened, it is sponged over with a damp sponge to remove the background and leave the brushwork pattern raised but intact. Resist materials used for this process are either hot wax or shellac, both of which will burn away during the bisque firing. Latex resist will not work properly

since it is fragile and will not take repeated washings with the sponge.

The choice of resist depends on how many layers might be required. Hot wax is more fragile than shellac and generally dries much faster, but the shellac surface is harder and will take more washings. Shellac can be purchased in the paint and varnish departments of most hardware stores. Brushes used for shellac need to be cleaned after use in a brush cleaner solvent.

Working on fine porcelain with layers of washed shellac resist is a primary surface enrichment method used by Arne Åse of Norway (see page 93). He often uses this process with delicate coloration from the use of soluble colorants (see Chapter 11).

Washed resists can be done on any clay. Textured, sandy or grogged clays can produce some particularly interesting results from dry surface washing; the heavier the texturizing materials in the clay, the more animated the surface will be. The process of throwing grogged clays usually brings the finer clay particles to the top, leaving the heavier particles in the core. Resists on that top coating will leave a fine surface, where washing away the background will expose the grog or sand. The result can be a very beautiful combination of rough and smooth surfaces, which can be further enhanced with

Photo: Judi Dyelle

Photo courtesy of the artist

Gay Smith, USA, "Crossed Jar," porcelain, thrown, altered, faceted or cut with wire tools when wet on the wheel, soda fired, 8-½" x 6-½", 2003.

Robert Turner, USA, "Owerri II," stoneware, glazed, 2000. Promised gift of Dr. and Mrs. Marlin Miller, Jr., Schein-Joseph International Museum of Ceramic Art, Alfred University.

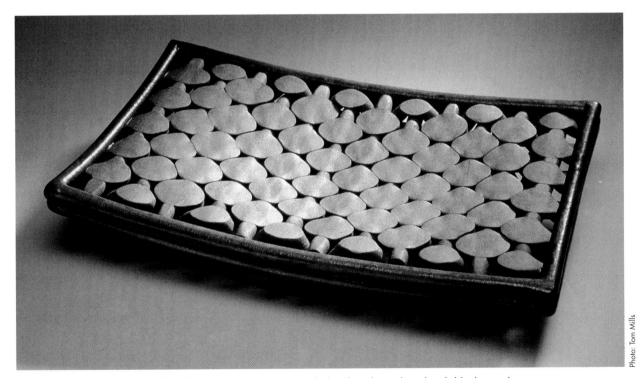

Photo: Tom Mills

Jan Schachter, USA, "Woven Plate," stoneware, woven extruded coils, edges glazed with black wood ash glaze, 3-½" x 10-½" x 18", 2001.

Photo courtesy of the artist

Hank Murrow, USA, "Bowl," porcelain, wire cut.

terra sigillatas (see Chapter 9), glazes or various firing processes.

Burn-Aways

The reverse of putting grog or sand in clay to create uneven raised and gritty surfaces would be to include organic materials that burn out, leaving an intriguing surface of pitted, holed or seemingly insect-eaten surfaces. Additives and combinations of such materials as sawdust, coffee grounds, broken nutshells, uncooked popcorn, millet, rice, pearl barley, dried seeds, lentils, etc. all will produce very interesting burnout materials that leave great textures often reminiscent of travertine marble. Some synthetic products, such as polystyrene or nylon beads and fibers, also can be used to burn out and create texture.

Good ventilation in the kiln area is a must when doing burn-aways because noxious smells often develop.

Although not strictly burnout materials, glass beads

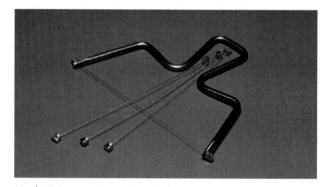

Hank Murrow's wire cutting tool.

can produce interesting surfaces. Depending on the final firing temperature, small, fine glass beads (sometimes referred to as seed beads) can be incorporated into the clay or added to the surface. If added to the surface, they should be rolled in place with a small roller or printmaker's brayer. As the temperature in the kiln rises, the beads will fuse and melt. The higher the temperature, the greater the melt, until a fluid vertical linear pattern forms, controlled by volume and gravity. The closer to

Clive Tucker, Canada, "Rainbow Cookie Jar," thrown porcelain, sprayed glazes, fired to cone 6 in oxidation, chattered on the wheel with trimming tool, 8" x 12", 2002.

Photo by the artist

Lee Middleman, USA, "Sunflower, Winter Series," high-fire white stoneware, thrown and textured, double glazed, electric fired to cone 10, 26cm x 15cm, 2002.

Photo: Tom Mills

Linda McFarling, USA, "Yanomi," white stoneware, faceted, thrown, red slip and sprayed ash, salt and soda fired, 4" x 3-½" x 3-½", 2003.

vertical the object is, the more the melted beads will run. Glass beads are available in a wide range of colors, sizes and prices. The textures may be further enhanced by subsequent layering of terra sigillata, pigment, glaze, wood ash, salt or soda deposits. To protect the kiln shelves, be careful to place the objects on a fire clay pad or piece of old kiln shelf covered with alumina hydrate or kiln wash made of 50 percent kaolin and 50 percent silica.

Sandblasting

Sandblasting, grit-blasting and air-erasing are surface enrichment procedures more often used in the decorative processes of glass than clay. These same processes are used for cleaning buildings and engraving grave markers. A high-pressure jet of sand is projected at an object, removing the surface through abrasion. In clay or glass studios, sandblasting usually is done in specially designed cabinets with glove inserts for holding the object, a window for viewing it, lights for illuminating the progress and a nozzle for directing the

Richard Hensley, USA, "Teapot," porcelain, molded with drips, cone 10, 13" x 6" x 6", 2002.

jet of sand either through a fixed nozzle or a spray gun. Safety glasses and dust masks always should be worn when sandblasting.

Various types of sand can be used for coarse or fine jets. The sand jet literally eats off the surface of the clay or glaze — or whatever comes in its path.

To create images by sandblasting, objects usually are masked with masking, duct, or other tape to resist the abrasion. Patterns and designs are made with a resist of some sort, either a latex sheet as used in stonemason's workshops, or with masking tape. Unless a major amount of cutting is being done, masking tape is quite resilient, as its slightly spongy surface bounces as the abrasive sand hits it. Larger images can be cut from heavy plastic or a rubber sheet and temporarily glued to the surface of the object with rubber cement.

An air-eraser is basically a miniature spray gun or airbrush with a hopper for erasing compound mounted above the hardened steel or tungsten spray tip. This tool for doing fine, well-controlled work is held like a pen and pointed at the surface approximately 3" or 4" away. A pressure release button controls the force of spray.

Mathew Metz, USA, "Box," terra sigillata, sgraffito on porcelain, wood fired, salt glaze, cone 10.

91

William Brouillard, USA, "Carved Casserole," stoneware, cone 10 reduction, 14" x 14" x 10", 2003.

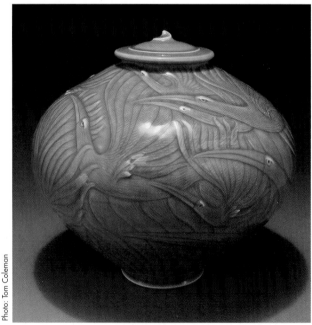

Elaine Coleman, USA, "Crane Jar," incised porcelain with added porcelain to surface, blue celadon glaze, fired cone 10 in reduction, 11" x 11", 2003.

Erasing compounds usually are made from fine zircon or alumina sand that is sprayed under pressure at the surface of the object. A small, one-quarter horsepower compressor is fine for work that is suitable for the air-eraser.

Sandblasting and air-erasing can create very interesting surfaces that look like they may have been etched with acid. Used very lightly, the sandblasted surface can appear as though a fine mist covers the blasted areas, while heavy blasting can eat completely through considerable thicknesses of clay or bisque. Using sandblasting, you can remove the skin of glaze or cut right down into the clay.

Different qualities can be achieved by sandblasting at different times in the making process. If it is done at the bone-dry stage, the edges will be soft and rounded. When done on either bisque or glazed ware, the edges are likely to be sharp and crisp. Sandblasting into colored clays can produce interesting effects. For example, the unglazed surface of a porcelain clay stained with a black

Sandra Byers, USA, "Open Light Dancer," porcelain, wheel-thrown, carved at leather-hard stage, calcium matte glaze, fired cone 9.5 in electric kiln, cooled slowly, 2-¾" x 2-½" x 2-½", 2003.

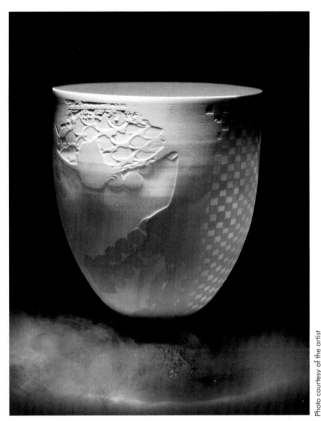

Arne Åse, Norway, "White Bowl," Limoges porcelain, washed shellac resist.

stain that contains cobalt and manganese will, after a reduction firing, have a different color than the core of the clay. Depending on the quantity of colorant in the clay, the surface will be black, dark brown or dark gray, and the core most likely will be blue or blue-gray. By sandblasting through the skin of the clay, the core is exposed, giving interesting black on blue results.

Sandblasting can be used to create a delicate textured surface when done very lightly over a glaze. It must be done with a great deal of care, as the process is very fast, and there is no reversing it.

For more information on sandblasting, refer to Chapter 19.

Late Classic 700 to 1000 C.E. Clay, paint. Three-dimensional figures applied to the walls of the vase. A Maya view of the heavens. The figures may represent constellations. Rollout photograph © Justin Kerr.

Maya Terminal Classic, 1000 to 1300 C.E. Clay, mold made, rubbed with red pigment.
Monkeys gather cacao pods as a man wrestles a monkey to take the pod. Rollout photograph © Justin Kerr.

CHAPTER 8

Marks of Impression

The subject addressed in this chapter is impressed patterns or marks, those made with stamps or a wide variety of tools and found objects. These include fired clay or plaster stamps, sticks, bones, fossils, shells, nutshells, linocuts, woodcuts, routed wood, natural wood and bark textures, stone surfaces, electrical and electronic circuitry boards, polystyrene grocery meat trays, carved fiber-printing blocks, roulette wheels, small gear wheels or cogs, clock and watch parts, textured rollers and rolling pins, paddles, strings and ropes, plastic mesh, shoe soles and just about anything that makes a mark by pushing it into the soft, receptive clay surface. Once you start to play with making a good impression, you always will be on the lookout for suitable tools and texturing devices to make marks that truly are individual and personal. The potential is endless.

Impressions generally work better when the tool is slightly porous, such as bisque-fired clay, wood or fiber. Metal, glass and other nonporous materials tend to stick in soft clay. To rectify this problem, it always is possible to make plaster casts from the original and press the clay into the cast. Clean up the rough edges, then fire to a hard but porous bisque state.

One of the great qualities of any type of impressed pattern in clay is that the impression can be greatly emphasized or enhanced by whatever goes on top of it. Depending on the desired result, this enrichment can be achieved with terra sigillatas (see Chapter 9), brushed or powdered colorants, pooled glazes and further surface development from firing processes such as wood, salt and soda. Glaze or color gets deep into the impressions, often making them look even deeper and more mysterious.

One artist who has utilized the impressed surface in a large body of her work and has written about it in depth is Lana Wilson of California. Here she describes the stamp-making processes she uses and teaches to others. This article first was published in "Claytimes Magazine" and is reproduced with permission. The illustrations are by Martha Naranjo.

Tools of impression.

STAMPS

By Lana Wilson©

There are three different piles of stamps in my studio: 1) keep and use; 2) almost good; and 3) in the trash. It is worth spending time making images and designs carefully. If the image is good, it will be reused many times.

I use any available clay except porcelain, because it cracks too easily. Some people like to mix plaster in a paper cup and then carve on the plaster to create stamps. I find plaster stamps wear down with use, but bisqued clay ones do not. Stamps less than $1/2$" thick easily break when pressed firmly into clay to make a fully detailed impression, so I make stamps about $3/4$" thick and in a square or a rectangular shape. One student made circular stamps that worked very well grouped together. No matter what shape stamps are, the edges need to be clean; edges show very clearly as part of the pressed image. The biggest convenient size seems to be about 3" to 4" square, but that size only applies to stamps pressed into clay. If you make a 7" square stamp, it actually functions best as a mold. You can put a slab of clay on top of it, then roll on the back of the soft slab to press the clay into the mold or stamp.

Useful tools to gather when making stamps include chopsticks, a Phillips-head screwdriver, double circles on the ends of some pens, square ends of wooden matches, jewelry, kitchen tools, shop tools, etc. To think of images and patterns, you might want to look at books about illuminated manuscripts of Ireland; Matisse's shapes in his Jazz series; plant and flower parts; ethnic jewelry books; fabric patterns from Japan, Africa and Bali; patterns on exotic fish and birds; geologic formations; etc.

Some of the basic fabrications for making stamps are listed below, but don't pay too close of attention to these directions. Start working and experiment profusely.

1. Select a patterned area from a large, decorated slab.

- Texture a large slab of clay by pulling a serrated edge across the surface; rolling a rock, seed or bamboo across the slab; or pushing different tools into the surface.

- Move an empty photo slide frame (or make a paper frame) over the textured slab until you find an intriguing design. Consider looking for a variety of sizes of marks or diagonal or checkered organization of the marks. Cut out any potential stamps you like.

2. Press tools or images into soft clay.

- Press a chopstick, tool or textured object into soft clay. You might try putting small balls of clay into the negative spaces or holes created by the chopstick impression. Press the tiny balls of clay with a Phillips-head screwdriver or the end

of a pen. This will secure the balls and also add detail to the stamp. Patterns can be random or a repeated design.

- Any object can be pressed into the clay. An image like this hand can be enhanced by pressing in tools with different tiny shapes.

3. Create multiple depth levels in stamps.

- Creating different depths in a stamp can be done by adding a coil on top or cutting away with a pencil or a loop tool. Attach the coil by rolling it firmly in place or scoring it.

4. Create raised, drawn line images.

- Drawing in clay makes a stamp that creates an appealing raised embossed line when the stamp is pressed into clay. Try drawing with tools of different end widths for richer variety of line quality.

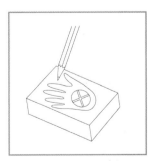

- Drawing on a concave curved slab means that further

variations of lines appear when you open the concave slab to a flat slab.

5. Carve in leather-hard clay.

* Make various sizes of 1" thick rectangles (or any shape) and let them set up until they are leather-hard. I speed up the drying process by using a hair dryer or heat gun (I wonder how many other clay people are as impatient as I am?). Use a carving tool to make lines at least $\frac{1}{16}$" deep. On leather-hard clay, you

have good carving control to make clean lines without the distortion or burrs that happen when carving in soft clay.

* Make V- or U-shaped carving lines in the clay to eliminate undercuts that can cause small rips in the image and difficulty in release.

6. Press cardboard into clay.

* An effective way to make an original image is to draw something on cardboard and cut it out. Press the cardboard image $\frac{1}{16}$" down into soft clay. You can turn the image over and have a right and left image.

* For more detail, press tools, like a square matchstick, inside the outline.

7. Make and use mother stamps.

Occasionally I make a stamp that doesn't make a good image when pressed into clay, and the only way to get a good stamp from it is to make a second stamp off the original. I use the negative stamp taken off the first (mother) stamp.

* Make an image the way you want the stamp to look. Unlike the negative image stamps made in Steps 1 through 6, this stamp will be the positive mother stamp.

* Bisque fire the mother stamp, then press it into clay. This second stamp, or negative, is the one you will use. Often I can't wait, and I press the unbisqued mother stamp into clay. Sometimes I break the original unbisqued clay stamp. But pressing the unbisqued stamp into clay also allows me to change the mother stamp, especially if it is leather-hard and not bone dry.

* Many stamps that are good as negative images can have a stamp made off of them, giving you a positive and negative of the same pattern.

8. Create roll stamps.

You've probably seen small bas-relief beads that can be rolled across clay to make repeated patterns. You can make larger versions of these by making even cylinders about 1" in diameter x 3" or 4" long. Press marks into this coil, and wait until it is leather-hard and carve into it. Here is another intriguing possibility to make a rolled image that does not repeat itself too often.

* Throw a straight cylinder about 4" diameter x 5" long. Or wrap a slab of clay around a glass jar or PVC pipe (covered in cut strips of newspaper so you can get the clay off) to create about the same proportions as the thrown cylinder. Both of these should have walls $\frac{3}{4}$" to 1" thick so you can carve into them later.

* Bisque the cylinder, then roll it across clay, pressing firmly. You can put a rolling pin or dowel inside the cylinder to help press down very firmly as you roll it over the clay. I find roll stamps very useful to do backgrounds where I want patterns that are not repeated.

People who throw can make several stamps the same size. One stamp can be pressed on the outside while another one is pressed in the same spot on the inside. It is helpful to have stamps in different sizes. A $\frac{3}{8}$" square stamp is useful for filling in small spaces left from solidly stamping clay with different sizes of stamps.

Stamps are like spaghetti dinners. The good ones take twice the time but are beyond twice as good. I still make about five stamps a week, and some are delicious.

Lana Wilson is an internationally respected artist, author and educator from Southern California. Her distinctive hand-built work is represented in public and private collections worldwide.

Sticks and Wood

Any piece of wood or stick that leaves an interesting impression is valuable. Building supply stores and carpenter finishing stores have a remarkable supply of wood moldings cut in lengths of profiled, milled stock. Small broken lengths often are available for a few cents. The range of shapes is huge, from simple quarter-round, half-round and dowels of different sizes to small decorative stock and larger moldings for architectural detail. Look at the profiles to see if they might suit your intended imagery.

Soft woods, such as pine or spruce, often are useful for creating raised grain pattern. The crosscut wood ends show both soft and hard tissue, or grain. If the wood ends are soaked in water for a few days, then brushed with a wire brush, the soft tissue will be removed, leaving the hard grain standing. Sometimes burning the end of the wood with a blowtorch will do the same thing, because the soft grain burns more quickly. Either method can produce good stamp or texture-making tools. Cut lengths of different diameter bamboo culms can be used for circular or near-circular impressions. Old Chinese brush handles work very well here.

Bones

The knobby ends of bones have been used to decorate pottery surfaces since prehistoric times in almost all early pottery-making cultures. The rocking movements of the bone have left graphic pathways across many a pot or shard. Different sizes of bones and bones from different parts of the bodies of animals or birds can create an unlimited range of marks. Some bones are quite fragile in use but can be hardened by firing them to a bisque temperature or above. I have a collection of animal bones that have been fired to cone 10. At this point they are almost as hard as porcelain and make really interesting impressions.

Fossils, Seashells, Nutshells, Etc.

Fossil and seashell impressions make wonderful images with their soft curves and radial patterns. A huge range of textural surfaces are found on fossils and shells. Since they are produced from calcium, they are hard and resistant to abrasion and breakage. They can be further hardened by firing to bisque temperature, but will likely break down if fired higher than cone 04.

Hard, textured casings, such as those from walnut, pecan, Brazil and cashew nuts, can be useful. Other natural texture makers, such as wood and bark, often include expanding radial patterns from worm, termite, carpenter ant and beetle chewings, providing much potential for natural pattern. When impressed into a soft clay surface, these markings offer intriguing glimpses into the world of nature.

Man-made textures from fiber also are valuable, particularly those with an open weave like burlap, lace and patterned crochet, or those with built-in raised patterns, such as corduroy or canvas. Heavily textured or embossed wallpapers also can be good sources of impressions on a large scale. These may often be available from paint or interior decoration stores or departments.

Photo by the artist

Halldor Hjalmarson, USA, "Bowl with Impressed Apache Trout," stoneware, bisque stamp of trout impressed onto wet clay, cone 10 reduction, 8" diameter.

Photo: Ken Mayer

Celia Rice-Jones, Canada, "Thrown and Altered Dish," stoneware, ash glaze over impressed surface, impressed textural handles, 10-½" x 9" x 2-½", 2003.

Photo: Julian Beveridge

Kathi R. Thompson, Canada, "Crustacean Pitcher," porcelain, 7" x 8". 1996.

Photo: Neil Patterson

Sandi Pierantozzi, USA, "Teapot," slab built, earthenware, 7" x 8" x 5", 2002.

Photo by the artist

Susan D. Harris, USA, "Armadillo Ewer," black stoneware, hand-built with thrown and press-molded additions, impressed decorations, reduction cooled, 9" x 15" x 3", 2003.

Photo courtesy of the artist

Katrina Chaytor, Canada, "Coffee Pot with Creamer and Sugar Bowl," cone 6, stain and glazes, coffee pot, 10" x 7" x 6", 2003.

Stone

The surfaces of rock and stone can be rather intriguing, having acquired a series of surface variations and abrasions through their geologic journeys over eons of time. Different types of rock — igneous, sedimentary and metamorphic — will break in a variety of ways, depending on their natural cleavage and the direction of the break. Sedimentary rocks, such as limestone, sandstone and shale, were formed from multilayering. They often leave particularly interesting surface texture, sometimes including fossils.

Linocuts, Woodcuts and Routered Boards

Linocuts and woodcuts are two simple forms of printmaking. The design is drawn on the surface of special linoleum, synthetic cutting blocks or plywood boards. The lines and textures are then cut into the surface using a combination of sharp knives and gouges. The tools and materials for printmaking are easy to find in most art supply stores. In making a print on paper, the top surface of the cut block is inked with a roller, the paper is laid on top and either run through a press or hand rubbed to develop the image left by the cut marks.

Pressing printing blocks into the clay leaves a raised or embossed line from the cut marks, and what would have been the printing surface becomes the background plane. These methods of decoration are very useful for repetitive patternmaking for tiles or any usage where repeat embossed patterns might be needed.

A carpentry tool called a router is wonderful for high-speed cutting of designs, lines and textures into wood. Routers have a wide range of cutting bits to cut many types and thicknesses of line. Routers can be used as speedy mechanical gouges to cut designs into the wood surface at predetermined depths, and these cut boards can then be used in exactly the same way as linocuts or woodcuts.

Circuitry Boards, Carved Textile Printing Blocks and Grocery Trays

The circuitry boards inside machines, such as computers, provide a wonderful resource of linear images with a contemporary flair, very much part of late 20th and early 21st century patterns. Because they tend to bend in use, it's best to glue them to a paddle or board. Clay can then be pressed onto the texture, or forms can be beaten with the textured paddles.

You often can find old carved blocks made for printing patterns on cloth in India or China. The wood is a very durable hardwood, perhaps teak, that has been cut so the background is removed, leaving a raised linear design for printing.

These carved blocks usually have paisley, floral or arabesque patterns for details and various grid designs for all-over decoration. When used on clay, the design is impressed into the surface, which is opposite of linocuts or woodcuts, where the background is pressed into the clay, leaving a raised cut line.

An array of regular dimpled, gridded and crosshatched patterns can be found on the polystyrene or Styrofoam meat and fish trays used by many grocery stores.

These also can be glued to wooden paddles or boards to give greater stability, or plaster casts can be made from them for a more durable surface.

Carved Bisque Molds

Wheel-thrown bowls trimmed to form an upturned hemisphere have been used for centuries to carve motifs into as a form of repeat patterning on the interior of bowls. The upturned hemisphere is carved with designs

Photo by the artist

Patrick Crabb, USA, "Chichen's Competition," press mold with extruded handle, details achieved from stiffened clay pressed against inside walls of box mold, 28" x 16" x 8", 2002.

Photo courtesy of the artist

Kathryn Finnerty, USA, "Flower Holder with Architectural Images," terra cotta, slab built, white slip, slabs are rolled onto plaster tablets that have been incised with designs, 15" x 8" x 4", 2003.

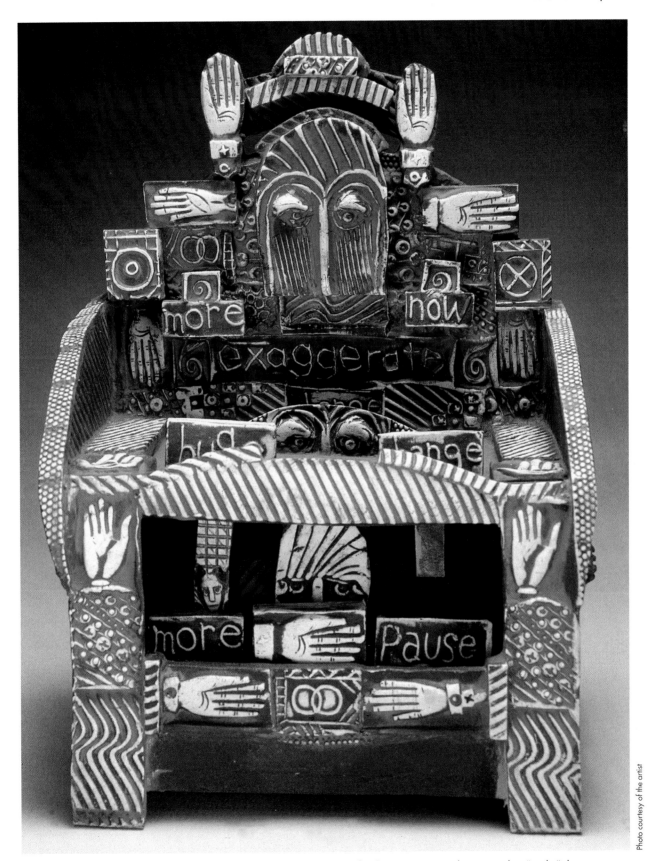

Lana Wilson, USA, "Altar of Changing Messages," white stoneware fired to cone 6, words are on clay "sticks" that can be picked up and turned around to show different words, 11" x 8" x 6", 1996.

at the leather-hard stage, left to dry, then bisque fired. The mold is placed on a potter's wheel, and a slab of soft clay is then applied to the mold and pressed down over the mold where the reversed impression of the carved design is transferred to the soft clay. Cut-in lines and concave carvings become raised lines and convex areas. A huge number of Chinese bowls from as long ago as the 10th century have been made this way. They are often hand fluted on the reverse side of the bowl and covered with translucent pale gray-green to olive celadon glazes. The depth of the carving emphasizes the color of the glaze.

Roulette Wheels, Textured Rollers and Rolling Pins

Lana Wilson talked about making ceramic roller stamps in her article earlier in this chapter. Rollers made with other materials can be very useful for the development of impressed or embossed images or patterns. Visit a paint store to find small, blank wooden rollers designed for smoothing wallpaper seam lines. Lines or texture easily can be cut into the wood with saws, knives or gouges, or burnt with wood-burning tools. If the wooden roller is varnished, the varnish should be removed with paint stripper to prevent the roller from sticking or sliding on the clay surface.

Printmaker's brayers, available in art supply stores, are rubber-coated rollers up to approximately 8" long and about 1" in diameter. The rubber surface easily can be cut or burned.

Some kitchenware stores sell patterned pastry rollers or rolling pins. The precut patterns usually are simple, but they can be very effective, particularly when later emphasized with glaze, terra sigillata or pigment or by firing processes that maximize the qualities of the raised or lowered surface texture.

Paddles, Strings and Ropes

Paddles are usually made from fairly thick plywood or wooden board up to $^3/_4$" thick and cut into paddle profiles with a jigsaw or band saw. The exact shape is personal taste. The surface of the paddle can be cut with saws, knives or gouges; soaked and wire-brushed; or burned and brushed to reveal the harder grain of the soft wood. The textured and patterned surfaces also can be glued on as described earlier.

To form interesting paddled surfaces, glue and/or

Photo: Tim Wickens

Chandler Swain, Canada, "Jug," stamped, stretched, cone 6 porcelain, stained with watery underglazes, covered with diluted glaze, 15" high.

staple dense rope or cord to the paddle faces. These paddles can be used on soft leather-hard surfaces and delivered with a sharp, quick hit to get the best impression.

Cords and ropes also can be draped on soft clay surfaces and rolled into place with smooth rollers. A well-known process of rolling short lengths of decorative rope decorative stamps, produce beautiful, subtle results. To experience the variety of this form of ceramic surface decoration, look at Korean pottery from the Koryo Dynasty (A.D. 918 to 1392) and early Punch'ong ware from the Choson or Yi Dynasty (A.D. 1392 to 1910).

Plastic Mesh Screens

Different sizes and thicknesses of polyethylene mesh can be used for grid-like, diagonal and scale-like indentations. Hardware, gardening and building supply stores often have many varieties and sizes of mesh that can usually be purchased by either the square foot or running foot. It's easier to handle small pieces of mesh, and since they don't deteriorate in use, they should last a long time. They are best placed on the soft clay and rolled into the surface with a small roller or brayer.

Silhouettes and Shoeprints

Shapes can be cut in cardboard, foam-filled cardboard, linoleum or rubber sheeting and also rolled into the surface of soft clay.

Shoeprints can be very interesting. Paul Soldner, one of the best known of American ceramics artists, often uses the combination of impressed figurative silhouettes taken from contemporary magazine photographs glued to thick card and impressed into clay that has been literally stomped on with heavily textured running shoes. Fired in low-fire salt or soda firing, Soldner's images represent current issues.

Etcetera

It should be obvious by now that almost anything can be used to make impressions in soft clay. Further manipulation of the impressed image can be made by stretching the image through, throwing out and extending soft clay slabs on a hard surface, sometimes coated with a powdered clay that has been sieved onto the working surface. A small kitchen strainer is ideal for this. This process encourages decorative cracking and granulation of the clay surface.

John W. Hopkins, USA, "Jar with Leaf," porcelain, cone 10, 18" x 8" x 8".

on the clay surface, then filling the resulting impressions with white or black colored slip inlay is known by the Japanese name of Mishima, although it was in Korea where the (Punch'ong) process was first developed. When covered with clear, translucent or celadon type glazes, these inlaid textures, often in conjunction with

Photo courtesy of the artist

Claudia Bergen, Canada, "Mr. Spratt's Extended Family," porcelain paper clay, slab and coil construction, oxidation fired cone 6, 16-¾" x 5-½" x 2-½", 18" x 5-½" x 2-½", 22-½" x 6-¼" x 2-½", 2001.

Jim Etzkorn, Canada, "Platter," rope corded, incised, sprigged, and stamped, cone 10 reduction, 12" diameter, 2002.

Les Miley, USA, "Porcelain Jar with Lid," wheel-thrown, indentations and stamped impressions, cone 9 reduction, turquoise glaze, 8" x 6", 2003.

Richard T. Notkin, USA, "20th Century Solutions Teapot: Nobody Knows Why — Yixing Series," stoneware, glaze, 9-⅜" x 15-⅞" x 11", 2003.

Tom Turner, USA, "Large Lidded Jar," porcelain, thrown in two sections, joined, carved and stamped, assimilated ash glaze, green and white glaze trailed dots, lid had three bird sentinels protecting a gold egg, 16" x 13".

Clays that are a different color than the working clay can produce rich and varied surfaces. With forms thrown on a wheel and coated with powdered clay, the piece can be further shaped from the inside, but be careful not to touch the outside decorated surface. Brushing the surface with sodium silicate, quick-drying the surface with a heat gun or blowtorch until the surface no longer is tacky, then expanding the form from inside can give the expanding form an aura of instant antiquity. These photos of Randy Brodnax's work show the process in action.

A soft clay cylinder just thrown, has a cleaned surface, then is impressed with various tools.

The surface is painted with sodium silicate solution.

A soft decorated form is expanded on the wheel from inside while being dried with a heat gun on the outside.

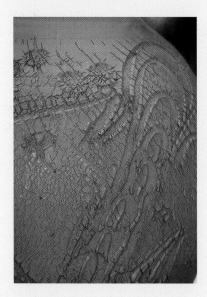

The surface shows decorative cracking detail from the heat gun and expansion.

Randy Brodnax, USA, "Textured Vase," raku, 2003.

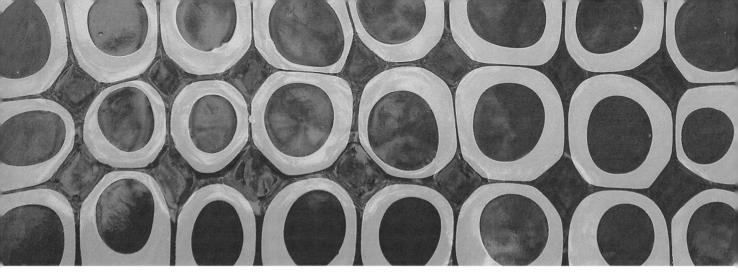

Traditional slipware process — dotting in the wet state. Photo: Judi Dyelle

CHAPTER 9

Marks of Liquid Clays

This chapter looks at the use of liquefied clays, including terra sigillata, slip and engobes or underglazes. These range from a solution almost as thin as water to coatings that may be thick enough to be applied with a palette knife. The thickness depends on what the artist is trying to achieve. Each variant has its own set of possibilities and historical origins, from the thin sigillata coatings on early Classical Greek and Roman Arretine or Samian wares, to palette-knife painting with thick slips on ware from late 19th and early 20th century European Paté sur Paté, to Art Nouveau-inspired art pottery made by Rookwood in Cincinnati and Weller Pottery in Zanesville, Ohio. Traditional European methods of trailing, combing, marbling, feathering,

Photo: Judi Dyelle

Slip, tools and slip trailer.

dotting and mocha diffusions, and the Oriental ones of Mishima, Hakeme or Onda style often use liquefied clays in thicknesses ranging from super thin to super thick. Each artist needs to find the type and viscosity of material that suits the imagery and technique to the best effect. If you put a dozen slipware potters in the same room, I'm sure they would disagree on the optimum viscosity. Like most things in ceramic surfacing, ultimately it depends on what you want to say, which will control how you best say it.

Terra Sigillatas

Colloidal slips, or terra sigillatas, produce a tough, satin-surfaced, semi glaze-like skin, which can be polished to a high sheen before being fired, usually between cone 08 and cone 1, depending on the clays being used. Ball clay terra sigillatas can be fired to cone 10 to produce a beautiful ivory-like surface but with some loss of sheen. When colored, they can be used almost like a watercolor over either dry or leather-hard clay, or even over bisque. Some artists even use sigillatas over both unfired glaze and fired glaze surfaces for variations of dry surfacing. There is no end to the possibilities that can be achieved by playful experimentation with any liquid clay process. In the pre-Columbian Paracas culture of northern Peru, slips were mixed with resin to achieve a deeply textured surface reminiscent of tooled leather.

The most common forms of sigillata are made from

Photo: Ernest Mayer, The Winnipeg Art Gallery

Curtis Benzle, USA, "Home Again," vitreous porcelain with refractory stain added, no glaze, slab built, fired in sagger lined with a flint wash, imagery from slip painting or Nerikomi technique, 5" x 5", 2003.

refined red clays, although many different clays work very well. The type of clay will, of course, affect the color. Sigillatas often are reduced, either during the firing or in post-firing, where the extremely thin film of slip accepts carbon very rapidly, turning to a rich black.

The following basic terra sigillata, creamy-white when oxidized, usually will absorb carbon and give a rich black when reduced.

Terra Sigillata Recipe

Ball clay	10.5 lbs. (4.77 kilograms)
Water	3 gallons (11.35 liters)
Household lye	1.7 oz. (48 grams) (deflocculant)

The weight ratio of clay to water is approximately 4:10. The clay and lye are poured into the water, thoroughly mixed and allowed to stand for 48 hours.

Caution: Lye is caustic soda. It should be handled with great care. Other deflocculants can be used, but lye works particularly well. Once the lye is mixed in, the slip solution quickly loses its caustic qualities.

After the material has settled, any decomposed organic matter that might show up as a dark gray, dark brown or black layer at the top of the solution should be removed and discarded. The thin, watery slip remaining is the sigillata and should be siphoned off, leaving heavier particles at the bottom of the container. The heavy clay material usually is discarded, and only the slip with ultra-fine particulate is used. I find this thick layer below the sigillata often will thicken up with the addition of a little vinegar and be fine for palette knife work.

The slip is best when sieved several times through a fine screen, up to 150 mesh, to make sure only the finest clay particles are in the solution. When the slip is in the correct solution, 100cc should weigh between 108 and 112 grams. It can be applied at any stage, but is perhaps best applied to bone-dry greenware by brushing,

Cheryl Tall, USA, "Oceanna," coil built, high grog sculpture clay, surfaced with metallic oxide, terra sigillata, engobes, glazes fired to cone 04 electric kiln, 38" x 22" x 29", 1997.

Photo: Gary Castle

Alexandra McCurdy, Canada, "Rectangular Box with Eight-Pointed Star" detail, slipcast porcelain fired in oxidation to cone 9, slip-trailed design using colored slip on greenware, transparent glaze overtop, 10cm x 13cm, 2003.

Photo: Mary Dixon

Pam Birdsall, Canada, "Serving Plate" detail of feathered colored clay slips, wheel-thrown brown earthenware clay, white slip, feathered floral decoration in center done with colored slips, rim glazed clear, dark blue, and green transparent glaze sponged overtop, 35cm diameter.

dipping or spraying. If applied to wet or leather-hard work, the slip likely will run off the surface. To aid the slip in adhering to the clay, it may be helpful to lightly spray the work with water, which opens the pores and may allow a better bond to take place.

When the slip has lost its wet shine, but before it dries completely, it can be polished with a chamois leather or cotton material as desired. As long as they are not scratchy, the inside of old fleece sweatshirts work beautifully. Polished sigillatas can be over-painted with a regular decorating slip to achieve a shiny/matte variation. If fired in the raku process and reduced in a combustion chamber, the effect will be of matte black brushwork over a satin to shiny black background. The visual effect is somewhat similar to black-on-black Pueblo pottery from San Ildefonso in New Mexico, pioneered by Maria Martinez and Popovi Da.

Sigillatas can be colored by the addition of the usual coloring materials to a maximum of 8 percent. Some colorants will likely be coarser in particle size than the slip, and they may not pass through the sieve. Coarse colorants or opacifiers can be ball milled to improve the fineness of the particles. They should be sieved with the slip for thorough mixing to take place. They also will have some effect on the firing temperature and reduction characteristics.

For the usual terra sigillata sheen, the above sigillata recipe is best when fired to cone 05. Sigillatas are usually fired between cone 08 and cone 1, although they can be fired higher or fluxed with calcium borate or frit to lower the fusion temperature. Flux additions will tend to bleach out some of the color, though, and personal decisions need to be made on the degree of compromise that is acceptable.

Colorants and opacifiers are best added to the slip before sieving. Mixing dry color to wet slip sometimes is difficult for accuracy, but a liter of liquid terra sigillata is approximately one kilogram in weight. A dry material weighed to 100 grams and mixed with the slip would approximate a 10 percent color saturation.

The application of sigillatas usually is very thin, almost like water, as it takes only one layer of the thinnest slip to produce results. Used this way, the slip will not cover or obliterate any surface textures or imperfections on the surface of the clay, such as grog holes, scratches or textural markings. This characteristic can be an advantage or disadvantage, depending on the desired result. Terra sigillatas make a superb base for other painting techniques used over them.

Slips and Engobes

Slips and engobes are more or less the same thing, and some confusion exists over the use of the two words. Slips are predominantly liquefied clay; they usually are applied on wet to dry greenware. Engobes usually have a lower clay content and also can be used on bisque-fired ware. The word slip generally is used to describe any clay in liquid form. All slips and engobes can be colored with oxides, carbonates and stains (see Chapter 11). Sometimes very crusty surfaces can be made by applying slips and engobes over the fired glaze surface and refiring.

To produce slips for casting into plaster molds, the ingredients for slip are mixed with water to which 1 percent to 2 percent of a deflocculant, such as sodium carbonate (soda ash) and/or sodium silicate, has been added. Slips made with deflocculant require much less water to achieve the same degree of fluidity as those without deflocculants.

Casting slips give extremely good properties for use as a drawing medium in a fine-to-medium aperture trailer. Since there is much less water in the deflocculated slip, it will leave a crisp, raised line drawing when applied to leather-hard surfaces (see Figure 9.16). To remove sharp points or develop a low relief, raised line slip drawings can be flattened slightly by rolling the surface with a small rubber-coated roller or printmaker's brayer.

Slips used for decorating usually are mixed with water only, unless specific qualities of fluidity or viscosity are desired. For these qualities, a flocculant such as vinegar or Epsom salts can be used for increased viscosity or thickening. Or a deflocculant, as mentioned above, can be used for increased fluidity. Decorating slips traditionally are used to coat the surface of clays in a variety of ways. They can be made from naturally occurring clays or from mixed materials and colorants to provide a range of decorative effects. They can be applied to wet, leather-hard or dry clay bodies, depending on the technique being used and the dry strength of the body. The slip decoration usually is covered with a glaze after bisque firing, although many people prefer to leave the slip patterns unglazed.

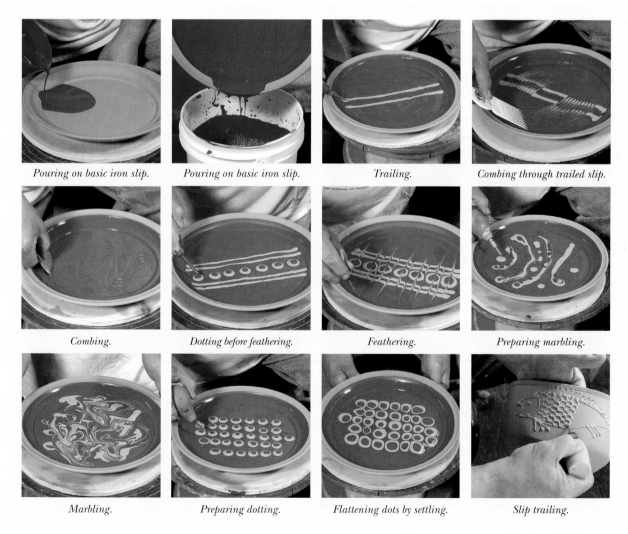

Pouring on basic iron slip.   *Pouring on basic iron slip.*   *Trailing.*   *Combing through trailed slip.*

Combing.   *Dotting before feathering.*   *Feathering.*   *Preparing marbling.*

Marbling.   *Preparing dotting.*   *Flattening dots by settling.*   *Slip trailing.*

Traditional English slipware processes.

Photos: Judi Dyelle

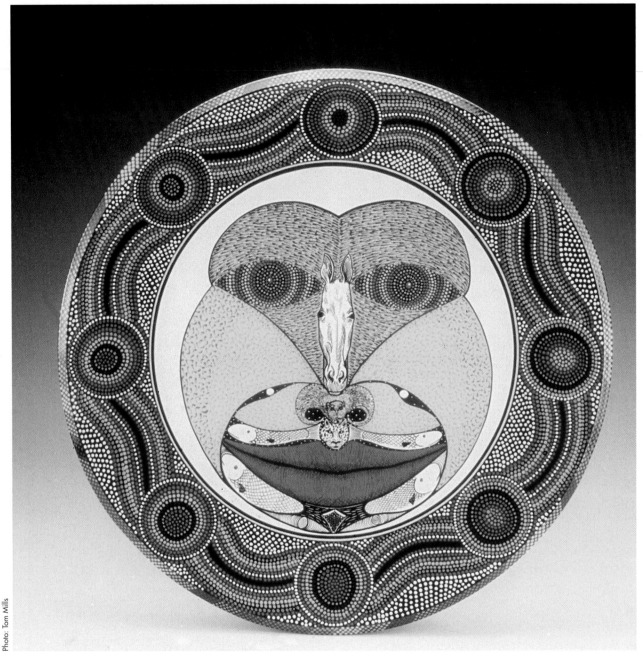

Photo: Tom Mills

Patrick L. Dougherty, USA, "Soul Dreamer," wheel-formed white earthenware, painted with underglazes, trailed on using bulb syringe with hypodermic needles, brushed, clear glaze and oxidation fired to cone 04, 4" x 25-½", 2000.

Slips can be used to coat another clay to make it lighter, darker or colored. They also can be used as a coating through which designs can be cut or scratched, resisted with wax or latex or layered with other slips to create a wide range of potential imagery.

Slips form the major decorative processes of a number of Oriental pottery styles, such as Punch'ong from Korea; Mishima, Hakeme and Onda ware from Japan; and various slipware styles from Hubei, Guandong and Yixing in China. Mishima (Punch'ong) was described in the previous chapter, as it is a combination of impression and slip inlay. Hakeme and Onda styles of surface decoration depend on brushed slip. Hakeme uses a large, coarse brush made from long pine needles or stalks of rice tied in a bundle about 1" in diameter. Pressure on the brush during application creates a

Jan Edwards, USA, "Robin's Garden No. 1," incised drawing on terra cotta clay slab, inlayed and painted slips, stains, commercial underglazes, multiple electric firings to cone 05, 14" x 16-½", 2002.

highly textured, multilinear mark that often forms the background to further painting with regular brushes and pigment. Slip decoration from Onda uses wide, flat brushes and a near-stippling process where the brush is raised and lowered on the turning form without ever leaving the surface. The distinctive pattern that results is like small waves circling the form. It typically uses a white slip on a darker clay. The Chinese processes are somewhat similar to a number of traditional European decorating processes such as combing, feathering, marbling, trailing and dotting. These processes simply are varied manipulations of liquid clays. An exception is mocha diffusions, where an acidic element mixed with colorant is introduced for decorative effect.

Mocha Diffusions

This intriguing method of surface decoration initially was developed and used in the southwest of England, and later in parts of eastern North America, particularly Canada. It only was done on wares of a simple functional nature and on forms that were simple in shape, such as mugs, bowls, jugs, chamber pots, etc. The name has nothing to do with coffee, but is derived from the word Mecca, the center of the Muslim world in Saudi Arabia, where the finest moss agate gemstones are found. These gemstones show veined patterns reminiscent

Preparing slip for mocha diffusions.

Preparing slip for mocha diffusions.

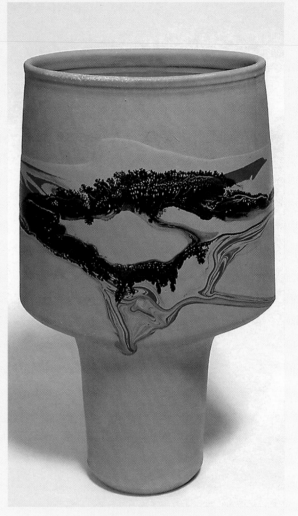

The finished mocha piece, while still wet. See the study of this piece in Chapter 21 to view the fired result.

of trees or ferns. The slow evolution is called dendritic formation, where acidic solutions, usually colored with manganese or iron, have permeated between layers of alkaline sedimentary rock. Compression and geothermal heating have hardened the stone into a gem quality. In nature these patterns may take hundreds of years to develop, but in ceramics the process is done in seconds. It is quite a simple process, but it demands exact timing and viscosity control. As with the natural occurrences, it depends on a reaction between acid and alkali. It must be done on leather-hard clay that hasn't started to change color in drying. The timing refers to the state of dryness. If the pot is too dry, it might crack or split;

if it's too wet, it might sag or slump. The viscosity refers to the thickness of the slip coating. If it's too thick, the acid/color mix won't move; if it's too thin, it will run excessively and become blurred. With practice it is quite easy to control.

Suitable Clays and Slips for Mocha Diffusion

Mocha diffusions traditionally were done on both red and white earthenware, but they can be done on almost any clay body and fired at almost any temperature. Clays with a high degree of sand, grog or lignite in them sometimes are prone to cracking from the extra wetting of the slip. From my experience, a clay body with a high

Photo by the artist

Bradley Keys, Canada, "Square Plate," thrown, cut and flattened, liquid clay slip, slip trailer on lip is wiped off to form a slight frame, multiple glazes sprayed in layers, 34cm x 34cm, 2003.

degree of ball clay or plastic kaolin, such as Edgar Plastic Kaolin (EPK), is the most ideal.

Various slip recipes are good for mocha diffusions. The most important factor is a high percentage of ball clay or other plastic clay. This basic recipe will fit most bodies and easily can be colored with stains or various oxides.

Slip for Mocha Diffusion

Ball clay	75
Kaolin	10
Silica	10
Feldspar	5

This creamy-white slip is good for all traditional slipware processes on most clay bodies from cone 04 to cone 12, in oxidation or reduction. The thickness should be like double cream, or room-temperature motor oil. A liquefied porcelain clay slip usually will not work well since a porcelain body typically contains a maximum of 50 percent plastic clay material, and the rest is nonplastic fluxes and fillers, such as feldspars and silica.

Acid/Color Mix

The mixture used to form the patterns is called "mocha tea." It originally was made by boiling tobacco leaves to form a thick sludge that then was thinned with water to a working consistency and mixed with color.

Photo: Peter Hogan

Bruce Cochrane, Canada, "Rectangle Bowl," press-molded form with thrown lip and foot, cone 10 salt-fired stoneware, crackle slip and green glaze applied with masked areas, 50cm x 30cm x 20cm.

It probably was originated by pottery decorators who chewed tobacco while they worked and spit in the paint pot, creating a murky brew. However, nicotine solutions are only a form of mild acid, and any form of mild acid will work, such as citric acid, lemon juice, urine, coffee, wine or vinegar, particularly natural apple-cider vinegar. The mix is made as a solution of acid mixed with colorant. Most colorants work quite well, although carbonates or stains usually are better than oxides, since they usually are a physically lighter precipitate than oxides. Heavy materials, such as black copper oxide, black cobalt oxide and black iron oxide, do not work well because the acid can't adequately hold the color in suspension. A ratio of about one heaped teaspoon of color to ¼ cup vinegar usually is a good starting point. However, a good deal of individual testing should be done to get the two liquids to work together to create significant dendritic patterns and to make things work correctly.

Mocha Method

The leather-hard object is dipped, poured or brushed with slip. While the surface is still wet, and

before it has begun to lose its shine, the acid/color mix is dripped or trailed into it. This is best done using a well-loaded brush held just touching the slip. If the viscosity of the slip and the acid/color mix is right, the feathering pattern will take place quite naturally, as the acid eats a fern-like pathway through the slip, pulling the colorant with it. Traditionally, the surface is coated with a thin coat of clear glaze or clear colored glaze, but this might cause the color to bleed out or become absorbed into the glaze, particularly at temperatures above cone 4. I prefer to use the technique on high-fired wares that don't need to be glazed, and I have been doing it that way for over more than 30 years. It is a technique that takes a while to get used to, but it can give interesting results when used sensitively. It also can be done quite easily on once-fired glazes, providing they have enough ball clay in them.

Where slips are stained with colorants, the color usually will bleed through the glaze, unless the glaze is totally opaque. The basic creamy-white slip recipe on page 108 will fit most clays and can be colored easily with any colorant or stain. I have used that slip recipe for many years and have found it to be very versatile and

Photo: John H. Stephenson

Susanne Stephenson, USA, "Yellow Beach," paper pulp in slip applied to leather-hard clay, bottom white and yellow slip sponged on, racked over with tied bundles of sticks, bisqued, black glaze and colored vitreous engobes rubbed in surface and washed off, 27" x 22" x 15".

Photo: Image-Ination

Ricky Maldonado, USA, "Vertigo 3 Vessel," coil built, carved, 17" x 19" x 17".

Photo courtesy of the artist

Diego Romero, USA, "Povi Drowning," earthenware bowl with gold luster, 10-¾" x 5-½", 2001. Exhibited SNC Cartier et Cie, 2001, Paris.

particularly good for traditional slipware techniques.

However, on some clays, particularly those firing at cone 2 or below, that slip can cause the covering glaze to craze. In this case more silica will be needed, and the slip can be adjusted.

The adjusted recipe should solve the crazing problem, but it also will bring about a lessening in plasticity and affect the fluid qualities necessary for some traditional techniques. These fluid qualities previously were assisted by the volume of ball clay. Some of this fluidity can be regained by adding a small amount of bentonite, macaloid, gum or deflocculant.

Adjusted Slip for Mocha Diffusion

Ball clay	40
Kaolin	20
Silica	20
Feldspar	10
Body frit (Ferro frit 3110)	10

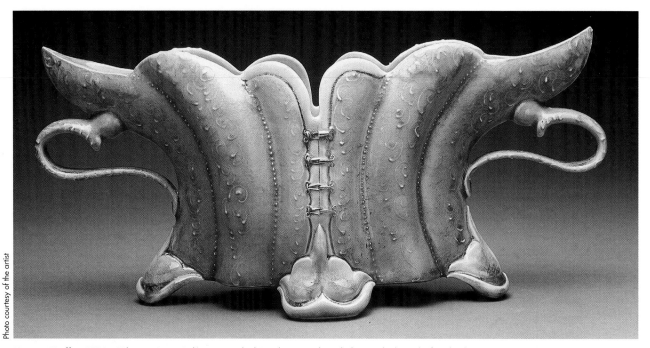

Photo courtesy of the artist

Kristen Kieffer, USA, "Flower Boat," thrown and altered, carved and slip trailed, soda-fired white stoneware to cone 10 reduction, electric fired to cone 6, hand-twisted kanthol wire clasps placed into leather-hard greenware through glaze firing, 14-½" x 7" x 5-½", 2003.

Engobes or Underglazes

The word engobe is used most often in North America and describes a wider range of uses in the development of the decorative surface. Underglaze is basically the same thing, and it can be colored with any colorant or stain. Many commercially made underglaze products are available, offering a wide range of color potential. They are applied easily by brush or spray. Whereas the simple liquefied slip commonly is used to coat greenware, an engobe can be formulated for use at any stage, including over bisque-fired ware. Engobes also often are used without a covering glaze, giving a wider potential for experimentation with the surface. An engobe or underglaze is more like a glaze in structure and may contain very little plastic clay.

Materials for making engobes fall into six groups: 1) Clays, with kaolin or calcined kaolin usually used in place of ball clay to counteract shrinkage; 2) Fluxes as used in glazes; 3) Fillers (usually silica); 4) Hardeners (borax, calcium borate, and various gums); 5) Opacifiers (tin, zircopax, titanium, superpax); and 6) Colorants.

The following three recipes for basic engobes give a good starting point for further experimentation. The engobes can be colored in any of the usual ways.

Basic Engobe Recipes

	CONE 04-3	CONE 4-6	CONE 6-10
Kaolin	20	15	15
Calcined kaolin	10	20	35
Talc	25	10	5
Calcium borate (or Frit 3110)	15	10	---
Nepheline syenite	---	10	15
Silica	15	20	15
Borax	5	5	5
Zircopax	10	10	10
TOTAL	**100**	**100**	**100**

Both slips and engobes can be formulated for a wide variety of temperatures, and the higher they are fired, the more vitreous they will be.

Vitreous slips basically are combinations of clays and other materials that will become tight enough on firing to almost resemble a glaze. They could just as well be called engobes or underglazes because they are usually halfway between slip and glaze. Although they generally are used on either unfired or bisque-fired ware, they also can be used over previously fired glazes and refired for further variations.

Photo: John Carlano

Robert Winokur, USA, "The Italian Hill Town," salt-glazed brick clay, slips and engobes, 16" x 40" x 9". Collection of the Los Angeles County Museum of Art, California.

Casting Slips on Greenware

Spraying casting slip on clay at the leather-hard state can develop pebbled surfaces unlike any other surfacing process. Spraying unevenly and allowing the casting slip to lose its sheen before the next spray pass builds extremely interesting textural surfaces. Several spray passes may be necessary to build up significant texture. Used in conjunction with rubber sheet or Tyvek® resists (see Chapter 13), it offers a wide range of possibilities. When the textured casting slip surface is sprayed from the side or at an angle with contrasting colored slips or colorant sprays, the result can be great illusions of organic surface undulations.

Irma Starr, USA, "It's a Twister (Wizard of Oz)," marbled slipware. Courtesy of the Nelson-Atkins Museum of Art, Kansas City, Mo.

Photo by the artist

Kate Maury, USA, "Porcelain Soy Bottle," slip-trail decoration, soda fired cone 10, 6-½" high, 2002.

Photo: Bill Wikrent and Marty Springer

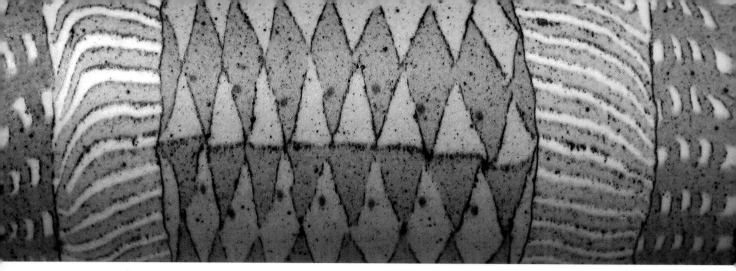

Detail of vase by Susy Siegele and Michael Haley, USA. Private collection. Photo: Judi Dyelle

CHAPTER 10

Marks of Colored Clays

Colored clays offer several decorative processes – some quite simple, others very complex. Either different naturally occurring clays or prepared clay bodies tinted with various colorants can be used. Colored clay work can be done at various temperature ranges, depending on the types of clays selected and the result required. In conjunction with other decorative processes and firing methods, a wide range of potential can be realized.

Egyptian Paste

The earliest historical use of color in clays was likely that done by the Egyptians some 5,000 years ago in the production of what we now call Egyptian paste. They used a paste body containing very little or no clay that was modeled, carved into simple forms or pressed into molds. Egyptian paste is basically a self-glazing, low-clay modeling material. It has a high silica and high soluble alkaline flux component and an abnormally low clay content. The soluble salts of soda ash, sodium bicarbonate, potassium carbonate and lithium carbonate migrate to the surface during drying, developing a powdery white scum. This scum melts during firing to form a glazed surface and a highly glassified core structure to the body.

Color can be mixed with the basic pastes. The colors that work best are those intensified by highly alkaline materials, mainly copper, cobalt, manganese, ochre and rutile, as well as mixtures of these colorants. The temperature range for firing Egyptian paste is between cone 012 and cone 04, usually in oxidation.

In formulating Egyptian paste, the clay content must be kept low to allow for sufficient glass-forming material to give an open, porous structure that will permit the migration of soluble ingredients to the surface. The material should contain about 60 percent nonplastic ingredients such as silica, sand, and feldspar. Clay can be added in amounts up to 20 percent, and at least 10 percent of some soluble soda compound is necessary. Soda can be added as soda ash, bicarbonate of soda, borax, or combinations of these. Coloring oxides are added directly to the batch. Copper oxide or copper carbonate, which give a beautiful turquoise color, are the favorite colorants; about 3 percent will give strong blue. Cobalt oxide, manganese oxide or many colored glaze stains also can be used. Coloring oxides also may be added in the form of soluble colorants, soluble sulfates or chlorides.

Egyptian Paste Recipe

Feldspar	40
Silica	20
Kaolin	15
Ball clay	5
Sodium bicarbonate	6
Soda ash	6
Calcium carbonate	5
Fine white sand	8
Bentonite	5
TOTAL	**105**

Julie Thompson, USA, "Boxes," ram pressed with inlaid colored porcelain and impressed patterns, cone 6 oxidation, glazed inside, and in impressions only outside, gold luster, 5" diameter, 2000.

At best, Egyptian paste is relatively nonplastic, and the forms made with it are, of necessity, simple. Bentonite or dextrine added to the material will partially overcome this difficulty. Objects made from Egyptian paste usually are fired to about cone 08. Jewelry or small sculptures made in this way can be very beautiful in surface and color. Beads can be fired strung on kanthal or kiln element wire in the kiln, which will prevent the slight scar that occurs if the bead is placed directly on a kiln shelf. Scars can be minimized by lightly dusting the shelf with alumina hydrate or kaolin. Different colors on the same piece can be achieved by inlaying pastes with various coloring oxides. Other than for jewelry-making, Egyptian pastes are not in common usage, but they form an important part of the ceramic spectrum, offering another possibility for self-expression.

Naturally Colored Clays

In the widest sense, all clays are colored. When fired, natural clays can vary from almost white to almost black and almost any yellowish, pinkish, grayish, reddish

Grace Nickel, Canada, "Light Sconce No. 7," earthenware with colored terra sigillata and oxides, glass, 43cm x 48cm x 15cm, 2001.

Photo: Harrison Evans

Barbara L. Frey, USA, "Look Ahead Teapot No. 2," porcelain, 7-¾" x 6-½" x 6", 2002.

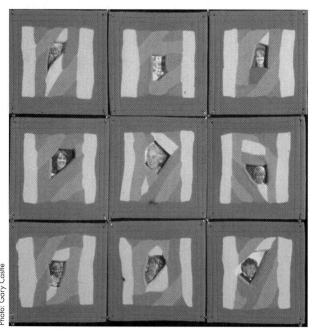

Photo: Gary Castle

Alexandra McCurdy, Canada, "Albert Bridge," colored porcelain, fired cone 9 oxidation, tiles sewn with brass wire and beads, photographs, 34cm x 34cm, 2000.

or brownish tone between black and white. Most of these tones develop naturally from contamination with iron oxide in one of its forms or combinations. In its earliest state, where coarse clay is the result of geologic degradation or the breakdown of feldspathic rock to kaolinite, it usually is light ivory or cream in color. It achieves its other naturally darkening tones during its journeys down rivers and into lakebeds, when it becomes contaminated by contact with other minerals, such as iron, calcium, titanium and manganese. The further it travels from the mother rock, the more contamination it acquires, and the darker it likely will be when fired. It usually becomes more plastic and malleable, too. As it settles into lakebeds, it forms layers of sediment, and over eons of time, layers build on other layers, creating a variable lamination. If you were to shovel down through several layers, you would see a variety of differently toned strata.

We could speculate that it was the sight of the natural layers of differently colored clays that was the idea source for Tang Dynasty potters of China to emulate in their marbled earthenware, starting about 1,400 years ago. To my knowledge this is the earliest use of laminated colored clays in mankind's ceramic history. Many of today's ceramic artists have turned their attention to the subtle variations of layered clays, either using naturally colored clays or adding colorants to light-colored base clays or porcelain.

A number of different names have been given to laminated colored clay processes, depending on where the process developed. In England they usually are referred to as *agateware* after the decorative, patterned gemstone. In Italy the use of colored clay often is referred to as *millefiori*, from a decorative glass-forming process meaning "a thousand flowers." In Japan the words *neriage*, *nerikomi* and *zougan* refer to different ways the colored clays are used. Always interested in why things are called what they are and the confusion surrounding names, I asked Thomas Hoadley, a long-time artist working with colored clays, about the Japanese names.

Hoadley told me, "When I became aware that colored clay work would be my primary life's work, I figured I should get to the bottom of the nerikomi/neriage question. I had been told that even in Japan the terms are mixed up. I spoke to a Japanese woman who lives here, and she explained that *neri* is a root word meaning 'to mix' and *age* is a root word meaning

Photo: Lucien Lisabelle

Lisette Savaria, Canada, "Les Elfes," porcelain, paper, addition of roses, 15" x 19" x 4", 2003.

to 'pull up.' This refers to the pulling up action in throwing clay on a wheel, hence neriage refers to wheel work with colored clays. *Komi* means 'to press into,' as in pressing clay slabs into a mold. Nerikomi thus means hand-building with colored clay, which in Japan I guess usually meant mold work. It has been expanded to include other methods of hand-building."

Neriage and nerikomi both use either naturally occurring colored clays or light-colored clays that are specifically stained to satisfy the artist's color requirement. Neriage, or agateware, is done by laminating different colored clays together and throwing them on a wheel to develop a swirling and spiraling blend of the clays.

Objects made this way can be left with the swirl pattern, or altered by various forms of cutting the surface, with fluting and faceting (see Chapters 6 and 7). Balls of laminated clays are best left covered in a plastic sheet so amelioration can take place.

Cutting across the grain of laminated clays will expose an infinite variety of random patterns. The type of pattern can be controlled both by the thickness of the layers and by how the laminations are placed when thrown on the wheel. If they are vertical to the wheelhead, they likely will produce fine, lacy patterns. If they are placed horizontally, much bolder patterns can be expected. If placed diagonally, a combination of both bold and lacy patterns might be expected.

Nerikomi is the process of laminating colored clays into blocks with a carefully controlled pattern developed through cutting, folding and rejoining the layered colored clays. Simply done, it might produce striated, checkerboard, zigzag, chevron or other easy geometric designs, as shown in the photos on page 127.

More complex designs exploring figurative, animal or floral imagery can be achieved by slicing through blocks of clay and inserting rods or lengths of previously colored and patterned clay throughout the length of the block, such as those shown on page 129. Sometimes a thin, black, slip layer is placed between clays to give further emphasis. When cut in slices across the pattern, the full image becomes visible. Slabs of patterned clay can be used on various forms of hand-building, or if cut

Neriage and Nerikomi

These images show the process for agateware, known in Japanese as Neriage. Colored clays are laminated together before throwing, and in the process of throwing get pulled into a random spiral. Cutting across the thrown spiral with wires, fluting tools, planes or knives exposes unrepeatable patterns of striations, similar to exposed surfaces of rocks blasted in road building.

1. Preparing colored clay for thrown agateware or neriage..

4. Fluting the outside of a thrown agate bowl.

2. Mixed colored clay before throwing.

5. Fluting the inside rim of a thrown agate bowl.

3. Using a plane tool to facet a leather-hard bowl.

6. Three different examples of fluting.

Whereas the agateware, or neriage, method produces random pattern, Nerikomi blockmaking allows carefully controlled pattern develoment that may be cut in very thin slices and used as a woodworker might use a veneer for decorative details in furniture. See the Siegele and Haley process images on page 129 to see this form of decoration in action with various pattern segments and the assembled finished object. In both methods the coloration is completely through the body, not just on the surface, and may be clearly seen on the interior of the object.

1. Preparing clay for nerikomi, three colors of porcelain.

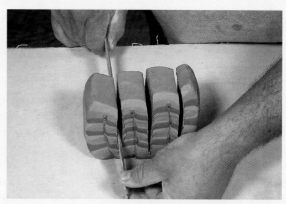

4. Cutting for the bracket pattern.

2. Assembling the sliced pieces.

5. Cutting the bracket pattern.

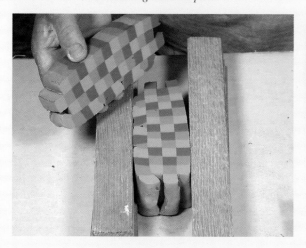

3. Checkerboard slicing.

6. Cutting a wave pattern.

Photo: Judi Dyelle

Photo: Steve Farmer.

Neil Forrest, Canada, "Trivet: Navigate No. 1", Egyptian faience, porcelain, grout and mortar, 21" x 9" x 9", 2000.

Photo: Eva Heyd

Marc Leuthold, USA, "Yellow and White Pair," carved pigmented porcelain, 8" high, 2002.

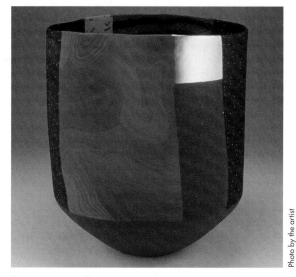

Photo by the artist

Thomas A. Hoadley, USA, "Nerikomi Vessel," colored porcelain, unglazed, electric fired cone 6, gold leaf, 9-¾" x 8-⅝" x 7-½", 2002.

extremely thin, can be employed as a patterned veneer attached to thrown, cast or hand-built forms.

Colored clay blocks are best left for a period of time for amelioration, where differences in the softness or hardness of the various clays can be equalized to one homogeneous mass.

Zougan refers to the sculptural process of layering varied clays in a random fashion, stacking them one atop another until the required height is reached, then wire or knife cutting the surface to reveal the stratifications. Pieces made this way can be hollowed out later or built around a removable form.

Color in Clays

Depending on the desired result, you can use stains, oxides or carbonates, either singly or mixed together, to add color to clays. Because of the opaque nature of clays, most colors will develop an opaque pastel-like quality, and the development of pure color is extremely difficult. Commercially prepared body stains usually are made with a clay base where the color is already diluted. They mainly are used in the sanitary ware industry for pastel-colored bathroom fixtures. Therefore, other coloring materials are better for the development of strong color.

A suitable dust mask should be worn when mixing

Susy Siegele and Michael Haley show the making of Nerikomi-style blockmaking for the production of limited edition objects. Here they are working on integrated surface design with colored clays that will be finished by a light wood firing.

1. Beginning to construct a figure from different colors of porcelain. The patterned piece will become a lady's dress.

2. The figure is turned upside down and feet laid in.

3. This is the complete figure before it's encased in background clay. A thin slice has been cut off to show the pattern more clearly.

4. The figure has been encased in a white background and is being lengthened and reduced in size.

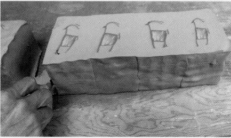

6. Antelope-like figures are constructed in a similar manner. The block now is joined to the figure block to create a new block from which mugs will be made.

5. The lengthened figure has been quartered and reassembled as a row of figures.

7. The completed mug block will be sliced into thin slabs. Each slab will be shaped into a cup or mug. A block this size will make 12 to 18 mugs.

8. The mug is finished after being single fired to cone 11, gas and wood kiln. The exterior has very fine spray of clear glaze and a bit of blush from the wood.

Photos: Michael Haley

Photo: John Cummings

Sylvia Hyman, USA, "Basket of Tin-Pan Alley Music," stoneware basket, porcelain scrolls, 7" x 12" x 8-½", 2003.

Photo: Dave Harrison

Dot Kimura, USA, "Untitled No. 2," 12-¾" x 6" x 6", 2003.

clays, particularly colored clays where airborne particles of heavy metals are likely to exist.

Mixing Colored Clays

Mixing colored clays can be done in a variety of ways, largely dependent on the volume being prepared. Colored clays can be made in test amounts simply by weighing out the dry ingredients of both the clay and colorant and soaking them in a bowl until they become liquid slip. They subsequently should be dried on a plaster batt and wedged to a plastic workable state. In larger volumes, the dry ingredients can be mixed in blungers, clay mixers or baths, either to liquid slip form (which generally makes for more thoroughly dispersed color) or to a plastic state ready for working.

There are a number of ways clays can be prepared. Some people believe the material must be ball milled, and for some colors this might be advisable. However, I have been using colored clays for at least 30 years, mixed only in the plastic state, with no problems. For those who are particularly concerned about developing an absolutely flat, unspecked clay or slip, particularly with cobalt-containing materials, ball milling for several hours is probably a necessity.

If you wedge dry colorants into the plastic clay, you undoubtedly will have specking of color in the final object. It also is almost impossible to work out exactly how much color you have in relation to the clay content. If you can't tolerate specking and want precise, repeatable color, the only satisfactory mixing process is the dry method, where an amount of dry clay is colored by a percentage addition of colorant. Always add dry colorant to a dry clay mix, then add water to turn it into a slip, and sieve it twice through a 60-mesh sieve. When thoroughly mixed, pour the slip onto a clean, absorbent surface such as plaster or canvas. When the water has been absorbed, wedge the stiffened clay until it's ready for use.

The amount of colorant needed to get a particular result will have to be determined through testing, because many colorants have quite different staining strengths when mixed into clay than when mixed into glazes. The type of clay also will have a profound effect on the color. White-firing clays give purer colors, and darker-colored clays give more muted tones. The percentage of colorant depends on the desired color. Anywhere from 0.5 percent to 20 percent by weight, but usually in the 2 percent to 10 percent range, is normal. Some colorants,

Max Blankstein, Canada, "Pile Driver" front view, 14-¼" x 9" x 4-½", 2003.

Photo: Lucien Lisabelle

Lisette Savaria, Canada, "Jaune Percée de Soleil," porcelain, paper, spray glaze, 12" x 19" x 4", 2003.

notably those containing cobalt and chromium, have great staining power, while others are often very pallid at less than 10 percent. Remember that you are putting the colorant into a very dense, opaque material. Putting a clear glaze over it will bring out the colors, much like soaking colored pebbles in water. Testing is done empirically in the "try it and see" approach (see "The Ceramic Spectrum," Chapter 17).

If you make your own clays, coloring them is very easy. If you use prepared clays, it is much more involved, and the preparation time is considerable.

Some colorants, particularly manganese, have a very strong fluxing effect in the body that can cause serious bloating or bubbling. These materials also can cause the clay forms to collapse, as they have little tolerance for over-firing and need careful watching. Work easily can be ruined through pyroplastic deformation.

Producing colored clays can be a very expensive process, given the current costs of some colorants. It is wise to thoroughly think through the desired result to make certain that colored clay is the most suitable avenue for achieving it. It is quite possible that a colored slip or engobe may be sufficient to do the job at a lower cost and with fewer potential problems.

The biggest problems that occur in developing colored clays lie in their use. Some colorants act as fluxes and will cause the clay to mature at a lower temperature. Some are refractory and will raise the maturing temperature. The problems generally arise when colored clays of an opposing nature are used together. The tensions that may develop can be strong enough to split the work apart, so a good deal of testing should be done to make sure this problem doesn't occur. If it does, the easiest solution is to add more kaolin to the over-fluxing clay and more feldspar or body frit to an over-refractory clay.

Finishing and Glazing Colored Clays

Most colored clay objects are improved immeasurably after the final firing by carefully cleaning the surface with fine wet-and-dry silicon-carbide abrasive papers under running water. Depending on the fineness of the body, a surface as smooth as eggshells or satin can be achieved, making the details of the patterned clay stand out further. Sandblasting also can develop further interest.

Colored clay works might be perfectly satisfactory and fulfill the artist's vision without any glaze coating. However, if a glaze coating is deemed necessary, glazes of all types can further increase the interest of colored clay processes. Glossy, satin, vellum and matte glazes all can be used, as can colored or opacified glazes. For example, agateware pieces made using colored porcelain clays containing copper can develop patterns that can be covered by tin-opacified glazes and fired at cone 8 to 10 in reduction. The result can give pink to red patterning on a white background. Different firing processes such as salt, soda and wood also will greatly extend the range of possibilities. The opportunities are infinite.

Part 3

PIGMENT PROCESSES

Maurice Savoie, Canada, "Luna Park," detail, porcelain mural with varied textures and low relief, color sepia, 1983.

Maya. Late Classic, 600 to 900 C.E. Clay, paint. Boxers wear helmets and carry conch shells as weapons (hand-to-hand combat in warfare). Rollout photograph © Justin Kerr.

CHAPTER 11

The Ceramic Spectrum and Electric Palette

This chapter is an extension of Chapter 5, particularly relating to the variables of ceramic colorants and basic suggestions for their use and development, mixing and application to develop a complete range of ceramic color. The ceramic spectrum has been divided into four segments: 1) Hot to Trot — the warm side (red, yellow, orange); 2) Play it Cool — the green/blue side; 3) Mood Indigo — the darker aspects; and 4) Electric Palette — colors and colorants that behave well in electric firing.

There are three charts in this chapter that give the basic controlling factors on the development of color in glazes — the warm, cool and dark sides of the spectrum. It makes little difference whether the color is included in the glaze or painted on top using the colorants specified. I usually include the color in the glaze for easy reference. When brushed over a glaze, there will be considerable variation. For example, brushwork painted on an uncolored glaze with a colorant or stain will yield variation of the color because of the way the brush first lays a heavy concentration of colorant. The colorant thins out as the tail of the brushstroke occurs, so there will be a range of color in a single brushstroke. The charts are listed in the following columns:

- Color required (basic color names from artist color charts);
- Colorant(s) needed to get that color;
- Orton cone temperature to get that color;
- Kiln atmosphere to get the color (oxidation or reduction);
- Percentage of colorant in the glaze base; and
- Comments on the controlling factors or parameters where the desired color is achieved.

Artists who choose to work in clay are at a disadvantage. Not only has biased tradition largely relegated the clay worker to the lowly position of artisan, but the nature of the medium makes it the most complex of any in the art world. Not only must the clay worker make a "canvas," but usually all of the "paints" as well. It is a tenuous balance of art and science, where, for production of much meaningful work, the ceramist needs to have an intimate knowledge of materials and their reaction with each other under variations of heat and kiln atmosphere. I am convinced that it is partly due to the medium's complexity that most clay workers tend to stay within a comparatively narrow framework of expression.

With few exceptions, squeezing paint out of a

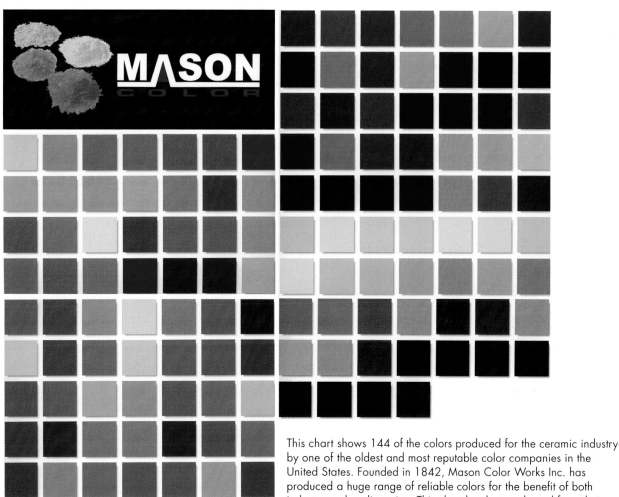

This chart shows 144 of the colors produced for the ceramic industry by one of the oldest and most reputable color companies in the United States. Founded in 1842, Mason Color Works Inc. has produced a huge range of reliable colors for the benefit of both industry and studio artists. This chart has been adapted from their regular color chart and reference guide to fit the space of this page. The full chart with product numbers and technical information is an extremely valuable reference for the studio artist in ceramics. Mason Stains are widely available through ceramic supply companies.

tube to mix desired colors by sight is a simple luxury unavailable to ceramists. Most of the time we are working blind or nearly blind. Glaze makers see what has been mixed only when glazes emerge from the kiln. There are methods available, however, that narrow the margin of error somewhat. The knowledge that three variables — glaze makeup, temperature and atmosphere — control all color development is the foundation on which all ceramic color and surface understanding is based. Your grasp of the complexities of material interaction has to come from acute observation, plus a little logic. In the past, it might have taken a generation for new developments to occur, but for our instant society, time becomes all-important, so we take many shortcuts that may lead us down blind alleys. Glaze recipes found in

books and magazines are an example of this. It often seems quicker and easier to use somebody else's recipe to clothe a form than to spend time working to make your own from scratch. But how often do published recipes and formulae really satisfy? It doesn't take long to begin to formulate intuitive understanding, and every series of tests you fire and analyze helps build the foundation for complete understanding. Glaze making is a creative act in itself, an integral part of the overall creative statement.

The potter's palette can be just as broad as the painter's, probably even broader if you consider all the textural variations and surface variations, from shiny and smooth to dry and rough. When you combine the numerous surface enrichment processes and the variables

THE HOT SIDE OF THE SPECTRUM: DARK RED TO ORANGE-RED

COLORANT	CONE	ATMOSPHERE	%	COMMENTS
Dark Red				
Chromium 012 to 01		oxidation	5% to 10%	Use in low-fire, lead-based glazes containing no zinc.
Copper	vary	reduction	0.5% to 5%	Best in glazes containing less than 10% clay content, and a high alkaline content. Needs good reduction. In low temperatures, it can be reduced during cooling. Good reds as low as cone 018.
Cadmium/selenium stains	010 to 05	oxidation	1% to 10%	Glazes need to be formulated from frits such as Ferro 3548 and 3278 for best results. Lead glazes can also be used. No tolerance for over-firing. Use only in well-ventilated areas, as even the fumes are highly toxic.
Iron	vary	both	5% to 10%	Good in many glaze bases at all temperatures. Can be improved with the addition of 2% to 5% tin oxide.
Nickel	4 to 10	oxidation	5% to 8%	Use in barium-saturated glazes.
Burgundy				
Iron – See Dark Red, Iron.				
Copper – See Dark Red, Copper.				Owing to the unstable nature of copper, this colorant can produce a wide range of results. Very controlled reduction firing and cooling are important.
Maroon				
Chrome/tin stains	vary	oxidation	1% to 5%	Use in glazes with calcium. There should be no zinc in the glaze.
Copper	vary	reduction	0.5% to 5%	Best in high alkaline glazes.
Crimson				
Chrome/tin stains – See Maroon, Chrome/tin stains.				
Copper + titanium	8 to 10	reduction	1% to 5%	Try various blends of copper (1% to 5%) and titanium (2% to 5%).
Calcium/selenium stains	010 to 05	oxidation	0.5 to 5%	Best with special frits. See Burgundy.
Vermillion-Scarlet				
Chrome	018 to 06	oxidation	2% to 5%	High lead glaze with no zinc.
Cadmium/selenium stains	010-05	oxidation	1% to 2%	See Dark Red, Cadmium/selenium stains.
Uranium	010- to 05	oxidation	1% to 10%	High lead glaze needed; strict oxidation.
Indian Red				
Iron	vary	both	5% to 10%	Best in high calcium glazes; small amount of bone ash helps. Tin addition up to 5% also helps. Also works well in ash glazes.
Brick Red				
Iron	vary	both	5% to 10%	Similar to Indian Red. Tin to 5% helps.
Orange-Brown				
Iron + rutile	vary	both	1% to 10%	Various mixtures (up to 8% iron and 2% rutile) in most glaze bases.
Iron + tin	vary	both	1% to 5%	Various mixtures (up to 4% iron and 1% tin) in most glaze bases. Creamier than iron with rutile.
Uranium	010 to 05	oxidation	2% to 10%	Needs high lead glazes. An addition of 2% iron helps.
Orange-Red				
Chromium	018 to 05	oxidation	2% to 5%	High lead glazes; no zinc.
Uranium	010 to 05	oxidation	5% to 10%	High lead glazes.
Cadmium/selenium stains	012 to 05	oxidation	1% to 4%	Best with special frits such as Ferro 3548 or 3278 or both. Helps to opacify with zirconium.

of kilns and firing, ceramics easily is as expressive as the gamut of painting and printmaking methods combined. Different techniques can be closely equated to working in any of the two-dimensional media, such as pencil, pen and ink, pastel, watercolor, oils, encaustics or acrylics. We also have an advantage in that the fired clay object is permanent — unless disposed of with a blunt instrument! Our works may live for thousands of years — a sobering thought.

Because a number of colors only can be achieved at low temperatures, clay workers have, during the last thousand years or so, developed a series of layering techniques in order to have the usually improved fired strength of stoneware or porcelain and the full palette range of the painter. To accomplish this, low-temperature glazes or overglazes can be made to adhere to a higher-fired glazed surface and can be superimposed over existing decoration. To gain the full measure of color, you must fire progressively down the temperature range so as not to burn out heat-sensitive colors that can't be

THE HOT SIDE OF THE SPECTRUM: ORANGE TO PALE CREAM YELLOW

COLORANT	CONE	ATMOSPHERE	%	COMMENTS
Orange				
Chromium – See Orange-Red.				
Uranium – See Orange-Red.				
Cadmium/selenium stains – See Orange-Red.				
Iron	vary	both	1% to 5%	Use in tin or titanium opacified glazes.
Rutile	vary	both	5% to 15%	Many glaze types, particularly alkaline. More successful in oxidation.
Copper	8 to 10	both	1% to 3%	Use in high alumina or magnesia glazes. Addition of up to 5% rutile sometimes helps.
Orange-Yellow				
Chromium		oxidation	1% to 2%	See Orange-Red.
Uranium		oxidation	2% to 5%	See Orange-Red.
Iron	vary	both	2% to 5%	With tin or titanium opacified glazes.
Rutile	vary	oxidation	1% to 10%	Best with alkaline glazes.
Yellow-Ocher				
Rutile – See Orange-Yellow.				
Iron	vary	both	1% to 10%	Use in high barium, strontium or zinc glazes.
Iron + tin	vary	oxidation	1% to 5%	Various mixtures (up to 3.5% iron and 1.5% tin) in many glaze bases.
Iron + rutile	vary	both	1% to 5%	Various mixtures (up to 2.5% iron and 2.5% rutile) in many glaze bases.
Vanadium/zirconium stain	vary	oxidation	5% to 10%	Various mixtures in many glaze bases.
Chrome Yellow				
Chromium	018 to 06	oxidation	1% to 3%	In high lead glazes.
Uranium	010 to 05	oxidation	1% to 3%	In high lead glazes.
Praseodymium stains	vary	both	3% to 10%	Good in most glazes. Sometimes burns out in reduction firing.
Honey Yellow				
Iron	022 to 04	oxidation	5% to 8%	Use in lead-based enamels and glazes.
Imperial Yellow				
Iron	022 to 018	oxidation	1% to 3%	Lead-based enamels.
Lemon Yellow				
Praseodymium stains	vary	both	1% to 10%	Good in most glazes. Best in oxidation.
Pale Cream Yellow				
Antimony	010 to 02	oxidation	5% to 15%	Needs high lead glazes opacified with tin.
Iron + tin	vary	both	2% to 5%	Various mixtures (up to 3.5% iron and 1.5% tin) in high barium, strontium, or zinc glazes. Titanium opacification helps.
Vanadium	vary	both	2% to 5%	Use in tin-opacified glazes.
Uranium	012 to 10	oxidation	2% to 5%	Wide variety of glaze bases.
Rutile + tin	vary	oxidation	2% to 5%	Various mixtures (up to 2.5% iron and 2% tin) in a variety of glaze bases. Titanium opacification helps.

achieved any other way. Usually the lowest and last firing is for precious metals such as platinum, palladium and gold. See Chapter 20 for more information on overglaze enamels, lusters, and china paints.

Hot to Trot

On the hot side of the spectrum — red, orange, and yellow — there are many commercial body and glaze stains, in addition to the usual mineral colorants. Because commercial products vary from one company and country to another, I prefer to explore the potential of basic mineral colorants. However, ceramists looking for difficult-to-achieve colors might want to consider prepared stains, particularly in the red, yellow, orange, violet and purple ranges, which often are quite difficult with standard minerals, be they in the form of oxides, carbonates, nitrates, sulfates, chlorides or even the basic metal itself.

Minerals that produce reds, oranges and yellows are copper, iron, nickel, chromium, uranium, cadmium-selenium, rutile, antimony, vanadium and praseodymium. Variations in glaze makeup, temperature and atmosphere profoundly affect this particular color range, probably more than any other. The only materials that will produce red at high temperature are copper, iron and nickel, and the reds they produce are more muted, usually in the oxblood, crimson and plum range. Reds in the scarlet to vermilion range only can be achieved at low temperatures, although the recently developed inclusion of encapsulated stains shows promise for a wider range.

A number of ceramic color making companies produce what are either referred to as encapsulated stains or inclusion stains. These are made for the ceramic industry to produce colors that are stable at a range of temperatures. These stains contain normally fugitive colorants, such as cadmium/selenium, praseodymium, uranium and vanadium, that are chemically bonded to zirconium to give stability. Since these stains are complex to prepare, they tend to be expensive to purchase. However, if this is the color range with which you want to work, you may have to bite the bullet and go for it. It usually requires only a small amount of colorant to get a profound effect. If you find colors that you can't live without, it would be wise to purchase them in larger volume, as they have a tendency to disappear from the market on a regular basis.

The charts for the hot side of the spectrum on pages 136 and 137 show 17 colors and 49 variations that should help pinpoint mineral choices for desired colors. This is the sort of color chart listing that you find for watercolors, oils or acrylics, and it is readily available at art supply stores. In this way, it is probably easier to recognize the colors for which you are searching and to be able to work on glaze development for a given hue. Colors are listed with the minerals needed to obtain them, approximate temperatures, atmosphere, saturation percentage needed and comments on enhancing/inhibiting factors. Because of the widely variable nature of ceramic color, there are many generalities here. Where the word "vary" occurs in the column under cone, it signifies that the intended results could be expected most of the time at various points up to cone 10 on the Orton scale.

Without doubt, this "hot to trot" segment of the ceramic color range is the most elusive and difficult to control. Some colorants, like copper and cadmium/selenium stains, are, for various reasons, likely to volatilize and disappear in firing. Others, like chromium, may make abrupt color changes as the kiln temperature rises or the atmosphere changes. That is why most times when these colors are required, they are achieved with overglaze enamels or china paints (see Chapter 20). At the low-firing range (cone 022 to 018) of enamels, both lead- and alkaline-fluxed mixtures can provide much more stability than can be had at higher temperatures. Small amounts of iron in lead-fluxed enamels will give the imperial yellows of Ming Dynasty China. Large amounts of iron can give Indian red colors. Gold in the same sort of bases will give a range of pinks through to maroon. These are generally known as "famille rose."

Play It Cool

The cool side of the glaze spectrum (from yellow-green to navy blue) is considerably easier to produce and work with than the hot. Colorants that control this range create far fewer problems than almost any of the red, orange and yellow range. Some are temperature and atmosphere sensitive, but nothing compared with the idiosyncrasies possible with warm colors. For more details, see the charts for the cool side of the spectrum on pages 139 and 140.

The colorants known for creating cool hues are copper, chromium, nickel, cobalt, iron and sometimes molybdenum. For variations, some are modified by titanium, rutile, manganese or black stains. The usual three variables — glaze makeup, temperature and atmosphere — still control the outcome, though it is less obvious in this range. Very broadly, the color effects that can be expected are as follows.

Copper. Most of the green-blue range from copper requires oxidation firing. Exceptions are when the copper is above 5 percent of barium-saturated glaze or in combination with other colorants or opacifiers such as rutile, titanium or tin. In these cases the copper molecule seems to become coated by the opacifier, which shields it from color-altering reduction. The result is a green in reduction where you might expect a red. Copper is extremely sensitive to variation in fluxes and so probably has the widest range of possibilities of any of the basic colorants. It also is very sensitive to kiln atmosphere changes.

Chromium. The green color range that chromium causes in most temperatures varies from chartreuse or acid green through to the heavy, dull colors of army camouflage. Chromium is less affected than other

THE COOL SIDE OF THE SPECTRUM: YELLOW-GREEN TO TURQUOISE

COLORANT	CONE	ATMOSPHERE	%	COMMENTS
Yellow-Green				
Copper + rutile	vary	both	2% to 10%	Various mixtures in a wide variety of glazes, particularly those high in alkaline materials.
Chromium	vary	both	0.5% to 3%	In yellow glazes without tin or zinc.
Chromium	4 to 8	oxidation	0.25% to 1%	In saturated barium glazes.
Chromium	018 to 015	oxidation	0 to 2%	In high alkaline glazes with no tin.
Cobalt	vary	both	0 to 1%	In any yellow glazes.
Light Green				
Copper	vary	oxidation	0 to 2.5%	In various glazes except those high in barium or magnesium.
Cobalt	vary	both	0 to 2%	In glazes opacified with titanium, or containing rutile
Apple Green				
Chromium	vary	both	0 to 2%	In various glazes without zinc or tin. Good in alkaline glazes with zirconium opacifiers. Also use potassium dichromate.
Copper			1% to 2%	See light green; use in nonopacified glazes.
Celadon Green				
Iron	vary	reduction	0.5% to 2%	Best with high sodium, calcium or potassium glazes. Do not use with zinc glazes.
Copper	vary	oxidation	0.5% to 2%	Good in a wide range of glazes.
Grass Green				
Copper	010 to 2	oxidation	1% to 5%	In high lead glazes; sometimes with boron.
Chromium	018 to 04	oxidation	1% to 2%	In high alkaline glazes.
Olive Green				
Nickel	vary	both	1% to 5%	In high magnesia glazes; matte to shiny olive green.
Iron	vary	reduction	3% to 5%	In high calcium and alkaline, usually clear glazes.
Hooker's Green				
Copper + cobalt	vary	oxidation	2% to 5%	In a wide variety of glaze bases.
Cobalt + chromium	vary	both	2% to 5%	In a wide variety of glaze bases, no zinc or tin. Good opacified with zirconium or titanium.
Chrome Green				
Chromium	06 to 12	both	2% to 5%	In most glazes, no zinc or tin.
Dark Green				
Copper	vary	oxidation	5% to 10%	Many glaze bases, particularly high barium, strontium, zinc, or alkaline with a minimum of 10% kaolin.
Cobalt + chromium	vary	both	5% to 10%	Blends of these colorants will give a wide range of dark greens.
Cobalt + rutile	vary	both	5% to 10%	Dark greens with blue overtones.
Teal Blue				
Cobalt + rutile	vary	both	1% to 5%	In a wide variety of glazes.
Cobalt + chromium	vary	both	1% to 5%	In most glazes without tin or zinc.
Turquoise				
Copper	vary	oxidation	1% to 10%	In high alkaline and barium glazes. Bluish with no clay content; tends toward greenish tint with added clay.
Copper + rutile	vary	both	1% to 5%	In high alkaline and barium glazes.
Copper + tin	vary	oxidation	1% to 10%	In high alkaline and barium glazes; usually opaque

colorants by the glaze makeup, although it is particularly sensitive to glazes that contain zinc or tin. Zinc usually causes an abrupt color change to tan or brown. In the presence of tin, chromium causes a pink that is generally regarded as undesirable. Chromium is a powerful colorant that is probably best used in small proportions. In alkaline glazes, when used at less than 1 percent, quite delightful yellow-greens can be achieved; in barium-saturated glazes, brilliant yellow-greens are possible. Chromium is a refractory colorant; it tends to matte down fired glazes

THE COOL SIDE OF THE SPECTRUM: LIGHT BLUE TO NAVY BLUE

COLORANT	CONE	ATMOSPHERE	%	COMMENTS
Light Blue				
Nickel	vary	oxidation	1% to 2%	In high zinc or barium glazes.
Rutile	vary	reduction	1% to 5%	In a wide range of glazes; best with low (10% or less) clay content.
Cobalt	vary	both	0.25% to 1%	Use in most glazes, particularly those opacified with tin. Also use mixed with small amounts of iron.
Celadon Blue				
Iron	6 to 10	reduction	0.25% to 1%	In high alkaline or calcium clear glazes. Black iron is generally preferable to red iron.
Wedgwood Blue				
Cobalt + iron	vary	both	0.5% to 2%	In most glazes; small amounts of cobalt with iron, manganese or nickel yield soft blues. Added tin gives pastel blue.
Cobalt + manganese	vary	both	0.5% to 2%	
Cobalt + nickel	vary	both	0.5% to 2%	
Cobalt	4 to 10	both	0.5% to 3%	In high zinc glazes.
Nickel	4 to 10	oxidation	1% to 3%	In high barium/zinc glazes; likely to be crystalline.
Blue-Gray				
Nickel	vary	oxidation	0.5% to 5%	In high barium/zinc glazes.
Rutile	vary	reduction	2% to 5%	In a wide variety of glazes, particularly high alumina or magnesia recipes.
Cobalt + manganese	vary	both	0.5% to 2%	In most opaque glazes.
Cobalt	vary	oxidation	0.5% to 5%	In high zinc glazes.
Ultramarine				
Cobalt	vary	both	0.5% to 5%	In high barium, colemanite, and calcium glazes; no zinc, magnesium or opacification.
Cerulean Blue				
Cobalt	vary	both	0.5% to 5%	In glazes containing cryolite or fluorspar.
Cobalt + chromium	vary	both	2% to 5%	In most glazes except those containing zinc or tin.
Prussian Blue				
Nickel	6 to 10	oxidation	5% to 10%	In high barium/zinc glazes.
Mix cobalt 2 + chromium 2 + + manganese 2	vary	both	5% to 10%	In most glaze bases.
Navy Blue				
Cobalt	vary	both	5% to 10%	In most glazes except those high in zinc, barium, or magnesium.

and may make them crawl. When mixed with cobalt and used in small volumes, it can produce a fine range of teal blue through to deep turquoise.

Nickel. The green and blue effects achieved with the use of nickel generally are muted tones. Nickel is particularly effective when added in amounts less than 3 percent to magnesium glazes to yield a range of soft olive greens, and in high zinc glazes, where it can give a series of soft blues that often are crystalline. Most of the time, however, nickel produces grayish hues and is mainly used to moderate or tone down other colors.

Cobalt. For producing most blues, cobalt is the choice. Of all the colorants, it is affected least by the kiln's atmospheric conditions. It gives good, stable results that often are strongly affected by the choice of the glaze's opacifier. With titanium, cobalt will produce greens; with tin and zirconium, it will give pale, pastel blues. It is best to keep a cobalt glaze free of magnesia unless you want it to turn lilac, mauve or purple, depending on the volume introduced. Cobalt usually is added in small percentages, but it may produce surprising color changes at volumes in excess of 7 percent; e.g. abrupt changes from blue to mauve-pink, particularly in barium glazes. When mixed with other colorants, it can be part of reactions that yield a wide color range.

Iron. Colors in the green to blue range from iron are dependent on reduction, the basic glaze makeup, and the amount/type of iron used. Most iron greens and blues are formed in Chinese-style celadon glazes. Almost any clear cone 8 to 10 glaze fired in reduction will, with added increments of iron up to 5 percent, produce a celadon range that appears anywhere from pale gray-green to deep olive. If less than 1 percent black iron oxide is used (rather than red iron oxide), there is more likelihood of getting subtle blues. A similar amount of red iron in a barium-saturated glaze also can produce a soft blue. Blue Chün-type glazes predominantly are opalescent and usually are colored with a similar amount of iron, but the color is more dependent on the glaze itself; it should have some phosphorous content, either from wood ash or bone ash, and/or be somewhat laced with boron, either in the form of colemanite (Gerstley borate) or boron frit. The apparent blues in these glazes are caused by the refraction of light from the inner surfaces of myriad tiny bubbles. Ilmenite and rutile are iron and titanium compounds that also give somewhat opalescent blue colors in a wide range of glazes. Next to copper, iron produces the most variations in color.

Molybdenum. Though seldom used, molybdenum can produce interesting colors and effects. In barium- and zinc-based glazes, it produces subtle yellow-greens that often are mottled with dark brown or blackish spots.

Greens and particularly blues are probably the easiest range of color to develop, but also the hardest to employ sensitively. In their brighter forms they can quickly be overpowering, and unless used very carefully, they easily can become quite garish and crude looking. The chart of green and blue variations identifies quite a spectrum, but for those who wish to develop more such colors, there also are a great variety of commercial stains available. The zirconium/vanadium stains produce a pleasant series of duck egg through baby blue to mid-turquoise. Some zirconium/vanadium/praseodymium stains produce very good greens, depending on the glaze. Remember that the colors developed from all ceramic stains are subject to the same variables — glaze makeup, temperature and atmosphere — that affect any other colorant. The color that may be on available samples often will be only an approximation of what you find on firing.

The next segment brings the glaze color spectrum to full circle by starting at indigo and working around to purples and plums. Some colors are outside the spectrum proper, such as brown, gray and black, so we will finish with them.

There are other ways to achieve many of the colors. What I give here is a good basis from which to start. I developed these charts because I needed to know how to achieve specific colors to fully realize the imagery I wished to use. The results have proved invaluable to me, and if they don't get to the absolute color I want, they at least narrow the field of experimentation, saving a great deal of time and frustration.

Mood Indigo

The indigo-to-purple part of the color wheel is small but significant. The colorants that produce this range are nickel, cobalt, manganese, umber, iron, chromium, rutile, ilmenite, copper, iron chromate and black stains. In short, you could say that the colorants needed include just about the whole group used for all the other colors in the spectrum. The only ones I haven't talked about previously are umber, ilmenite, iron chromate and black stains.

Umber. Along with sepia and sienna, umber is a high-iron colorant with small amounts of chemically combined manganese. It is closely related to red and yellow-ocher, and, like ocher, is an iron colorant that has been chemically leached by contamination with calcium. Umber is very useful as a color moderator, and, on its own, can do what you would expect a mixture of iron and manganese to do, namely give a range of browns.

Ilmenite. Another iron colorant, this time chemically combined with titanium, ilmenite is similar to but darker than rutile, which also is a chemical combination of iron and titanium. Ilmenite generally is used to modify other colorants, but it can produce fine colors of its own in the more muted ranges. Because it is a naturally occurring mixture of two minerals, Ilmenite sometimes can give an extra zing where you might be using iron on its own. In granular form, ilmenite and rutile often are used to speckle clays and glazes in oxidation firing.

Iron chromate. Within this colorant, iron is chemically combined with chromium. Wherever you might wish to use these two colorants together, iron chromate alone may suffice. In oxidation, brushwork done on tin-opacified glazes often will produce a black line surrounded by pink.

Black stains. Formulated from a variable mixture of other colorants, black stains usually are rather expensive, because they are saturations of colorant materials. Various companies produce black stains, usually from a

THE DARK SIDE OF THE SPECTRUM: INDIGO TO PINK

COLORANT	CONE	ATMOSPHERE	%	COMMENTS
Indigo				
Nickel	vary	oxidation	8% to 15%	Use in high barium/zinc glazes. Also likely to crystallize.
Cobalt + manganese	vary	both	5% to 10%	Various mixtures in most glazes.
Cobalt + black stain	vary	both	5% to 8%	Various mixtures in most glazes.
Violet				
Cobalt	vary	both	5% to 10%	In high magnesium glazes.
Nickel	vary	oxidation	1% to 10%	In some saturated barium glazes.
Manganese	vary	both	5% to 10%	In high alkaline glazes.
Copper	4 to 6	oxidation	8% to 10%	In some saturated barium glazes.
Purple				
Copper	6 to 10	both	8% to 10%	In high barium and barium/zinc glazes.
Copper	8 to 10	reduction	1% to 5%	In copper red glazes opacified with titanium.
Nickel	vary	oxidation	5% to 10%	In some high barium glazes.
Cobalt	vary	both	5% to 10%	In high magnesium glazes.
Manganese	04 to 10	oxidation	5% to 10%	In high alkaline and barium glazes.
Iron	8 to 10	reduction	8% to 10%	In high calcium glazes; likely to crystallize.
Copper + cobalt	vary	reduction	2% to 8%	Various mixtures in many glazes.
Chrome 1 + tin 9 + cobalt 0 to 1%	vary	oxidation	2% to 8%	Various mixtures in many glazes
Mauve or Lilac				
Cobalt	vary	both	1% to 5%	In high magnesium glazes.
Nickel	vary	oxidation	1% to 5%	In some saturated barium glazes.
Pink				
Cobalt	vary	oxidation	1% to 3%	In high magnesium glazes opacified with tin. Also in very low alumina content glazes.
Copper	vary	reduction	0.2% to 2%	In copper red glazes with titanium.
Copper	6 to 10	oxidation	0.2% to 3%	In high magnesium or high alumina glazes.
Copper	8 to 10	reduction	5% to 10%	In copper red glazes opacified with at least 5% titanium.
Chromium	vary	oxidation	1% to 2%	In calcium glazes opacified with 5% to 10% tin.
Iron	vary	oxidation	1% to 5%	In calcium glazes opacified with tin.
Rutile	vary	both	5% to 10%	In high calcium and some ash glazes.
Nickel	018 to 010	oxidation	1% to 3%	In high barium glazes with some zinc.
Manganese	vary	both	1% to 5%	In alkaline glazes opacified with tin/titanium; also in high alumina glazes.

combination of iron, cobalt, chromium, manganese, iron chromate and sometimes nickel, which are mixed with fillers and fluxes such as clay, feldspar and silica. The best blacks usually contain cobalt and may cause some glazes to have a bluish tint. I use the following recipe.

Black Stain Recipe

Chromium oxide	20
Cobalt carbonate or oxide	20
Manganese dioxide	20
Red iron oxide	20
Feldspar (any)	8
Kaolin (any)	8
Silica	4
TOTAL	**100%**

This mixture is best ball milled for a minimum of four hours to limit its tendency toward cobalt specking and to make sure that the colorants are thoroughly mixed. Because any black stain is a very concentrated mixture, only small amounts normally are needed to cause a strong effect. In a clear glaze, a maximum of 5 percent should produce an intense black. In opaque glazes, more stain than that may be needed. Black stains and white opacifiers mixed together will produce a range of opaque grays. Stains, like other ceramic materials, are subject to the three variables: glaze makeup, temperature and atmosphere.

Outside the color wheel are tones of brown, gray and black. These also moderate other colors. A color wheel could, I suppose, include the range of opacifiers,

THE DARK SIDE OF THE SPECTRUM: BROWN, GRAY AND BLACK

COLORANT	CONE	ATMOSPHERE	%	COMMENTS
Brown				
Iron	vary	both	3% to 10%	In most glazes.
Manganese	vary	both	2% to 10%	In most glazes.
Nickel	vary	both	2% to 5%	In high boron, calcium and lead glazes.
Chromium	vary	both	2% to 5%	In high zinc glazes.
Umber	vary	both	2% to 10%	In most glazes.
Ilmenite	vary	both	2% to 10%	In most glazes. High calcium may yield a bluish tint.
Rutile	vary	both	5% to 10%	In most glazes; golden brown.
Gray				
Iron	vary	reduction	2% to 4%	In many glaze bases; gray brown.
Iron chromate	vary	both	2% to 5%	In most glaze bases without zinc or tin.
Nickel	vary	both	2% to 5%	In most glaze bases; gray brown.
Copper	8 to 10	both	3% to 10%	In high magnesium glazes. Warm gray in reduction; cold gray in oxidation.
Cobalt + nickel	vary	both	1% to 5%	Blue-gray in most glazes.
Cobalt + manganese	vary	both	1% to 5%	Blue-gray to purple-gray in most glazes.
Black stain	vary	both	1% to 5%	Shades of gray in most opacified glazes.
Black				
Iron	vary	both	8% to 12%	In high calcium glazes, the Tenmoku range.
Copper	vary	both	8% to 10%	In a wide range of glazes.
Cobalt	vary	both	8% to 10%	Blue-black in most glazes except those high in zinc and magnesium.
Manganese	vary	both	8% to 15%	Brown-black in most glazes.
Copper + manganese	vary	both	10% to 20%	In most glazes; sometimes lustrous.
Uranium	vary	reduction	5% to 10%	In most glazes.
Cobalt + iron + manganese	vary	both	5% to 10%	Various mixtures in most glazes.

since they also have a strong role in affecting color. The toning influence of brown, gray and black is just as much opacifying in result as are the white opacifiers, such as tin, titanium and zirconium compounds such as Zircopax, Opax, Superpax and Ultrox. Slight additional increments of any of these colors will render most glazes, colored or not, progressively darker as they are added.

This brings us to the end of the color circle. The possible variations are infinite because of the vast range of material intermixtures that can be formulated. If you haven't begun to explore the colorant area of ceramics, I hope these notes will help you find a direction and lead you to as much fun as I have had learning about them. If you already have substantial knowledge of colorants, I hope I've added to your ideas about color formation.

Ours is a magical art form, dealing with transforming a motley collection of powders and grits into something akin to gems and jewels. There is no sleight of hand in this magic, just work, observation and intuitive decision making. Sometimes the process may be boring, but the result always is enlightening. It is worth remembering that when you are at the end of your tether or up to your ears in glaze tests and still haven't found that elusive gem, don't give up or compromise — the next one may be your diamond!

Fired Up, Wired Up

The potential for development of the ceramic surface, particularly the ceramic glaze surface, is absolutely infinite. If you were to change your mind about how to use the technology every second day, an 80-year lifetime wouldn't be long enough to explore all the possibilities. This section is about exploring the development and use of glazes in the electric kiln.

Learning the ceramic medium is a long building process. It is far better to thoroughly understand a small area of work and apply that knowledge to the next stage of development. After a while, it becomes so ingrained as to be almost intuitive. It is like learning any other form of language. Telling a story means learning about grammar, words, word order, phrases, sentences and paragraphs. Without the basics, there is no communication. Pottery making and its decoration are among the earliest forms of human communication. Exploration and experimentation build accrued knowledge, and the range of knowledge expands both as understanding increases and as the need arises. The limitations that we place on ourselves normally relate to the three basics: kiln type, temperature and atmosphere.

If you were to make a world survey of the types of kilns used by clay workers, it's almost certain that electric kilns would outnumber all others by an extremely large margin. And yet the ceramic literature specifically aimed at the electric kiln user is limited to a very few books and a larger but still limited array of magazine articles. Most of the books that do exist don't do justice to the subject, tending to look with a very narrow perspective at a few clay bodies and a few basic glazes for a strictly limited range of temperatures. It often seems to be forgotten that there are potters all over the world variously working at 37 or so cones (from cone 022 all the way to cone 15) that make up the workable range for the making and decorating of pottery. So much can be done at each temperature that such arbitrary limitations tend to squelch the personal and creative aspect of glaze and color development. There is more to life than a recipe, no matter who originated it!

In the early period of the contemporary studio movement, from the 1920s to the 1960s, potters chose to use reduction-fired kilns, as most of the popular glazes came from Oriental origins and, at that time, the Oriental aesthetic generally was deemed the most sophisticated. Oriental kilns primarily were fired with wood. This fuel usually gives an alternating atmospheric condition, reducing when being stoked and shortly after stoking, then oxidizing as the fire burns more fiercely and efficiently. Because most urban centers do not allow the use of polluting devices such as reduction-fired ceramic kilns, most urban potters use an electric kiln as the alternative. However, what started as a method of convenience has become the reliable preference for many, regardless of where they live. I personally prefer to use each firing method for what it does best and how it allows me to complete the ceramic cycle from concept to reality.

There is a different aesthetic evident in oxidized clay works; for many it is clean, clear and infinitely preferable for use. Your aesthetic sensitivity, vision and experience will have some effect on how you relate to oxidation. For those weaned on high-fire reduction kilns, working with oxidizing kilns, particularly in temperatures below cone 6, often requires a total aesthetic rethinking before any real degree of satisfaction is achieved. These potters often work like mad trying to emulate the naturally occurring effects of the combustion kiln and throw all manner of damaging things (mothballs, naphtha, propane gas, oil-soaked rags, charcoal and small pieces of wood) into their electric kilns to get the same effects. I know, because I've been there!

It is far better to learn what works best in oxidation and make the most of what the uncontaminated kiln has to offer. The oxidation atmosphere, in fact, offers a richer palette of color than the reduction kiln. The lack of carbon makes the colors more vibrant. At the same time, it is quite easy to modify the colors to a more muted tone if that's what is required. Surface variations easily can be adjusted through a firsthand knowledge of the behavior of materials, particularly the fluxes. Small amounts of some of the least-used fluxes, such as lithium, cryolite, fluorspar, bone ash, pearl ash, wood ash, magnesium carbonate and amblygonite or low-solubility spodumene, can produce extremely interesting results. In a glaze without colorants, or in conjunction with other colorants or stains, a small percentage (1 percent to 5 percent) of titanium dioxide can enliven even the most boring looking oxidation glaze by forming micro-crystals that give visual surface or color breakup.

Any technical ceramics book or article is bound to have a great many generalities included, as that is the nature of the medium. It is difficult, if not impossible, to be precise when ceramic materials fuse and melt at such a wide variety of temperatures. Pinpointing an exact temperature as the optimum point for a given color or color range often is impossible due to all of the variables that come into play during fusion. The general range of our total color palette has been laid out in the charts. It is hoped that this will give you a fairly good view of the overall possibilities of working with standard metallic mineral colorants. For more specific colors, it might be better to look into the use of stains, underglaze colors or even overglaze enamels or china paints.

As you may have noticed, a great deal of what constitutes the mineral color range occurs in oxidation firing. Much color variation can be achieved at a wide variety of temperatures using the same volume of colorant in either very similar or completely different glaze bases. Unless you are being temperature specific, much of what you might wish to explore is subject to the variables of the glaze and any slips or engobes that may be used to develop the total surface. Most ceramic surfaces are, in fact, a gradual layering of materials or compounds that interact both with each other and, to some extent, with the clay body as they fuse. In oxidation firing, the layering of different glazes is likely to produce the most satisfying results as the material fusion becomes most interesting. Putting one slip, engobe or glaze over another by the usual application methods of dipping, pouring, spraying, etc., allows a great deal of interaction between glaze materials, colorants and opacifiers. Sometimes parts of layers will be hidden or lost in the process. Often this is beneficial to the final work; sometimes it is infuriating. However, it is part of what makes the challenge of ceramics so rewarding and exciting.

In looking at the electric palette, or the way colorants behave in oxidation glazes, you must be aware of the temperature to which the glaze is fired, as well as the makeup of the glaze itself, in order to speculate on color accuracy. Because the range of commercially prepared stains is so variable, I only am concerned here with the usual metallic colorants. If you know the colorants that make up the various prepared stains, it should be possible to discover what stains might be affected by what sort of glaze, and which fluxes might be needed to predominate so shade card accuracy can be achieved. Here I only state the effects of the single metallic mineral colorant in its oxide form because the basic fired behavior of oxides, dioxides, carbonates, sulfates and nitrates usually is quite similar. The pattern of color variation is the main concern. If I succeed in piquing your interest to delve further into glaze and color control, you undoubtedly will find out that many other variations and subtleties are possible. All colorants and opacifiers can be intermixed, so the total color potential of the medium is awesome. Even if you only use the most basic mineral colorants of iron, cobalt, copper, manganese, nickel, chromium and rutile, the potential is vast. Most colorants are used in saturations of 0.25 percent to 10 percent, depending on the strength of color desired. If it is understood that there is a huge variation in color that can be achieved from almost any of these common colorants, you can state the following generalities and simplifications.

Iron. In oxidation, iron will give a range of color that includes yellows, tans, reds, browns and black. It can be added to high- and low-temperature barium, strontium and magnesium recipes. Iron-containing, lead-based glazes will lean toward the yellow to yellow-brown range. In zinc-based glazes, cream to ocher colors develop. In boron-based glazes, opalescent blue to black can be achieved. In calcium-based glazes, pale yellow to black is possible, while additions of bone ash or wood ash can help in developing olive green to Indian red.

Cobalt. Cobalt is the most powerful and least variable of colorants, and it normally gives various hues of blue, although lilac, mauve and purple can be developed with magnesium-based glazes. Saturations of 7 percent to 10 percent in barium, strontium and some talc and wood ash glazes can give vibrant pink. In most glazes, this degree of cobalt saturation will yield blue-black to black; in zinc-based glazes, soft blue-gray colors can be achieved.

Copper. Copper is the most variable colorant. In lead-dominated glazes, it produces grassy greens; in barium and strontium glazes, turquoise blue to purple; in magnesium glazes, orange, salmon pink and gray; in zinc glazes, soft turquoise green; in high alumina glazes, gray; and in boron and alkaline glazes, mottled turquoise.

Manganese. In most glazes, manganese yields variations on brown, from soft fawn to dark purple-brown. In barium-, strontium-, and alkaline-based glazes, it can give reddish purple; in magnesium glazes, it can give a soft, mushroom pink.

Nickel. Nickel can give a wide range of colors, from flesh pink to red, green, blue and purple. It most often is used as a modifier of other colorants. In barium- and strontium-based glazes, it can yield pink to mauve to red-purple to mottled purple-green; in high magnesium glazes, it can give acid greens to olive; in zinc glazes, blue to purple, often crystalline.

Chromium. In most glazes, chromium generally gives opaque, dark-green colors. In high-lead glazes fired below 1,740°F (950°C), it can give a range of bright yellows, oranges and reds. These would be unsuitable for food-safe surfaces. In barium and strontium and other highly alkaline glazes at saturations of less than 1 percent, it can give acid and chartreuse greens. In glazes containing zinc, chromium invariably turns brown, usually tan. In conjunction with tin oxide in glazes containing approximately 20 percent calcium carbonate, it can produce a range of pinks to crimson reds. It can also volatilize during firing to turn adjacent tin-opacified glazes pink. The volatilized chromium also can impregnate kiln brickwork, releasing color into subsequent firings.

Rutile. In most glazes, rutile gives a range of cream or tan through to muted yellow, orange and pink colors. In conjunction with tin oxide, it may produce strong yellows. It has a particularly strong effect on other colors, turning cobalt green, iron gold and copper yellow-green, often with a micro-crystalline surface.

Mixing either two or more of these seven basic mineral colorants can produce a limitless range of color variations. Combining this potential with the added possibilities that come from cross-blending with different opacifiers, this group can produce most of the spectrum. There are a few times when the use of stains is particularly beneficial, usually for the bright yellow range or for very specific colors that might be needed for color matching. However, the price of prepared stains usually is quite high, and similar effects can be achieved using standard colorants at a considerably lower cost.

It really doesn't take a tremendous amount of testing to come up with a personal glaze palette to satisfy your oxidation needs. For any particular temperature range, adding colorants to a few variously fluxed white or colorless glazes with differing surface qualities will produce a wide response. A small amount of experimentation time used wisely with excellent record-keeping can produce wonders.

Patination

Patination is the name given to the changes that usually occur on metal surfaces as they age, alter and decompose. It often is used to describe the familiar green coloration, or verdigris, that occurs on copper roofs or ancient bronze sculptures. Since the ceramic surface is capable of being developed in an almost limitless fashion and employs mainly metallic oxides to do it, it is reasonable to expect that there are many ways to explore these thin coatings. Patinas are particularly appropriate for use on textured surfaces or sculpture, giving great visual depth to forms and markings. They usually are darker than the clay body, but they can be developed as a light patina to emphasize depressions on a dark clay.

In this case they probably would include white clays, pale terra sigillatas and light-colored opacifying agents. Patination is best done at temperatures above cone 4, where the colorants begin to fuse with the clay.

Patination by Colorant

Almost any mineral colorant can be mixed with water and a little gum or a terra sigillata and applied to the surface of an object with a sponge. The colorant will find cuts, lines and depressions to fill, where the color will become deeper or lighter, depending on the colorant selected for the job. Once a full sponging has been done, a damp sponge or cloth can be used to remove any excess from the surface so that maximum contrast can be seen between the surface and the depression that holds the color. The following colorants are particularly useful for patination. Some are best applied over white clays or porcelain, or over a white slip or terra sigillata.

COLORANT PATINATION OR COLORANT WASHES
- **Red-brown:** iron oxide; ochre; umber; iron and tin mixed
- **Dark brown:** manganese; iron and copper mixed; nickel
- **Greens:** chromium; titanium and cobalt mixed; prepared stains
- **Bronze-gold:** manganese 7 + copper 3 mixed
- **Blues:** cobalt; cobalt and tin mixed; prepared stains
- **Yellows:** rutile; rutile and tin mixed
- **Oranges:** rutile and iron mixed; iron and tin mixed

Patination by Fluxes

This can be done by making thin solutions of fluxes mixed with water and applied by sponge in the method described above. Fluxes that work well include frits, calcium borate, barium/lithium mixtures, and mixtures of calcium borate with rutile.

Patination by Glaze

Most glazes can be used in this way to emphasize highlights and depressions in the surface. Where a colorant patina usually will be matte in surface, a glaze patina will usually be glossy. They can be done with many forms of glaze, particularly those that have dramatically different characteristics when either thick or thin.

Maya. Late Classic 600 to 900 C.E. Clay, paint. A hunter with a blowgun shoots a water bird with a fish in its beak. The bird drops the fish, and another bird retrieves it. Rollout photograph © Justin Kerr.

CHAPTER 12

The Mark of the Brush and Soft Stamp

Some of the softest, most expressive and eloquent marks ever to grace ceramic surfaces have been made using tufts of hair, fibers of plants, whiskers of mice and bunches of feathers! Simply bound together or attached to a handle, these ordinary fibrous materials produce marks of astonishing variety and beauty. Combining soft-stamped decoration with brushwork can produce extremely interesting and complex imagery. Through the process of layering between pigments, slips and glazes, multilayered effects can impart a richness equal to painting and printmaking.

Brushes

From the broad, flat, bristle brush for expansive

An assortment of brushes.

Brush marks with varied brushes.

Photo: J. Jones

John Ikeda, Canada, "Slab Container," 4" x 4" x 7", 1998.

Onglaze painting (majolica style) and glaze trailing

The base glaze coat with the first brush mark of a different glaze.

Iron brush decoration.

Continuing the iron brush decoration.

Trailing white glaze over.

More glaze trailing.

The fired and completed teapot.

Photos: Judi Dyelle

148

Chandler Swain, Canada, "Dinner Plate," stained slips on cone 6 porcelain, sgraffito, 10".

painting of anything from pots and houses, to the most minute, hair-tipped stick for the tiniest of details, the brush has been part of the ceramic tool kit for millennia.

The enormous variety of commercially available brushes is bewildering, and you really need to try many of them out with ink or water to get a feeling for their potential and how they feel in the hand. The type of brushes you need depends on the work you plan to do

with them. For broad expanses, house-painting brushes from 2" and larger do a great job. For calligraphy (from the Greek words "kalos" and "graphein," meaning "beautiful writing"), specialized animal hair or hair from a particular part of the animal most commonly is used. Perhaps some of the most exciting and vital calligraphic marks on American ceramics of the 20th century were made by Paul Soldner, who used the severed tail of a roadkill raccoon! Ultimately it isn't the type of brush

Photo: Jeremy Jones

Ian Symons, Canada, "Hatchway," red earthenware, white slip, sgraffito, painted with colored glazes, glaze fired to cone 04, 26cm x 32cm x 14cm, 1995.

you have, but how you use it that matters. It would be impossible to write in a single chapter a total view of all the variations and qualities that brushes embody, as it would about any single group of tools in the ceramist's tool kit. The photograph on page 147 shows a few common brush variations and the type of marks they make. Every brush has three essential methods of use: the tip, or point; the side, or drag; and the full-bodied stroke.

In bristle brushes, there is little absorbency in the coarse hair that takes up a charge of ink or color, so the marks from these brushes usually will be short, staccato or stippled. In long, fine-hair brushes, the mark may be long and sinuous from a single charge of ink or paint. A charge is the amount of ink, paint, pigment or glaze that may be held by the brush as a sort of reservoir that is released gradually as the tip, side or full brush moves across the paper or ceramic surface.

Many brushes now are made using synthetic materials, like nylon. Though not as good in use as many varieties of natural hair brushes made from sable, elk,

Photo: Brian Oglesbee

Bruce Winn, USA, "Cup and Saucer," porcelain, glazed, 8.2cm x 14cm, 1992. Museum Purchase, Corsaw Collection, Schein-Joseph International Museum of Ceramic Art, Alfred University, 1992.

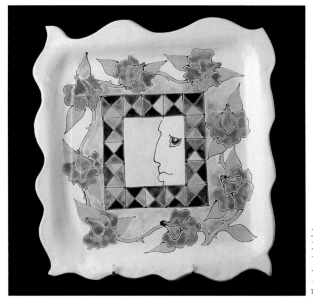

Angela Gallia, USA, "Rose Platter," earthenware, colored wax resist applied with a slip-trailing bottle then painted with a stain, 14".

Jim Smith, Canada, "Dog and Rabbit Vase," Nova Scotia earthenware clay, white slip, sgraffito drawn decoration, brush painted colored stains, oxides, sulfates with clear glaze over all, 30cm x 20cm x 15cm, 2002.

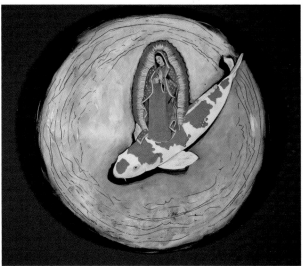

Jenny Lind, USA, "Platter," painted engobes, cone 03, 16", 1998.

goat, dog, deer, camel and even horse hair, synthetic hair brushes usually are a perfectly serviceable and less-expensive alternative. Synthetic brushes also are slightly more resistant to the abrasive qualities that are a natural part of all ceramic pigments, surfaces and glazes. Unfortunately, brushes do wear out over time, usually at the most inopportune time. If you have a favorite brush, especially of a particular make and number (usually branded into the shaft), keep careful note of the information. It might be a good idea to always keep a second one in stock in case of loss or damage. Favorite brushes tend to become like extensions of your hand. If the company that makes them suddenly ceases production, it can be a major trauma. A few years ago, a brush I had

used for years suddenly died of old age and overuse. It was a fude, wonderful for big, floppy marks. The center fell out without warning. The company that made it had sold out to another company and discontinued the line. After diligent research and testing many look-alikes, I finally found that the new company had a small stock of these brushes left, so I bought the whole lot to keep me covered for the rest of my life as a good insurance policy. A good brush can be that important!

Linda Arbuckle, USA, "Tea Pot – Green Balance," majolica on terra cotta, 12" x 4-½" x 13", 1999.

sharp knife to a brush, the results of customized brushes are marks that often have much more surface interest, movement, vitality and individuality.

Brush alternatives, such as cellulose sponge brushes, will hold a good charge of color, but they usually need to be soaked in water before using. Sponge brushes can be customized with scissors or a red-hot needle tool. Sometimes plant fiber brushes are made using yucca, bamboo, cedar bark or flax. Although plant fiber brushes make great marks on paper and ceramic surfaces, the abrasive ceramic materials shorten their lifespan. Plant fiber brushes generally will hold a minimum of charge, giving a very broken stroke.

At most stages in the cycle of a ceramic object's development, the surface is quite absorbent, and the liquid will be sucked from the brush much more quickly than when working on most forms of paper. For people new to painting ceramic surfaces, this often leaves the brush without enough charge to finish the stroke. Unfortunately, double stroking a brush mark usually leaves a mess, and most of the time, it is not removable because ceramic colorants tend to stain through layers into the absorbent surface. Practicing brushwork on newspaper or newsprint rolls approximates the ceramic application quite well. New brushwork patterns worked out on absorbent paper give the painter a feel for the type of charge needed and the speed of stroke required. Brushwork almost is like a dance, where the movement of arm, wrist or fingers transfers energy to the finest tip of the brush. Like dance, it takes time and concentrated effort to learn brush control. Freedom of interpretation and movement comes only after much practice. Variations in pressure, speed, lift, drag, flow and direction will develop an enormous range of expressive marks. Taking courses in Oriental brush painting, calligraphy or noncharacter calligraphy on paper is a great way to learn the disciplines of the brush, but these disciplines will need to be adjusted when applied to ceramic surfaces. Besides the absorbency of the material to be painted, the ceramic surface often is vertical, whereas paper is normally horizontal. A three-dimensional object presents different problems in brush movement than a flat, horizontal plane. The way the brush is held in these two scenarios also is quite different. When painting on paper, the brush often is held toward the end of the shaft, away from the brush tip, with much of the brush control coming from wrist movement. In ceramic

The more you work with brushes, the more demanding you will become on their performance. Hair brushes for watercolor, Oriental brush painting or ceramic painting also come in a wide variety of shapes, from long and thin (often called pencils and liners) to short and fat (often called fudes) and specifically shaped such as fan, dagger, angled and squared (often called sign writer's brushes). Each shape has things that it does best, and it is up to the user to explore the potential of each variable. Brushes can be customized by cutting away part of the brush hair with a sharp-pointed knife or razor blade. Partially removing the side hairs by cutting the hair approximately halfway between the tip and ferrule, leaving the center hairs at the original length, will produce very interesting combination brush marks. Removing a few selected hairs from a fan brush will result in much more linear, textured and broken marks. Although it may seem like sacrilege to take a

Photo: Bruce Spielman

Duane Perkins, Canada, "Jar," porcelain, slip and glaze trailings, brushwork with glaze; oxides, stencils, wax resist, multiple glazes, 16-¾" x 10-½", 2002.

Michael Cohen, USA, "Three Trays," sponge printing of iron slip on blue glaze, foreground 15" x 5", 1994.

painting, the brush usually is held on or just above the ferrule, almost in the middle of the shaft, where there is a physical balance and firmer control. A full- or lower-arm movement typically is used, unless you are working on small-scale objects. There usually is a slightly tighter grip to balance the natural tendency of absorbent clay or bisque to pull the moving brush to a dead stop.

Many artists take great pride in making their own brushes. I find this much more difficult and frustrating than I am prepared to accept. I prefer to use the brushes made by someone else who knows what he or she is doing. For a custom-made brush that will last many years, I usually prefer those made by Keith Lebanzon Brushes (www.brushman.net). When an artist uses brushwork for a large percentage of his work, it becomes just as much a signature as signing the name. A brush that allows the artist to develop a very personal repertoire of marks is a special investment. Sometimes handmade brushes are very expensive and are almost like works of art themselves. Since brushes vary greatly, they should be tested with water before purchase, if possible. Some brush makers

will custom-make brushes for a client's personal use. If you plan to make your own brushes, the type of hair and the part of the animal's body the hair is from are extremely important. The most resilient hair that will retain its spring normally is from the nape of the neck, where there is less friction. Often, small bundles of soft fur act as a charge reservoir and are surrounded by longer, more resilient hair to form a long, thin point. The amount and type of hair is critical to the brush's performance. If you feel that brushwork is to be the identifying mark that represents your work, the attention to the capabilities and the selection of the brush are critical, as is the care of the brush in cleaning and general usage. Whether you make it yourself, find it or purchase it, a good, responsive brush is worth its weight in gold!

Making Dots

A mark that goes well with brushwork but that brushes often don't do well is a round dot or square dot as an emphasis to brushwork. To make dots, try the various sizes of cotton swabs or cotton wool buds on a

Photo: E.G. Schempf

Lynn Smiser Bowers, USA, "Milk and Sugar Set," porcelain, cone 10 reduction, pitcher 9" x 8" x 5".

stick available at drugstores, pharmacies or electronics stores. Normally used for small cleaning jobs, from ears to tape-recorder heads, they can be dipped into the pigment and easily used for creating "punctuation" marks to brushwork. For larger or square dots, thin cellulose foam sheet can be stretched over short lengths of wooden dowel rod or square-section wood of different sizes and secured with thin copper or brass wire or an elastic band.

Brushes and Resists

Many artists like to use brushwork with various resist processes. Unfortunately, most liquid resists, such as latex or wax, will quickly clog or destroy a brush. To clean resist medium out of brushes, dip the brush in kitchen detergent and gently squeeze through the hair, then rinse it in warm water. To protect brushes from latex resists, it helps to dip the hair into kitchen detergent before the latex application and massage the detergent well into the hair.

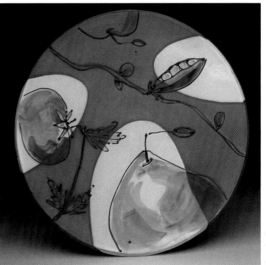

Photo by the artist

Wynn Wilbur, USA, "Mixed Fruit and Veggie Platter," majolica on terra cotta, 16" x 16" x 2", 2001.

Banding or Decorating Wheels

One of the most important additional tools for the painter of ceramics is a good quality, sturdy, well-oiled banding or decorating wheel. The best I have found

155

are the heavy-duty wheels produced by the Shimpo Co. The ideal size for most work is a turntable of 8" to 10" with a shaft height of 6" to 8". This type of decorating wheel allows the user's hand to fit beneath the head and give continual movement through twisting with the fingers. For banded decoration or horizontal lines around a form, the object is centered on the wheel. Then, with the wheel turning, the banding is done by holding the brush in place while turning the turntable with the other hand. For larger work, a 13" wide, low decorating wheel is very useful.

Preparing Pigment for Brushwork

Brushwork usually is done with either a single colorant and stain or a combination of colorants. A ceramic stain basically is a combination of mineral colorants, fillers, fluxes and opacifiers that are prepared to develop colors for the ceramic industry. They are made and used under carefully controlled conditions to give specific colors in conjunction with glazes of a particular type.

The ceramic artist is the beneficiary of huge amounts of industrial color research. Whether you use individual mineral oxides or carbonates, stains or blends of mineral oxides and carbonates, the process basically the same. The pigment is mixed with water to a smooth, brushable consistency, using either a tile and palette knife, a flat glass maul on a tempered glass

surface, or a mortar and pestle. Unless you want a gritty pigment to paint with, it is usual to grind the pigment to a thin, smooth paste. The finer the grind, the better it will work, and the less wear and tear it will cause on the brushes.

Sometimes gums are added as siccatives, or suspenders, to produce a smoother material and make the brushwork flow more easily. Gum additions also have the secondary benefit of hardening the unfired surface of the pigment, which otherwise would be quite fragile from returning to a powder on the surface as the water evaporates. Adding gum to pigments is particularly useful in schools and group workshops where there is a possibility of unwanted hands touching the work and smudging the decoration. Many different gum solutions can be used, such as gum arabic, gum tragacanth, carageenan, CMC and others. Powdered gums usually are mixed with boiling water, left to stand overnight and stirred until smooth. Sugar, molasses and syrup solutions also can be used. Ideally, the stickiness of the gums should disappear as soon as the brushwork dries on the surface. The gums or other suspenders will burn away in the firing and should have no residual effect on glazes.

The pigment pastes are thinned with water to suit the work. Gauging the saturation and thickness of the pigment is a trial and error process, since all colorants have differing strengths of coloration. Some materials can be used quite thickly, while others might bubble

Photo: Tom Holt

Sam Scott, USA, "Three-Piece Canister Set," wheel-thrown porcelain with overglaze brushwork decoration on clear glaze, reduction fired to cone12, 10-½" x 9" x 7-½".

Photo: Yosh Inouye

Kayo O'Young, Canada, "Jar," porcelain, wheel-thrown, crater glaze surface with brushed oxides and glazes, reduction fired cone 10, 13" x 16" x 47".

Photo by the artist

Katheleen Nez, USA, "Jeddito Black-on-Orange," lidded casserole, 11-¾" x 7-½", 2000.

Preparing the Surface for Brushwork

Brushwork can be done on raw clay, bisque or unfired glaze, depending on how the results are visualized. Each state has its own set of breakable rules of combat or engagement! The more experienced you become working at different states in the ceramic cycle, the more likely you are to find a specific niche that works better or feels more comfortable.

On leather-hard greenware, the absorption of water into the surface is minimal, so the pigment will stay wet longer. On dry greenware, the water content of the pigment is drawn into the clay surface. On top of a freshly applied glaze, the pigment's water content will be sucked in the same way as on dry greenware, but if the glazed surface is left to totally dry out before painting is done, the pigment's water content will be rapidly sucked from the brush and may even cause the glaze to lose adherence to the clay body.

Painting on the unfired glazed surface is the preferred state for many, whether it be on low-fired

at the same saturation. Some pigments work perfectly well on one glaze but not another. Keeping notes of what works and what doesn't is a particularly useful habit. It's best not to rely on your memory, as memory can play tricks!

157

earthenware in the form of majolica or on higher fired wares and adapting the majolica process. Low-fired majolica glazes often have a clay content of less than 10 percent and may need some surface hardener to make it possible to paint without danger of the glaze lifting and possibly causing crawling or a separation from the body. If it is fragile or friable, the glaze surface can be hardened by adding a small amount of gum, bentonite or macaloid to the glaze in the dry state before the glaze is mixed. The ware also can be sprayed with a sugar or starch solution to harden the surface and make brushwork easier to control. Sprayed glazes usually have less adhesion than glazes applied by other methods (see Chapter 16).

High-temperature glazes for stoneware or porcelain usually have a clay content of 15 percent or more, either in the form of ball clay or kaolin, or a combination of the two. This makes the unfired glaze surface much harder for the application of brushwork and other surfacing processes and allows a far better adhesion to the underlying clay body. Other than problems caused by excessively thick saturations or applications of color, high-temperature glazes produce an ideal surface to paint on without a further hardening coat. If the glaze is still fragile or friable, the same hardener applications used for low temperatures work fine.

Soft Stamps

Soft stamps, cut or burned from cellulose upholstery foam or sponge, offer yet another exciting range of decorative possibilities in conjunction with pigments, slips or glazes. Cellulose foam comes in different hardnesses and thicknesses. The harder the foam, the less it will absorb the pigment, so medium-to-soft foam works best for most uses. Foam can be purchased from upholstery suppliers, and often off-cuts are perfectly suitable for making sponge stamps. If the sponge is to be backed and glued onto a ½" thick wooden board, a 1" thickness of foam will be adequate. For stamps that are not backed, a 2" thickness is ideal.

Soft stamps can be cut with scissors, knives or scalpels, or burnt with small, fine-point soldering irons or wood-burning tools. Burning foam should be done in a well-ventilated area or with a fan to blow the noxious fumes away. The burning or cutting depth should be at least ¼" to allow the development of a clear image.

For printing on surfaces with soft stamps, the sponge is dampened by saturating it with running water, then squeezing out the excess. Colorant is applied, either by painting the colorant on the design face of the sponge or by rubbing the sponge design face in the smooth pigment on a glass or tile surface. The stamp then is placed on the object being decorated, and, using light pressure, pressed until the image is transferred to the ceramic surface. Too much pressure likely will end in a spoiled image, and too much pigment possibly will lead to bubbling. Sponge stamps can be used to develop a positive image, as above, or to develop a negative image by the pattern removal of slip, pigment or glaze using the same damp sponge with no colorant in it. The dry sponge is soaked in water, squeezed out and gently pressed to the surface where the pattern removal is to be done. The dampened slip, pigment or glaze then is lifted from the surface, attached to the face of the stamp. This is a good way to develop "ghost" images.

Robin Hopper, Canada, "Vase Southwest Series" — detail. Porcelain with terra sigillata, black/bronze pigment brushwork fired in oxidation at cone 9. Trailed with chrome red glaze and refired to cone 08. Photo: Judi Dyelle.

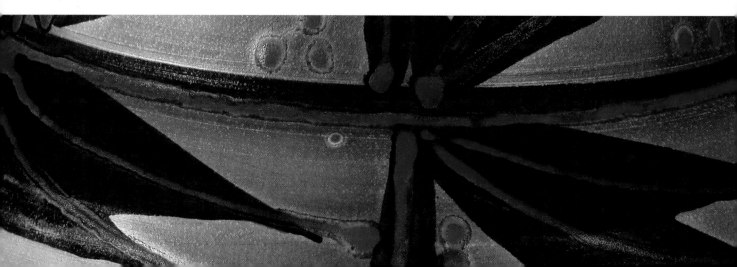

Maya. Early Classic, 300 to 500 C.E. Clay, resist fired and incised.
An abstract scene of the watery otherworld with the water lily monster and lotus blossoms. Rollout photograph © Justin Kerr.

CHAPTER 13

Marks of Resistance

Creating barriers or protective coats between layers of the ceramic surface during the decorating stages is done with resist materials. Most of the time, resists used in ceramics repel water or water-based materials, such as pigments, slips and glazes. The most effective repellents for water are wax, oil, rubber or resinous varnishes, such as shellac. The type of resist you choose can be critically important. Resist processes might use petroleum products, such as hot wax, wax crayons, candles, floor wax and petroleum jelly; rubber products, such as latex solution, rubber sheet, rubber cement or latex house paint; sheet products, such as acrylic sheet and screening; or fiber products, such as paper, Tyvek®, masking tape,

graphic tapes and adhesive-backed profiles or cutouts that can be used as stencils, a form of selected resist. The type of resist used for any given process depends on a combination of personal preference, what's to be resisted, the surface being protected and at what stage in the ceramic cycle it's being done. Resists can be used both to protect imagery and to create it.

Petroleum-Based Resists

Hot Wax

Petroleum-based waxes are heated to form a liquid that usually is applied to the ceramic surface by dipping

Arne Åse, Norway, "Panel," Limoges porcelain, shellac resist and sponging in multiple layers.

Arne Åse, Norway. Assorted brushes for shellac resist and sponging in multiple layers.

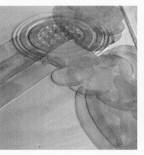

Arne Åse, Norway. Limoges porcelain, layered shellac and washings after the shellac dried.

Arne Åse, Norway, applying shellac to a porcelain surface.

Photo: Jo Åse

Photo: Alain Gauvin

Mahmoud Baghaeian, Canada, "Lidded Jar," bisqued piece glazed, liquid wax emulsion applied, washed with wet sponge, glazed again.

Photo: Frank Pedrick

Chic Lotz and Sandy Frizzell, USA, "Lodge Pole Pine," wax resist, electric fired to cone 6, 16" x 2", 2001.

Photo: Seth Tice-Lewis

Brad Tucker, USA, "Platter," stoneware, design carved into dry glaze, over-sprayed with contrasting glaze, black slip on rim, 18", 2003.

Photo: Diane Kenney

Julie Johnson, USA, "Black Box," terra cotta, cone 03, 8" x 6-½" x 6", 2003.

or brushing. They usually are available in a number of different hardnesses or melting temperatures, depending on what they are being used for. They often are available directly from petroleum companies as the base product for candle making.

I find the temperature rating of 110/120°F to be the most satisfactory. Wax that's too hard easily can be softened by the addition of light machine oil. If you prefer it perfumed, you can add scented coal oil, the kind used in home oil lamps. Heating is done best with an electric frying pan with a heat sensor, but you should always be vigilant. Second-hand electric frying pans often are available in thrift stores. Great care should be taken to avoid overheating, as hot wax is an

Marc Egan, Canada, "Plate," dark burning earthenware, glazed using cuerda seca technique, outlines painted with mixture of wax emulsion and iron oxide then glazed, wax separates different colors of glaze and oxide fuses with clay during firing, creating a dark dry clay line, fired cone 2, 30cm, 2002.

extremely volatile material and can spontaneously ignite if overheated. I nearly burnt down a studio with hot wax in an electric frying pan that an assistant forgot to turn off. Fortunately, there was hardly any wax left in the pan when it caught fire. Make sure there is adequate ventilation in the working area. Although wax fumes are not toxic, they can be extremely nauseating and may cause severe headaches. An extractor fan in the studio

wall is a good idea, as is situating the wax working area close to an open window or door.

Almost as soon as hot wax touches a cool surface it will harden to a tough coat. Doing brushwork with wax resist usually requires a speedy application, or the wax will cool and congeal in the brush before it gets onto the pot. To extend the working time, add oil to the wax in small increments until it's the consistency you

161

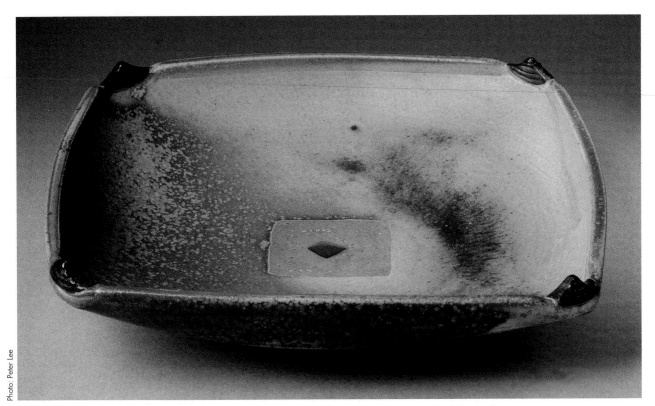

Photo: Peter Lee

Jeff Oestrich, USA, "Plate," thrown and cut, wax resist decoration, soda fired, 3" x 10" x 10", 2002.

like. The only drawback to doing this is that it makes the wax decoration more fragile and unable to tolerate much abrasion. There are times when a very soft wax is beneficial, mainly for cutting and scratching through before applying a wash of color to create sgraffito line drawings or colorant inlay. Soft wax won't chip as easily as hard wax.

Once a brush is dipped into hot wax, it is just about useless for any other purpose, and there are really no solvents that will clean wax thoroughly. Excessively hot wax or extensive use also can frizzle real brush hairs and completely melt synthetic ones. There are brushes made specifically for hot wax, which usually are used for resist painting on silk. They can be purchased from batik and silk painting suppliers.

Wax Crayons and Candles

These can be especially effective for drawing on a hard surface, such as bisque or bone-dry clay. Any form of wax crayon or candle can be used. Crayons and candles most often are colored by organic dyes, but occasionally they may be colored with an inexpensive mineral, such as iron oxide. Candles incorporating mineral colorants, such as iron, copper, rutile, chromium, cobalt, etc., can easily be made specifically for ceramic use by dipping a string in a mix of colorant and hot wax until a candle forms. You also can roll cooling wax into a crayon shape as it begins to solidify. If the wax is too hard, some light oil can be added to the mix.

Cold Liquid Floor Wax and Petroleum Jelly

Cold liquid floor wax is best applied to bisque-fired ware and used with thin coatings of glaze, colorant or terra sigillata. It quickly will penetrate the surface of bisque, leaving a thin layer of resist. Floor wax and petroleum jelly can be combined to thicken the mix, but it often will take considerable time to dry to the touch and be ready for further coatings.

Rubber-Based Resists

Rubber-based products, such as latex solution, rubber sheet, rubber cement or latex house paint, all are very useful and fairly inexpensive methods of forming resists. Artist's latex solution, rubber sheet and rubber cement usually can be purchased at art supply stores. Latex house paint is available from hardware stores. Latex

Photo: Ken Mayer

Gillian McMillan, Canada, "Pope's Hat Plate and Pedestal Bowl," earthenware, painted with brightly stained slips, clear glazed, terra sigillata on all exposed clay, plate 18", 1996.

Photo: Michael Dismatsek

Carol Rossman, Canada, "Shallow Bowl," bisqued bowl with burnished terra sigillata finish, areas masked before matte glaze airbrushed on, tape removed before raku firing, 11-¼" x 2-½", 2000.

solution and latex paint are best when applied by brush and can be thinned with water if necessary.

Resists can be done at any stage, depending on how you visualize using them. Remember to thoroughly clean the brushes with warm water and soap as soon after use as possible, making sure to massage out the congealing residue that usually builds at the ferrule. When looked after properly, brushes will last for years; if improperly looked after, they may last just days. Any form of brushed-on resist normally will shorten the life of brushes as well as take some of the "spring" or resilience out of the hair. This ultimately will lower the responsiveness of the brush in doing decorative brushwork.

Rubber sheet can be purchased from hardware stores or hobby shops in a variety of thicknesses. It can be temporarily glued to the ceramic surface with rubber cement. Old rubber cement usually can be rolled off the ceramic and rubber sheet surfaces quite easily. Rubber sheet is a particularly useful material for making masks for sandblasting or air-erasing. Thin sheets easily can be cut into profiles using scissors, scalpels, craft knives or box cutters (see Chapter 19).

Acrylic Sheet and Screening

Fine acrylic sheeting and screening also work well for covering large areas that need to be protected or textured. The super-thin sheet used by dry cleaners is very useful for forming barriers in layered decoration processes.

Fiber Products

Fiber products, such as oiled paper, Tyvek®, masking tape, graphic tape and adhesive-backed profiles or cutouts all are very useful, particularly where there isn't a great amount of abrasion taking place in the resistance being

Photo: Peter Hogan

Marc Egan, Canada, "Bowl," earthenware, wax resist, glazed using cuerda seca technique, outlines painted with mixture of wax emulsion and iron oxide then glazed, wax separates different colors of glaze and oxide fuses with clay during firing, creating a dark dry clay line, 10cm x 39cm, 2003.

done. They will have a short life when sandblasted, but they likely will resist water-based materials for a considerable time.

Paper cutouts often are used in slipware applications. For extensive use and reusable masks, a synthetic paper called Tyvek® is extremely useful. It is occasionally available from art supply stores, but more often it will be found in hardware or building supply stores. Its main use is to protect buildings during construction. The material is extremely tough, almost impossible to tear with the hands and waterproof. It easily can be cut with scissors and held in place with rubber cement.

Masking tapes usually have one adhesive-coated side and one slightly textured surface. They can be stuck to the surface quite easily as long as it is at a bone-dry or later stage. Masking tapes come in a wide range of widths and easily can be cut into shapes to form profiles.

Photo by the artist

Brian Gartside, New Zealand, "Waikato River Design," stoneware, marks by resist using masking tape, 400mm.

Chris Staley, USA, "Teapot," stoneware, design applied with liquid latex as a mask, dipped in black and white glazes, latex removed, wax applied on design and glazed again, 9", 2000.

Erin Furimsky, USA, "Iron Breast," hand-built porcelain, cone 6, carved, silkscreen, china paint, 7" x 6" x 6".

They will not last long under heavy abrasion, but they are easy to work with. Similar to masking tapes, but offering extremely fine linear possibilities, are the range of graphic tapes used in graphic design. They are flexible and give lines as fine as $1/16$" wide. With most graphic design now being done on computer, these fine tapes may be hard to find, but at the time of writing, they were still available.

Another group of available adhesive-backed masks or stencils are the wide range of precut paper shapes or stickers often used by children. Differing sizes of circles, stars, squares, ovals, rectangles and other shapes, in conjunction with linear tapes, present an enormous range of possibilities for graphic expression on the ceramic surface. If they are difficult to remove before firing, they will burn away during the firing, usually leaving a small amount of cleanup to be done before applying a glaze coating.

The range of uses of resists is large, particularly when the varied states of surface are taken into account. Which method gives the best result depends on what is visualized and the types of layering used to achieve it. Much depends on the person doing the work and his or her particular preference for the tools available. Which method works best is dependent on the state of the object, the moistness of the clay or the cleanliness of the bisque. Resist processes, in conjunction with many of the decorative processes already described, open an unlimited range of possibilities.

Paul Donnelly, USA, "Lidded Jar," high-fire porcelain with celadon glaze, 11-½" x 11-½" x 10-¾", 2003.

Late Classic 600 to 900 C.E. Maya. Clay, resist. fired. A design with abstract frogs that appears on fabrics.
Rollout photograph © Justin Kerr.

Jack Sures, Canada, "Wide Bowl" detail, ceramic ink drawing on porcelain. Private collection. Photo: Judi Dyelle

CHAPTER 14

Marks of Pencils, Crayons, Pens and Trailers

For those who are excited about the graphic possibilities of the ceramic surface and enjoy the use of drawing implements that have something of a sharp, scratchy or linear nature, the marks made by pencils, pens, crayons and trailers likely will make them favorite tools of expression. Chapter 1, about the process of drawing and the nature of mark making, showed that these tools are the foundation of written or pictographic communication in Western civilization, whereas the brush is the foundation of mark making for most Eastern civilizations. Those who have grown up in the Western traditions usually feel more affinity with scratchy drawing tools than with the soft, calligraphic brushes. Fortunately, the range of ceramic decoration tools encompasses both soft and hard possibilities.

Ceramic Pencils

Regular pencils, with what we call "leads," actually are made from graphite of various degrees of hardness from 6H (extremely hard) to 6B (extremely soft). If these pencils are used to draw on the ceramic surface, marks made with them will burn away in the firing. Sometimes this is a convenient eraser of guidelines or grids for patterns and designs done with ceramic pigments. Guidelines also can be painted on with vermilion watercolor paint that also will burn away.

Pencils for ceramic use are made with combinations of refractory materials, clays, and colorants and are usually only commercially available in one level of hardness that would probably equate to an HB rating in a graphite pencil. HB hardness is midway between 6H and 6B. Companies that produce ceramic pencils have a habit of coming and going, but most ceramic supply houses usually will be able to find and supply them. Pencils are commercially available in a very limited variety of colors.

Photo: Judi Dyelle

Trailers, ceramic pens and pencils.

Sergei Isopov, USA, "Thin Line," porcelain, 17-½" x 15-½" x 15", 2002. In the collection of David and Jacqueline Charak, courtesey of the Ferrin Gallery, New York, USA.

Verne Funk, USA, "Split — Portrait of the Artist," whiteware wheel-thrown, underglaze pencil, glaze, 18" diameter, 1996.

Work with ceramic pencils normally is undertaken on bisque-fired clay that has been sufficiently hardened to withstand the pressure needed for satisfactory mark-making. Since the pencil "lead" may be quite fragile in use, the smoother the clay surface, the better the drawing. Bisque surfaces can be smoothed by sanding with wet and dry silicon carbide or aluminum oxide papers, or the surface of the greenware may be sprayed or brushed with a terra sigillata coating to provide a harder working surface. Ceramic pencils may be used on the ceramic surface just like their graphite equivalent on paper. Although sharpened points tend to wear quickly on the abrasive ceramic surface, the combination of pencil tip marks, side-of-pencil marks and the opportunity to create tones through finger-rubbing or smudging the soft image gives wide potential for drawn imagery development.

Photo: Richard Faller

Jenny Lind, USA, "Platter," cone 6, painted engobes, clear glaze, 22", 1997.

Photo courtesy of the artist

Jeanne Otis, USA, "Ephemeral Passage" detail tile No. 6, fired to cone 5, five times, smooth surface covered with white slip, multiple washes of overglaze color applied with a brush and sponge, underglaze pencil lines added last, 18-½" x 19" x 1", 2003.

Steve Irvine, Canada, "Jar," stoneware, wood fired, hand-built, trail glaze decoration on upper part, 27cm x 22cm x 22cm, 2001.

Andrea Freel Christie, USA, "Sugar and Creamer," porcelain, underglaze, glaze, 6-½" x 4" x 3-½", 2003.

If the commercial underglaze pencils are too soft for satisfactory use, it is quite easy to make your own and harden them to a more satisfactory and less friable state. Ceramic pencil drawings can be fired onto the bisque-fired clay to harden them before glazing, or, alternatively, they can be fired on unglazed high-fired clays, such as porcelain or stoneware, without the need for a glaze coating.

The selection of colorants or mixtures of colorants used in the coloring of the lead will control the effectiveness of the drawings at high temperatures, but most will tolerate cone 10.

Making Ceramic Pencils, Pastels, Crayons and Watercolors

Note: I wish to thank Jeanne Otis for her research, and Arizona State University for permission to restate their work. It has been expanded from the original text.

To make ceramic pencils and pastels, use a porcelain-type slip with 50 percent white firing ball clay or plastic kaolin. For dry strength in the green state, 3 percent macaloid or 5 percent bentonite should be added.

Ceramic Pencil Slip Recipe

White firing ball clay	50
Potash feldspar	25
Silica	25
TOTAL	**100**
Macaloid (or 5% bentonite)	3
Colorant (maximum)	15

The materials, including colorants, should be dry sieved through an 80-mesh screen to ensure thorough blending. For color, you can use mineral oxides, carbonates and prepared stains. A variety of combinations will produce a wide range of colors, although it is important to select colorants that won't burn out at high temperatures; not many will, but cadmium/selenium and potassium dichromate are likely to do so. The amount of colorant can be up to 15 percent. More than that will cause loss of plasticity in the raw state, making it difficult to form the pencils. The more colorant used, the more intense the color.

Mix the dry materials with approximately 45 percent

Photo: Ross Mulhausen

John McCuistion, USA, "Pond Series," cone 04 oxidation, 18" diameter, 2000.

water, to which 1 percent of sodium silicate per 100 grams of dry material mix has been added. This will slightly deflocculate the slip, giving additional green strength while also intensifying some of the colorants.

Form the pencils by drying the colored slip to a plastic state, and then either rolling out coils or extruding lengths of the desired thickness. These then can be left as pencil lengths or cut into shorter (1" to 2") lengths. When dry, fire the pencils to between 800°C and 950°C, depending on the desired hardness. Lower firing will produce softer lead; higher firing, harder lead. The short lengths can be placed in a claw grip drafting pencil (the

Koh-I-Noor No. 48 drafting pencil can hold leads up to ¼" in diameter).

Pastels normally are used from the greenware state and are not prefired unless they prove too friable for convenient use. To make pastels, use the basic recipe above and simply form the clay into coils or extrusions to the desired size for use. If they prove too fragile, they can be fired to between 600°C and 800°C without making them excessively hard. Ceramic pastel drawings should be fired on the ceramic object to harden them before a glaze is applied; otherwise, the powdery surface likely will be spoiled in glaze application or handling.

Lynda Katz, USA, "Covered Jar," thrown, altered, and hand-built porcelain, glaze-trailed decoration, 8" x 5" x 4", 1997.

Photo by the artist

Lynda Katz, USA, "Bayou Boogie Woogie," thrown and faceted porcelain, underglaze pencil drawing with luster glazes, 13" x 4-½" x 4-½", 1984.

Surface powder also might cause crawling through lack of glaze adhesion.

To make wax crayons, mix the dry recipe above with ordinary commercial wax resist. Form the crayon, and let it dry. Since the crayon will contain some latex, it also will have a slight resist effect on the work, particularly when used on bisque-fired ware. For a crayon with greater resist ability, stir colorants into wax, let cool, roll the wax into rods of different widths, and cut the rods in convenient lengths.

Underglaze Pens

Underglaze pens are like super-fine trailers containing an "ink" that gives good flowability for drawing. They are available commercially from a number of producers, or you can make your own with the fine trailers that are available. You also can dip any form of "nibbed" pen, from fine-pointed mapping pens or quills to sharpened bamboo, into ceramic ink.

Black Ceramic Ink Recipe

Calcium borate	30
Potash feldspar	30
Ball clay	25
Silica	15
TOTAL	**100**
Bentonite	5
Mason Stain 6600 or other black stain	10

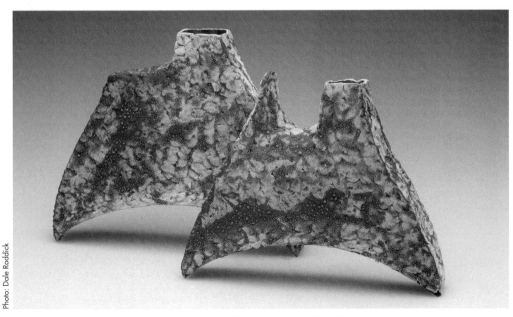

Judith Graham, Canada, "Urns — C Series," 8-½" x 10" x 2-½", 2002.

Thoroughly dry-mix these ingredients, then add a mixture of water and 5 percent sodium silicate (100 milliliters water to 5 grams sodium silicate). Pass it through a 100-mesh sieve two times. The ink is then thinned for appropriate use and should be usable at all temperatures to cone 12. It can be thinned to produce pen and wash-like drawings or used with a ceramic watercolor or glazes. Other colorants also can be used with this base.

Watercolors

Ceramic Watercolor Recipe

White firing ball clay	50
Potash feldspar	25
Silica	25
TOTAL	**100**
Macaloid (or 5% bentonite)	3
Colorant (maximum)	15

Photo: Julie Larson

Julie and Tyrone Larson, USA, "Pineapple Tile," porcelain, slip-cast tile by Tyrone, sprayed base glaze with glaze painting on top of raw base glaze by Julie, painting applied with trailers, cone 7, 12" x 16" x ½".

Photo: John Brennan

Jan Schachter and Margaret (Peggy) Forman, USA, "Evala," vase form, porcelain, black slip, rutile wash, cobalt chloride wash, underglaze pencil, etching, re-bisqued to set drawing, transparent glaze, 7" x 2-¾" x 3", 2003.

Photo by the artist

Paul Lewing, USA, "Summit Lake — Mt. Rainier," porcelain tile, cone 4 oxidation, colored glazes applied with slip trailer, extruded border with sprayed glaze, 33" x 21", 2003.

For watercolors, the materials are thoroughly mixed together, then enough water is added to make a slip, which is sieved through an 80-mesh sieve and poured onto a plaster surface. When dry to the touch, watercolor cakes can be made by forming rounds or squares of the colored slip and letting them dry completely. They then can be used like ordinary schoolbox watercolors by wetting the surface with water and applying with a brush.

Trailers

A wide range of trailers for slip, ink, glaze or overglaze uses are available from ceramic suppliers, kitchen stores and drugstores. They usually consist of a rubber or neoprene bulb or container and a nozzle with a fine-aperture tip, or sometimes multiple tips. The simplest to find is usually either a hair coloring applicator bottle or a child's enema rubber bulb from a drugstore.

Ceramic suppliers often have fine-tipped trailers, sometimes with interchangeable tips of differing aperture. The aperture of the tip required depends on the thickness of the material being squeezed through. Thin inks will go through a fine tip without clogging, but a wide tip may be needed for slips or glazes to flow properly.

As with any tools, you will need to practice to get the correct "feel" to achieve the best results. Keep a thin needle tool nearby when working with trailers, because the fine ones tend to clog quite easily.

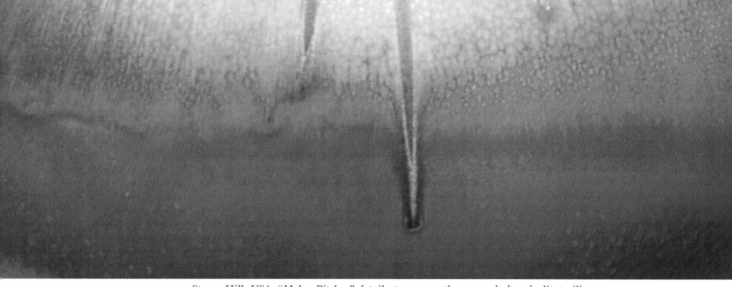

Steven Hill, USA, "Melon Pitcher" detail, stoneware, thrown and altered, slip trailing, sprayed multiple glazes, single fired, 13" x 9" x 8", 2002. Photo by Al Surratt

CHAPTER 15

The Mark of the Spray

The earliest artistic use of a spray of color most likely occurred when Neolithic rock painters put their hands flat on rock faces and blew color through hollow grass tubes to create silhouette images of their shapes. These individualistic images occur through many prehistoric sites in many parts of the world. Blowing pressurized air through a tube and across another tube immersed in liquid still is the principle behind most spraying processes.

Spraying glazes, pigments and slips can be done with a variety of tools, from simple to complex. The choices range from an angled-mouth atomizer or a bent tube to

Photo by the artist

Peter Lane, UK, "Pair of Birds," stoneware, thrown and modeled, copper carbonate sprayed, removed with dry brush in places, under a dolomite glaze, electric kiln, 22cm high, 1999.

a highly sophisticated and expensive compressor, spray gun or manifold spray gun and spray booth, extraction fan and air filtration equipment. The extent to which you invest in equipment depends on what you want to achieve and what is necessary to achieve that. Some spraying methods can be done at negligible cost. For others, the costs can be considerable, but if spraying gives you the results you visualize on a consistent basis, the expense is more than justified.

The most primitive process of energizing molecules of liquid into a simple spray is done with a medium-bristle nailbrush or a soft toothbrush. Irregular spray patterns made by dipping a brush into liquefied pigment and pulling a knife blade toward you across the brush surface still offers an animated surface. Bristles of a suitable flexibility will eject droplets of liquid color as they are bent back by the knife blade and, upon release, spring forward to project the liquid on the surface under pressure. Primitive as it may seem, this still can be a useful method for developing an uneven spray pattern on the object, particularly for small details where an uneven spray has more visual vitality than an even one.

The simplest air-propelled spray is done with a mouth-blown atomizer, which is basically two tubes, usually metal, that are at a right angle (90 degrees) to each other, with the blowing tube set slightly back from the edge of the reservoir tube. As air is blown through the blowing tube, it causes a venturi effect, where suction on the reservoir tube pulls the liquid to the top of the tube. The pressure of the breath then propels the liquid into a fine, but unsophisticated, spray. A simple

version can be made with an 8" length of ¼" flexible or copper tube bent at a right angle, approximately 3" up the tube, with a fine hole drilled or filed at the bend. The 5" section becomes the blowing tube, and the 3" section is the reservoir tube.

Atomizers are available at art supply stores at low cost. It always is useful to have one available for small amounts of detail spraying, particularly where resists are used (see Chapter 13).

Slightly more sophisticated, yet still inexpensive, spray applicators are used by gardeners to spray liquid fertilizers or pesticides. These sprayers work by a pump-action pressure chamber that sucks the liquid up a tube from the reservoir and propels it forward through a fine-apertured brass or plastic nozzle. If the spray is extremely fine, it may clog with heavier materials, like glazes and slips. Apertures can be drilled to allow heavier particles to pass through more easily, but the larger the aperture, the more scattered the spray pattern.

A small, updated version of the atomizer and simple pressure sprayer is a disposable spray gun that uses small, pressurized gas cylinders with a built-in atomizer unit attached to a glass reservoir bottle. The gas used is aeron A-70/DME (50/50) propane (21.5 percent) dimethylether (50 percent) that is not harmful to the ozone layer. These convenient sprayers are great for thin, water-based solutions of colorants, stains or soluble colorants, but they will not work with heavier glaze solutions. They are ideal for small-detail spraying jobs. They should be cleaned by spraying through with clean water after each use. They are produced by Preval Sprayer Division, Precision Valve Corp., and are available from paint suppliers and hardware stores.

Compressed Air Spraying

Airbrushes and spray guns need air compressors to propel the glaze or colorant from the reservoir to the gun tip and onto the work. Some airbrushes and spray guns have the reservoir below the trigger and work through a venturi system that pulls the liquid up through a tube in the reservoir. Others have the reservoir above the gun, where the fluid is fed by gravity. It is largely a matter of personal preference as to which to buy.

Depending on the type of spray equipment you are using, the compressor would be of different sizes with a wide range of possible pressures. Airbrushes generally only need small compressors, while spray guns

Photo: Judi Dyelle

Spray equipment.

Photo: Allen Cheuvront

Nan Smith, USA, "Clarity," detail of sculpture, airbrushed underglazed and glazed earthenware, 18" x 14" x 12", 2003.

Photo: Yosh Inouye

Diane Nasr O'Young, Canada, "Basket," kaolin-based glaze, flattened coil construction, pinched and pierced, fired cone 10, 6-½" x 5" x 25-½".

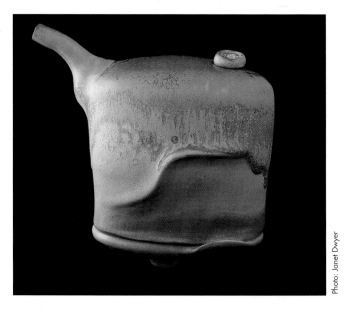

Photo: Al Surratt

Photo: Janet Dwyer

Steven Hill, USA, "Melon Pitcher," stoneware, thrown and altered, slip trailing, sprayed multiple glazes, single fired, 13" x 9" x 8", 2002.

Meira Mathison, Canada, "Soya Bottle," layered lithium glazes, ash sprinkled, sharp tool pushing from inside to make curved lines, lines manipulated to delineate marks, fired downdraft kiln, cone 10.

Steven Hill, USA, "Oval Covered Jar," thrown and altered, slip trailing, sprayed multiple glazes, single-fired stoneware, 10" x 10" x 6", 2000.

Tom Coleman, USA, "Footed Vase," thrown and altered white stoneware, added handles, numerous Shinos, porcelain slip and sprinkled ash, 11" x 11" x 3", 2003.

Billye Singer, USA, "Canister Set," stoneware, wheel-thrown, sprayed with two glazes, sprinkled with mesquite ash, cone 10 reduction, 9" x 7".

need large ones to work efficiently. Suppliers of spray equipment should be a good source of information on what is needed, if you tell them what you are doing with the tools.

It is much easier to become proficient with an airbrush or spray gun than with a paintbrush; many operators become quite expert after only a few hours of practice. The basic approach for both tools is similar, although the thickness of the material being sprayed by airbrush likely will be thinner than with a regular spray gun.

Approved safety dust masks should be worn at all times when spraying glazes. Many ceramic materials and colorant solutions are toxic, carcinogenic or silicotic and can lead to respiratory and other health problems if sprayed extensively. Safety masks can be purchased through paint suppliers, ceramic suppliers and industrial safety equipment companies. Make sure you tell the supplier what you are using it for and which dusts are likely to be in the atmosphere. Although safety masks don't perform well on bearded people, it still is worth filtering out as much dust as possible.

In learning to spray, the tendency often is to hold the gun too close to the work, causing excessive wetting and buildup, leading to flowing glaze rivulets or, alternately, moving the gun too fast so that an inadequate coating is deposited. Keep the gun tip at least 6'' away from the object being sprayed, and paint in long, even strokes, covering in a series of moves. Make each stroke separately and release the trigger as you finish each stroke (the instant the gun has stopped moving in one direction and before it starts on the return stroke) to prevent the glaze or slip from piling up. The best coverage comes from several passes over the spray area, with occasional thickness testing with the point of a needle tool.

For general spraying, try to get into the habit of keeping your gun pointed squarely at the work throughout the whole length of your painting stroke. Many spray glazers continue spraying into the air at the end of each stroke to clear the nozzle, like turning a can of spray paint upside down and spraying just propellant through the nozzle to clear excess paint. This generally is referred to as "feathering out." This tip cleaning process causes much of the mist or fog commonly associated with spraying glazes. Occasionally lubricating the following points will ensure longer life and smoother operation: material needle, air valve and fan control needle packings, material needle and air valve stem, springs and trigger bearings.

Mix your glaze for spraying as thick as the gun will handle with reasonable speed. Too thin a liquid causes mist and has a tendency to run after application. The more body there is in the glaze or slip, the heavier the coat that can be applied. All materials for spraying must be finely sieved, preferably through at least a 100-mesh sieve. Be sure to use a clean paddle to stir the liquid. Lumpy slips and gritty glazes will quickly clog the gun, causing all manners of frustration.

Reasons for Inefficient Gun Performance

- Bent fluid needle not seating properly;
- Worn fluid needle or damaged tip in the fluid block;
- Broken or distorted needle valve spring;
- Fluid needle binding due to over-tight packing felt; or
- Foreign matter collected inside fluid block where fluid needle seats, or in some cases on the needle.

Leakage in Needle Packings

Packings become hard and smooth from constant use. Periodically remove them and work them in a little oil. In most cases, this will keep them usable longer. Check the hose connections for proper seating and snugness to prevent air leaks and inefficiency.

Spray Booths

If you are only doing a small amount of spraying in the summertime in a large, nonurban area, it is possible, but not particularly satisfactory, to do it outside where breezes will disperse the spray mist. Always remember to spray in the direction the wind is going!

This is not an environmentally sound practice for extensive use. If you are doing a lot of spray glazing, it is better to work indoors with a proper spray booth, complete with an extractor fan and interior light. You easily can make a spray booth with a few woodworking tools, or you can purchase a commercial one to fill your needs. The extractor fan should be placed behind a removable and washable or replaceable screen, so that most particles are trapped in the screen. Commercially produced spray booths are available in a range of sizes to suit any situation and budget.

Spraying Casting Slips on Greenware

Spraying leather-hard clay with casting slips can develop pebbled surfaces unlike any other surfacing process.

By spraying unevenly and allowing the casting slip to lose its sheen before the next spray pass, you can build extremely interesting textural surfaces. Several spray passes might be necessary to build up significant texture. Used in conjunction with rubber sheet or Tyvek® resists or stencils, it offers a wide range of possibilities. When the textured casting slip surface is sprayed from the side or at an angle with contrasting colored slips or colorant sprays, it can give great illusions of organic surface undulations.

Some thoughts on spraying are given here by Steven Hill, an artist who has chosen to spray glazes for almost all of his working life.

SPRAYING GLAZES

By Steven Hill©

First published by "Pottery Making Illustrated," March/April 2002

While I love the surface potential spraying gives me when I'm glazing, I hate the hassles associated with the process. I put up with this love/hate relationship because spraying permits me to blend multiple glazes together seamlessly and also gives me the ability to isolate colors on the rims, handles and feet of my pottery. I have always responded to the surface variations that occur naturally on pots fired in atmospheric kilns (wood, soda, salt), and spraying gives me a means of introducing comparable transitions across the surfaces of my single-fired reduction stoneware pottery. For years I used the technique of spraying in combination with both dipped and poured glazes; however, in my current work, spray guns are my primary vehicle for applying glaze.

The affinity I feel for spraying began in my childhood. My father always had some kind of project going around our house, and these projects often were finished with flat black spray paint. Through my father's guidance, I learned how to spray in short bursts to get even coverage and keep the paint from running. As a result of this early experience, spraying glazes has always felt natural to me.

Although most of my experience has led to positive results, the one aspect of spraying that has frustrated me for 20 years is judging glaze thickness. In the beginning, most potters err on the side of applying glaze too thinly. It is helpful to watch for

Photo by the artist

Teri Silva, USA, "Covered Jar," earthenware, gloss glazed interior, airbrushed with slips masked with natural ferns and sprayed multiple coatings, fired cone 05, 18" x 6".

subtle clues, such as how wet the surface of the pot gets during spraying or to test for glaze thickness with a needle tool. Most of the time, a combination of experience and intuition is enough of a guide, but glazes with a narrow range of acceptable thickness, such as ash glazes, can be difficult to get consistently right.

My first experiment with spraying glazes was with a manually operated "flit" gun (made for applying weed killer) in the mid-'70s. By the late '70s, I was using a small, continuously running compressor that was nearly as irritating as a small dog barking at my feet. Eventually I acquired a compressor with a 30-gallon tank and located it in the next room to keep the noise down. I use anywhere from 20 to 80 pounds of pressure, depending on the gun I'm using and the thickness of the glaze I'm applying. Since the gun is never in constant use, the capacity (in cubic feet per minute) of the compressor is not too important. Most portable compressors with an air tank are quite adequate.

My favorite type of spray gun is an automotive siphon feed touch-up gun with a top-mounted trigger. This type of action is similar to holding a pencil or a brush, and I have better control of detail than with a full-sized gun. For most applications, this is a good compromise between the fine control and small capacity of an airbrush and the large capacity, broad coverage and corresponding weight of a full-size spray gun. I have also experimented with HVLP (high volume, low pressure) spray guns. They are more efficient, creating less overspray and therefore reducing the amount of glaze fog in the air. Although they are more environmentally friendly, they do not have as fine control and must be used with a pressurized cup.

Although most of my experience has been using guns with cups attached, there are some real advantages to a remote pressurized paint pot. Over time, using a heavy spray gun contributed to a case of tendinitis in my elbow. Locating the glaze container on the floor takes away most of the weight and thus relieves stress on the arm. These remote pressurized pots are large capacity (two quarts to five gallons) and potentially give better control of the spray pattern and volume of glaze applied. Changing colors is much more time-consuming, however. If money wasn't a factor, I'd have 15 remote pots set up, each with its own dedicated glaze!

The biggest problem with all automotive spray guns is wear. Due to the abrasive nature of glazes, the fluid tip and needle wear down over time and need to be replaced. Using a spray gun specially made for ceramic glazes, such as the "Critter," can minimize this costly maintenance. These guns operate by a simple atomizer principle and have no internal parts to be worn down by the abrasive action of glazes. Although ideal for classroom situations where they routinely are abused, this type of gun typically provides a coarser spray without the fine adjustment potential of an automotive gun.

For health reasons, using a well-ventilated spray booth is essential. Although there are several brands of commercial booths available, a good one can be made from plywood and a wall-mounted ventilation fan. I have seen plans in various ceramic publications. A simple way to experiment with spraying without the cost of a booth is to spray outdoors in fair weather with the spray directed downwind, but this is not environmentally sound or practical for a permanent setup. A properly fitting respirator with a HEPA filter should also be worn at all times while spraying.

In spite of the added equipment expense and hassle, I remain firmly committed to the process of spraying glazes. Spraying has given me the flexibility to blend multiple glazes or to isolate and change colors from rim to neck to body to foot. Freed from the hard edges of dipped and poured glazes, which often seemed arbitrary and interfered with the clarity of my forms, spraying has given me the potential to apply glaze so that it reflects and emphasizes the various form changes on my pottery.

I began single firing while attending a salt glaze workshop at the Memphis Academy of Arts, taught by Peter Sohngen, in the summer of 1972. It was the first time all the various processes of pottery making fit together in a coherent way for me. In a week's time we threw, decorated, glazed, fired and unloaded kilns. I was a junior in college and pretty much at the mercy of a rather dogmatic regime in the ceramics studio, so this way of working was a total revelation for me. I swore that summer that I'd never glaze another bisque pot again, and I've stuck to that now for 31 years!

Spraying is ideal for single firing, since it involves less handling of fragile ware and also because much of the water evaporates from glazes between the tip of the spray gun and the pot. Thus, many of the potential disadvantages of raw glazing are avoided when spraying.

Steven Hill has been a studio potter for more than 25 years. First working out of a basement and then a backyard studio, since 1998 he and his wife, Susan, have owned Red Star Studios Ceramic Center in the Crossroads Arts District of Kansas City, Mo.

Part 4
GLAZE PROCESSES

Photo: Tony Clennell

Tony and Sheila Clennell, Canada, "Box," thrown and squared, ash deposits, 10" tall.

Robin Hopper, Canada, "Metchosin Mists" landscape plate, detail — slab-built porcelain, multiple glaze application fired in reduction at cone 10. Photo: Judi Dyelle.

CHAPTER 16

Marks of the Glaze and its Application

Almost every ceramic object shown in this book represents an extensive personal journey for the artist who made it. The journey included a lengthy period learning the making processes — hand-building, throwing, slipcasting, extruding and various combinations that give structural solidity to a vision. Surface marking may be part of the initial vision, developed as an offshoot of the process of making or decided on at any stage in the path from wet clay to formed and bisque-fired ceramic. If you haven't thought about it before, this is the time to visualize the completed object and work toward that vision.

Getting to the bisque-fired stage without any surface enrichment limits the possibilities for a few decorative

Photo: John Carlano

Rain Harris, USA, "Amber Poison Bottle," multiple fired slipcast and altered porcelain, luster and crystalline glaze, 12" x 8" x 4", 2002.

Tom Turner, USA, "Vase," paddled, carved, blue tea dust glaze, flambe over with iron on top, bird sentinels, 8" x 8".

processes, but there are still masses of options available. These go from glazing the ware in various ways to giving the kiln a major role in processes, like pit firing, wood firing, salt and soda firings (see Chapters 17 and 18) or the reduction chamber for raku.

Beyond the firing process are still more options,

as will be seen in Chapters 19 and 20. A limitless and sometimes overwhelming range of possibilities exist.

In a complex medium such as ceramics, most people tend to focus on a small range of the possibilities and then branch out as they become more aware of aspects of the medium that touch a nerve with their visual experiences

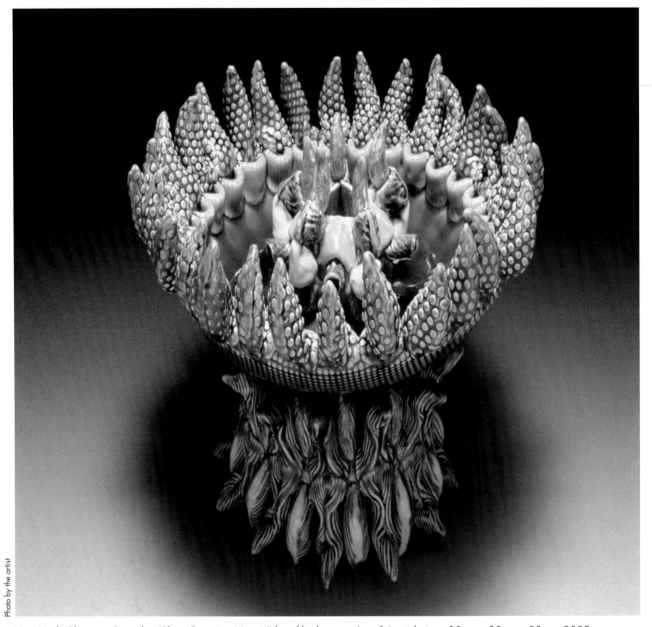

Photo by the artist

Ying-Yueh Chuang, Canada, "Plant Creature No. 4," hand-built, cone 6 to 04 oxidation, 30cm x 30cm x 23cm, 2002.

and offer personal directions. Invariably, as you become fluent in one part of the ceramic language, you'll make contact with or be exposed to a wider range of potential in surface enrichment. Developing a personal idiom in a medium that has worldwide history of at least 10,000 years is intimidating, but it is done on a daily basis by artists who have managed to create an individual stamp by the way they combine elements of ubiquitous ceramic experiences with personal vision.

After the length of time ceramic objects have been around, you might think that everything that can be done already has been done. This is far from the reality of this medium, which probably has seen more innovation and technical change in the last 50 years than during the previous 5,000. This new technical information, in combination with a myriad of both making and surfacing processes, continues to give us an inexhaustible palette. There are always variations on a theme. The more you know, the more you can say with your language. If the language is the ceramic medium and your knowledge of it is extensive, the more options that exist for new and exciting avenues of personal growth. Being aware

Sally Resnik Rockriver, USA, "Geochemical Landscape," crystalline glaze, 10" x 14", 1993.

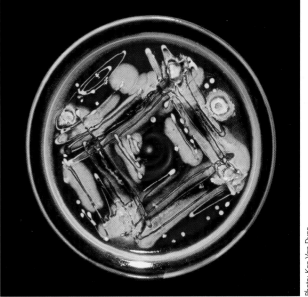

Winthrop Byers, USA, "Flashed Platter," stoneware, wheel-thrown, sprayed shiny black glaze on rim and back, copper red and wood ash glazes in center, flashed by flame during the firing, cone 11 reduction, 16-½" x 2-½", 1999.

Gail Russell, USA, "Plate," wheel-thrown porcelain, copper red glaze with iron, iron/rutile mixture brushed on, white glaze trail, burned out small acorns and soybeans create opalescent dots, larger 'auroras' created by burned out burr oak acorns placed on plate before firing, 12" wide.

of what has been done historically, as well as what's happening today, gives the contemporary ceramic artist an enormous lexicon or library of resources that previous generations of ceramists did not have. The combination of museum collections, art gallery exhibitions and the enormous research possibilities of the Internet just serve to increase the depth of the well of research and inspiration sources from which we can draw.

Working with glaze applications on ceramic surfaces has been done for approximately 4,500 years, initially with low-temperature glazes developed in the Middle East. With the development of high-firing kilns in China about 3,000 years ago, the range of possibilities caused by melting fusible minerals onto clay surfaces to make them waterproof also offered wide decorative possibilities at the same time.

After early man discovered how to make useful objects of fire-hardened clay, functional objects, ritual objects and objects made for contemplation soon followed. Mankind's natural curiosity about his local environment ultimately led to using many local minerals as glaze and color ingredients. Through millennia of trial and error and heating and melting minerals onto clay surfaces, a wide spectrum of glaze possibilities emerged. This same process still is being done by ceramists all over the world in the hunt for the elusive "who-knows-what."

A large part of the contemporary ceramic artist's work lies in personal research of the inexhaustible range of the ceramic surface. Glaze and color development represent challenging areas of this medium that offer

Photo by the artist

Alan Lacovetsky, Canada, "Flying Pelicans," platter, wax resist brush painting, celadon/kuan type glaze over iron red kaki glaze, wood fired, 2-½" x 14", 2002.

the greatest opportunities for personal growth. Chapter 5 gave a few pointers for personal glaze development, and Chapter 11 gave a wide coverage of ceramic coloration taken from my first book, "The Ceramic Spectrum." That book offers the contemporary ceramist guidance to learn about materials empirically and to make glazes and other ceramic coatings based on that knowledge. Once you are in the habit of glaze testing based on intuitive understanding of the materials involved, you inevitably will be faced with a blank surface that calls for glaze enrichment.

No matter how eager you might be to begin splashing on your newly concocted glazes, there are a few details that must be put in order first. The surface of the clay form should be cleaned of any dust or grease that might spoil the finished object. A large enough volume of glaze or glazes to do the job must be mixed to a suitable thickness. You must determine the type of work, clay, firing temperature, atmosphere and prefiring surface treatments. You probably also will have to decide the type and thickness of the glaze to be used, its coloration and/or opacification and any post-firing surface enrichment techniques.

The application of the glaze follows these decisions. They will, to some extent, have predetermined the application methods that will be used to achieve the desired result, including brushing, dipping, pouring, spraying, stippling, spattering, sponging, trailing, glaze intaglio and multiple glaze application. Many ceramists use various methods on the same piece to achieve a specific effect.

The thickness, or viscosity, of a glaze often gives remarkable variations in both surface and color. Diverse application methods can be used to beneficially exploit these variations. Once again, it is only by personal experiment that real understanding of the potential of any single glaze can be realized. Ceramists have been known to explore the particular qualities of a single glaze for years, sometimes even a lifetime. Certainly with many glazes, the thick and thin variables can be so extreme that, in conjunction with firing variations, a whole palette can be made from a single glaze, in subtlety, color and surface texture. High-temperature Shino glazes are perfect examples of this.

The working thickness, or specific gravity, of glazes can be monitored by the use of a simple hydrometer (like wine-makers use), if such control is required. A

Yoshiro Ikeda, USA, "Tea Pot," coil built, fired at cone 3 and cone 03.

Kate S. Maury, USA, "Moth Wing Jar," thrown stoneware, wax resist, gas fired, cone 10 to 12 reduction, 9-½" x 6-½", 1999.

hydrometer easily can be made by attaching some form of lead weight to one end of a piece of wood dowel or flat wood, such as a ruler. It should be varnished to facilitate washing. The wood can be marked with any form of calibration (inches, centimeters, etc.) to show the specific gravity of the glaze solution. Immerse the marked wood, weight downward, in the glaze when the optimum thickness has been decided. The thinner the glaze, the more the weight will sink into the liquid; the thicker the glaze is, the less it will sink. Note the ideal calibration reached on the stick beside the recipe for future reference.

The possibilities of glaze application are many. Following are processes that particularly relate to the glaze and its application methods. Since the development of the ceramic surface usually is a combination of different layers, processes mentioned throughout this book can be employed with glaze coatings on top to further increase the visual and/or tactile interest of the object.

Brushing and Roller Coating

Brushing often develops an uneven surface, purely due to the nature of the process. It generally is best done on unfired ware, because this ware is less likely to "suck" the wet glaze from the brush, which often happens when brushing glaze on bisque-fired ware. For this reason, brushing often is used to glaze once-fired ware in cases where a defined brush quality is required or where streakiness doesn't matter or may be encouraged.

Depending on the desired result and the area to be covered, almost any brush can be used, from soft hair artist watercolor brushes to various types of house painting brushes, or even homemade ones made with dog or other animal hair.

Chinese brushes are useful for glaze brushing where a streaky result is undesirable. These have a number of bamboo shafts joined together to make a soft brush up to 6" wide. This type of brush can be cut to different widths. Large, soft Japanese brushes called *hake* also function in a similar fashion.

Glaze brushing usually is best done with a well-charged brush to cover the maximum area in a single sweep. If it's necessary to go over an area several times, the result almost inevitably will be streaked unless the glaze is sufficiently fluid to disguise the brush marks.

If you want a flat surface, brushing probably is not the best way to glaze the piece. Both cellulose and sponge household paint rollers are less likely to leave streaky surfaces, although some texture probably will show. For further textural interest, rollers easily can have designs or patterns cut or burnt into the surface to leave an imprint as the glaze-charged roller is pushed or pulled across the ceramic surface. Inexpensive lambswool and cellulose sponge rollers come in a variety of widths and diameters and are available through hardware or paint stores.

Brushing and Roller Coating Advantages
- Able to cover large areas with small amounts of glaze;
- Good for fragile or once-fired pieces; and
- Good for details on decorative pieces or overlapping areas.

Brushing and Roller Coating Disadvantages
- Likely to be streaky;
- Bisque-fired ware sucks the liquid from the brush; and
- A very slow method of glazing.

Rollers, sponges, and stamps.

Rikki Gill, USA, "Square Dance" porcelain.

Photo: Judi Dyelle

Photo: Bonita Cohn

Photo: Peter Lee

Linda Sikora, Canada, "Covered Jar," porcelain, polychrome glaze, wood, oil, salt fire, 14" high, 2002.

Dipping

Dipping wares into pots or buckets of glaze is probably the most common glaze application method used by ceramists. It is fast and easy, and dipping generally gives a coating of even thickness. It is the most useful glazing process for production work, where speed and efficiency are important.

If the glaze runs during application, it can be removed with a knife to ensure a smooth coating for any further painting. Touch up unglazed spots (from where you hold the piece) with a brush or your fingers. For small to medium pieces, dipping tongs are very useful. The work is held by a claw grip, and although the tongs leave marks to be touched up by brush, the marks are usually very small and easily removed.

Dipping Advantages

- Ease of application;
- Evenness of coating; and
- Speed of application.

Dipping Disadvantages

- Large volume of glaze needed.

Pouring

Pouring and dipping often are done on the same piece: The inside is poured, and the outside is dipped. Pouring can be done with a variety of tools, such as cans, pitchers or long-spouted pots such as indoor plant watering cans, to various forms of ladles.

All pouring vessels have their own qualities of flow, and individual requirements will dictate the best tool to use for the job. I personally prefer a narrow-spout aluminum teapot bought at the local hardware store.

Glazes for pouring usually should be prepared a little thinner than those used for dipping, as there is almost inevitably a certain amount of overlap, and excessive thickness easily can cause the glaze to run. Pouring can be used for a wide range of decorative effects, particularly when glazes of different characters and colors are used over each other, and the thickness variations and glaze interaction are used to advantage.

Pouring Advantages

- Small amounts of glaze may be used; and
- Speedy and free decoration techniques.

Sam Scott, USA, "Black and White Lidded Reliquary," wheel-thrown porcelain with lid and handles, black matte glaze poured on the surface, reduction fired cone 12, 12" tall.

Photo: Tom Holt

Ginny Conrow, USA, "Porcelain Bowl," 8" x 7" x 6".

Photo: Roger Schreiber

Gay Smith, USA, "Tripoint Jar," porcelain, wheel-thrown and altered, raw glazed and single fired to cone 10 in soda kiln, surface is faceted, dipped in copper glaze when leather-hard, fired in soda kiln where glaze surface is fluxed and fumed by the impact of sodium sprayed into kiln, reducing flame, 7-½" x 7-½", 2003.

Donna Polseno, USA, "Small Footed Box," cone 6 porcelain, layered glazes with wax resist pattern, 5" x 5" x 6", 2003.

David Beumee, USA, "Teabowl," wheel-thrown porcelain, brushed with Shino glaze over Blackbird slip, 4-¼" x 4-¼", 2002.

Patrick Horsley, USA, "Boat Vase," thrown and altered, slip trailed, matte black glaze sprayed front and back, pattern drawn with soft pencil, wax resist, matte black cut away/washed off in spots, dipped in silver black glaze, 11" x 4" x 12".

Pouring Disadvantages

- Likely to be uneven, with glaze runs.

Spraying

Spraying is a good application method, although it usually takes quite a lot of experience to achieve even coatings and to learn to judge the thickness necessary for an adequate covering. Spraying can be used to glaze the whole piece or just small areas.

When spray glazing, much material is lost in the atmosphere as floating dust. Because many glaze materials and most colorants are toxic, spray glazing is best confined to a ventilated spray booth with the glazer wearing a safety mask.

Most glaze materials are quite abrasive and are likely to cause severe wear to the nozzles of spray guns. To minimize this problem, carbide spray tips are available. All equipment should be carefully cleaned after every use.

Glazes used for spraying can be ball-milled to ensure that the particles of material are pulverized as finely as possible. They normally are used in a much thinner consistency than in other application methods. The glaze can have a deflocculant added, such as 1 percent sodium silicate solution. This will minimize the water content, lower the likelihood of excessively wetting the piece and prevent the glaze from "washing" or flowing from the surface. Is it usual to apply several thin coatings, gradually building up the thickness to give the desired result. If the piece is to be glazed all over, particularly when an even coat is required, it is advantageous to place the piece on a banding wheel.

Spraying probably wastes more material than any other glazing method. If you are doing a lot of spraying, particularly with expensive materials, some sort of waste retrieval system might be worth thinking about.

The nature of spraying usually results in a broadcast of color. If intricate patterns are desired, masking techniques such as latex, paper or wax resist should be employed (see pages 202 and 204).

Spraying Advantages

- Ease of handling, particularly for once-fired or fragile work;

Photo: Sean Scott

Gail Kendall, USA, "Tureen," drape molded and coil built, 11" x 9" x 16", 2003.

- Eliminates glaze runs and overlapping in the unfired glaze;
- Ease of color gradation; and
- Small amount of glaze required.

Spraying Disadvantages
- Atmospheric pollution and respiratory health hazards;
- Waste of materials;
- Cost of equipment;
- Equipment maintenance;
- Difficult to control spray, except with expensive units;
- Difficult to gauge correct thicknesses; and
- Need for masking in pattern control.

Note: See Chapter 15 for more information on spraying.

Stippling

Stippling is a form of application done with the edge or tip of a brush, or with a sponge. Stippling is a good way to apply glaze or color when you want a broken texture. The best type of brush to use is a house painting brush or an artist's bristle brush used for oil painting. Be careful of the amount of glaze charged into the brush. Since stippling uses the edge or tip of the brush, it usually is held vertically. If the brush is overcharged, the glaze is likely to run out.

Spattering

Spattering is more or less a form of spraying, where, because of the nature of the tools used, a broken and uneven spray is achieved. Sometimes, bad, inefficient or worn out spray guns inadvertently do the same thing!

The usual tool for spattering is a toothbrush or similar form of stiff-bristled brush. The bristles are dipped into the glaze, and the brush is held near the area to be sprayed. A knife blade then is pulled across the bristles, toward the decorator or away from the work, forcing the bristles to bend, spring back and release the glaze or color in an uneven spray. Spattering can be a very effective way of coloring a specific area.

Sponging

Sponges can produce interesting glaze textures.

Both natural and synthetic sponges can be used to soak up the glaze and apply it to the work. Synthetic sponges can be cut or burnt into patterns, which then can be used to create overall repeat patterns or patterns for simple and fast production. If the sponge is sufficiently fine grained, quite delicate patterns can be made in this way.

By overlaying the sponge marks or stamps, it is possible to develop great depth in the decoration. Although the sponge will deteriorate in time, it will have quite a long life if washed carefully after use.

Trailing

Glaze trailing is a way to draw on the ceramic surface in a linear fashion. Like slip trailing, it can be done with a variety of tools. Almost any squeezable plastic bottle with a fine aperture tip will do. In the cleaning, it helps if the bottle or other tool has a removable cap or nozzle. In the Orient, trailing is done with a tool made from two pieces of bamboo. A thin length is used for

Photo: Istvan (Steve) Pinter/Graphex

Mary Fox, Canada, "Desert Riches," wheel-thrown earthenware, lithium compound sprayed, oxidation fired, mounted in Vancouver Island sandstone, 32.5cm x 19cm, 2003.

the trailing end, which is joined to a short, wide bamboo reservoir.

Glazes for trailing are best used in a thicker than normal consistency. In firing, trailed glazes usually will flatten and spread to some extent. If a detailed drawing is required, it often is better to trail the glaze on the unfired surface, then bisque fire, or on a bisque-fired surface before applying the main glaze. Trailed glazes applied over other glazes tend to be fragile during handling because the raised portions are knocked off easily. If the drawing spreads too much in the firing, it might be a good idea to consider alternate techniques, such as brushwork or underglaze pencils, to develop the required images.See Chapter 14 for more information on trailing.

Multiple Glaze Application

Multiple glaze application refers to the use of two or more glazes over each other, which can be applied in a variety of ways to achieve a particular result. Most often, similar glaze bases are used in multiple applications because they melt in similar ways and are less likely to cause difficulty in application. However, it doesn't have to be done that way, and very different glaze bases applied together can provide rich results.

In the application of multiple glazes, it is important that the work is done in a relatively short time to prevent one glaze from drying out before the next is applied. If drying does occur, it is quite likely that the glazes will flake off, or crawl. Crawling glazes can produce interesting reticulated lizard skin patterns that can be controlled. They occur most often when a glaze with a high clay content is put over a glaze with a low clay content. As the second glaze dries, the clay causes greater shrinkage to occur, and the places where crawling is likely to occur are established.

Glazes for multiple application generally work best used in a thinner than normal consistency, unless excessive running or thick buildup of low flow is needed or desired.

Multiple glazing on vertical forms is likely to present some problems in the firing if the glazes are too thick, because they probably will run. Using thin glazes and minimizing the amount of overlapping at the lower part of the work should help discourage runs.

Glaze Removal Processes

Along with all the variables of glaze application,

Minako Yamane-Lee, USA, "Sunset I," wheel-thrown, altered rim, black and orange glazes sprayed to show the terrestrial ridges, as the sun rises, cone 10 reduction, gas kiln, 5" x 7" x 7", 2001.

Photo: Alan Decker

Chris Gustin, USA, "Platter," wheel-thrown stoneware, wax and latex resist methods, layering of glazes to build up surface, 24" x 25" x 4", 2002.

Photo: Dean Powell

there are many glaze removal processes that can add greatly to the richness and diversity of the ceramic surface. Some of these are used in conjunction with the glaze application, and some are done after the glaze firing.

Sgraffito

Sgraffito is probably the simplest form of removal. In sgraffito, a pigment, slip or glaze is scratched away to reveal the surface beneath. It can be done at various stages in the making and decorating processes. When done through pigment or slip on soft or leather-hard clay, it will have a different quality than when done through slip on dry clay. In the first instance, it will give a more fluid, sharp-edged line; in the second it will usually show a broken line through the grainy quality of the clay.

Sgraffito can be done through once-fired glaze, cutting down into the clay or through glaze down to bisque-fired clay. A variety of tools can be used, from sticks to knives and old dental tools. Sgraffito techniques can be compared in their visual qualities to pen and ink drawings, as both are essentially scratch processes. The fired result can have all of the expression and richness of this form of drawing.

Resist Processes

Resist processes can be done at various stages in the ceramic cycle. Chapter 13 gives a lengthier description of the diverse methods. Since resists primarily are used in conjunction with glaze decoration, a condensed overview of resists also is included here. The various forms of resisting glazes, slips or colorants all do basically the same thing, although with quite different qualities. The process makes possible the removal, or resistance, of one material from another by making some form of barrier that subsequent applications of glaze or color are unable to penetrate. This can produce a wide range of color, texture and glaze variation, because the resisted area will show one color, and the area where the glaze or color has not been resisted will show another.

Resists can be done on clay, on bisque or on the glaze, depending on the result required.

Wax Resist

This may be done with hot paraffin wax or candle wax, or with cold latex wax or wax emulsion. When using hot wax, it is often a good idea to add a small quantity of kerosene or thin machine oil to make the wax melt at a lower temperature. These additions also will produce a better flow from the brush when doing resist brushwork.

I prefer to heat the wax in an electric frying pan where the temperature can easily be controlled. If wax is overheated, it can quickly ignite. Overheated wax also is likely to be absorbed into the surface of the ware, losing its efficiency as a barrier.

Wax can be used on greenware and painted over with pigments to get an underglaze decoration, then bisque fired. The wax will burn out, leaving the pattern, and glaze can be applied over it. Wax also can be used on the bisque to keep glaze off entirely or to show the character of the clay body. It also can be used between layers of glaze or between glaze and colorants. Resist processes can be used in conjunction with any of the previously mentioned application processes.

Paper Resist

Paper resists usually are done better on leather-hard clay, using either slips or colorant brushed, poured or sprayed on. Absorbent paper, such as newsprint, can be applied to the piece by wetting with water, after which the slip or colorant is applied. When dry, the paper is removed, leaving a positive/negative image that can be glazed over or left as is. Masking tape also makes a good material for paper resist.

Crayon Resist

The underglaze crayons described in Chapter 14 also can be used to produce drawings that partially resist the glaze, depending on the thickness of both. They are best used on either bone-dry or bisque-fired clay. Children's wax crayons can be used in the same way. Some colors may stain, but lighter colors probably won't. You can draw with wax candles, as well.

Latex Resist

There are various forms of latex material on the market that can be used for decorative purposes. Almost any rubberized cement or glue will do very well. Some latex materials can be thinned with water, making them more versatile. Some will dry in a sheet that can be peeled off after the desired effect has been reached, allowing further work to be done on the previously resisted areas.

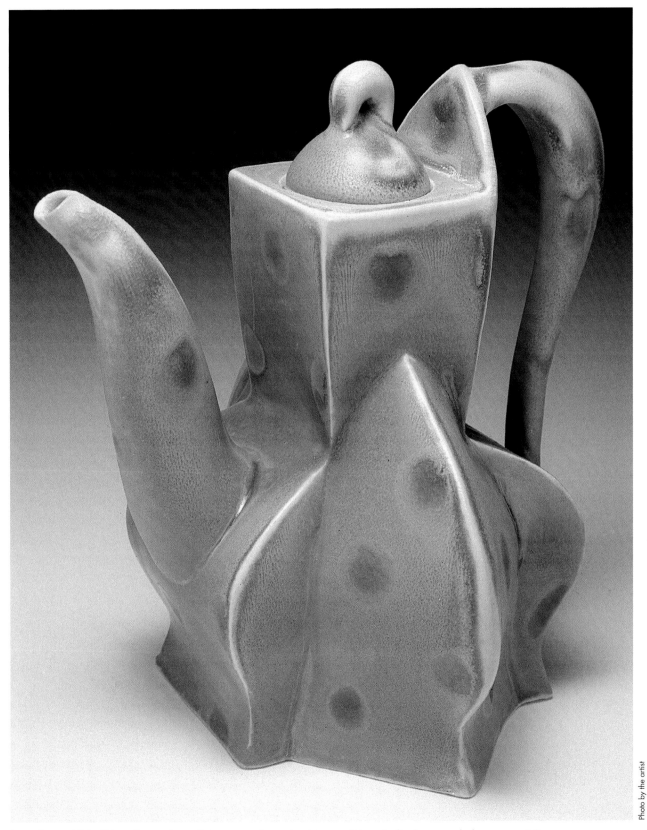

Sam Chung, USA, "Ewer," porcelain, slab construction, wheel-thrown lid, soda fired, sprayed glaze, cone 10, 6" x 5" x 5", 2003.

Photo by the artist

Sally Bowen Prange, USA, "Untitled," wheel-thrown with added slabs and incisions, barnacle slip, glazed with pink flashings from copper red glaze in same kiln, 8-½" x 7-½" x 7-¼", 2002.

Floor wax liquid and solid floor waxes also can be used for resists, although they generally are not as efficient as other resist materials.

Sponge Removal

Sponges can be used to produce negative images as well as a positive images, as described earlier. To achieve this, place a damp sponge, patterned or otherwise, on the slipped or glazed area until the area softens. Lift the sponge, removing the glaze or slip at the same time.

Sponges also can be used freely to remove slip or glaze coatings just by wiping the material away. The area of glaze removal can be left as is, where the thin residual glaze will usually fuse slightly, or it can be covered with another glaze. See Chapter 12 for more information on sponge removal.

Finger Wiping or Combing

Finger wiping or combing glaze is the reverse of finger painting. Removing glaze produces a negative image. Combs can be made of stiff rubber, leather or card. Wiping or combing can be done with slips or glazes in a very fluid, free movement. This works particularly well on glazes with a 20 percent or higher clay content and that stay fairly wet for a time after application.

For best movement, finger wiping and combing should be done while the coating is still semi-liquid. The process essentially moves some of the material, rather than removing it completely, giving a variety of thick and thin areas where the concentration of glaze has one effect and thinning of glaze another.

Glaze Intaglio

Glaze intaglio is the name given when one slip or glaze is removed by any method and another slip or glaze is put back in its place. It can be an extremely laborious process, but it is a way of obtaining very controlled designs in slip or glaze.

Intaglio usually is done with a variety of tools, knives, needles and so on to scratch away the material. The removal also can be done using a removable latex resist or by covering an area with hot wax on top of a glaze and removing this after subsequent application of another glaze. The resisted area then can be filled with glaze using either a brush or trailer.

The incredibly rich palette of glaze variation, combined with sub-glaze coatings and other marks or details, offer an even further array of possibilities when they are fired in various ways. The next two chapters look at firing variables.

Part 5

FIRING AND POST-FIRING PROCESSES

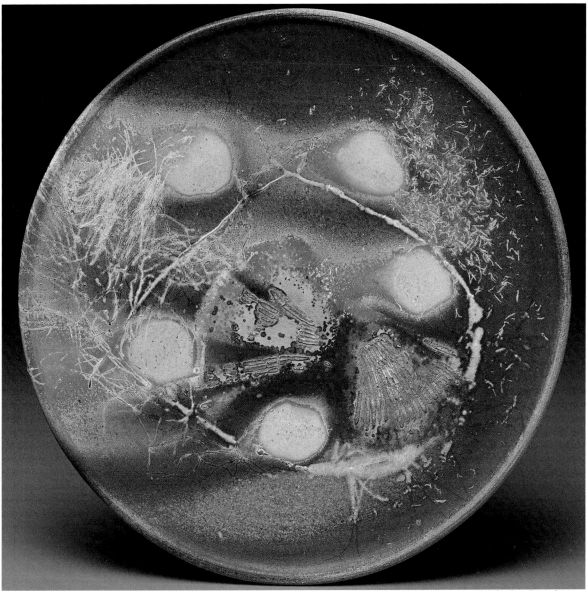

Photo: Janet Dwyer

Pat Webber, Canada, "Comet Series," platter, wood fired, horsetail and clamshell marks, matte crystals developed in the halo of the shell and wadding areas.

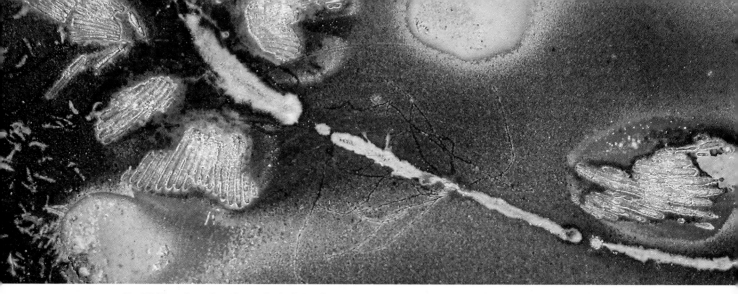

Pat Webber, Canada, "Comet Series" detail, platter, wood fired, horsetail and clamshell marks, matte crystals developed in the halo of the shell and wadding areas. Photo: Judi Dyelle

CHAPTER 17

Marks of Heat, Flame and Smoke

In most circumstances, the kiln has the final say in how your work appears. It can be the kiss of life or the kiss of death, or one of joy or despair. In the hands of experienced ceramic artists, firing becomes almost like a dance in partnership with the fire. Most kiln types require a period of time for the firer to develop an understanding of how best to plan the dance to get the best out of the partnership — when to lead and when to back off or be led.

From the normally inert oxidation atmosphere of the electric kiln through the active atmospheres of primitive firing, general reduction and post-firing reduction to the flame markings and fluid glaze of wood firing, surfaces can be altered in a variety of ways, either as special qualities in themselves or in conjunction with other surface development methods already mentioned or yet to come. This chapter is a collaboration between the author, Robin Hopper (RH), and Randy Brodnax

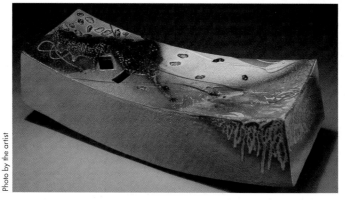

Photo by the artist

Tom Coleman, USA, "Ikebana Slab," hand-built white stoneware, porcelain slips, numerous Shino and ash glazes, fired cone 10 in reduction, 8" x 7" x 22", 2003.

Photo: Sibila Savage

Jane Burton, USA, "Idly Wild," coil built, burnished with polished rock, pit fired with copper wire and sheeting, steel wool, burlap, seaweed, salts, sawdust and oak, 24" tall, 2002.

(RB), an adventurous Texas ceramic artist who has explored more types of kilns, firing methods and surface development processes related to firing variables than anyone else I know personally. I have written it in part as a form of dialogue between two ceramic artists/educators who have spent their working lives intrigued by and consumed with understanding the incredible range of possibilities that constitute the ceramic medium and the roles that kilns and firing play in the final result.

A kiln (from the Latin *culina*, meaning kitchen) is a container for concentrating heat and transforming clay into pottery. The concept is simple. A kiln can be built in the form of a box, tube, cylinder, pit or several of these combined as a unit. The heat source can be radiant, such as electricity, where heat develops from the resistance of electrical current through wire elements, or it can be combustible through the burning of natural gas, propane gas, oil, wood, sawdust, dung or almost anything that can develop and hold high degrees of heat. Designing kilns to accommodate the variables of temperature and atmosphere and finding out what each type of kiln will do and what is the most suitable for a given product can be a lifelong learning journey.

From the viewpoint of the firing process, the easiest to use is the electric kiln. It is much like a super-insulated kitchen oven. You turn it on low for an hour or two, then either directly up to high or medium for an hour or two, and then on high for the remainder

Photo: Alain Gauvi

Mahmoud Baghaeian, Canada, "Peacock Raku," after raku firing, heat applied to desired area of surface, this produces colorful designs, torches of various sizes used for different effects.

of the firing. It can be shut off manually (after looking through the spy holes at pyrometric cones placed inside the kiln), using a pyrometer, or electronically through cone-bending kiln sitters or on computer programs. Many electric kilns are computer controlled and almost foolproof. By following the instructions in the manual, anyone can do it.

Great work can come out of electric kilns, as is evidenced by much of the ceramic work done over the last 75 years. However, since the kiln contributes little to the final quality of the ware, other than heat, it requires the ceramist to work extra hard to develop expressive imagery, creative surfacing solutions and extensive glaze development to create levels of interest

Photo: Cadwald Henry

Randy Brodnax, USA, "Fish Vase," raku with expanded texture plus commercial glaze application sprayed with ferric chloride before reduction.

Photo: Cadwald Henry

Randy Brodnax, USA, "Raku Lidded Jar," carbonized horsehair pattern.

found naturally in almost all other forms of firing. The electric kiln fires only in oxidation, unless the ceramist introduces burnable materials into the firing or glaze for some particular effect. The vagaries of combustible fuels and the fact that they can be made to smoke by limiting oxygen and creating a reducing atmosphere, plus the variety of ways they can be used and temperatures at which they can be used, offer the ceramist an enormous potential palette of possibilities. There are myriad ways to fire ceramics, and firing can be done in a variety of venues, including high schools, community colleges, universities, art and recreation centers, and potters' studios. No matter what type of work an artist produces, any combustion-firing kiln requires a considerable amount of sensitivity to fire for optimum results. How do you go about learning this?

Randy Brodnax (RB). Before I fire any combustion kiln there are several factors to consider — type of kiln, location, weather, type of fuel. Most important to me is to reach a mental state of sensitivity equal to the personality of the kiln. During the course of a calendar year, I fire at least 15 to 20 different kilns in locations from Texas to Canada and from high elevations in the Rocky Mountains to sea-level Mexico. In the beginning I was horrified — each kiln had a different personality! It didn't matter whether it was updraft, crossdraft, downdraft, gas, oil, wood or dung-fired, each one had its own nuances. As I acquired more knowledge about each kiln's temperament, I looked forward to the individual interaction with each kiln.

Thinking in a dynamic nature enables me to relate to the kiln's most sensitive characteristics. The location of the kiln, the elevation, the humidity and the types of fuel used all are dealt with in an incredibly sensitive manner. Learning to work with kilns to exploit the best qualities of each requires that you develop understanding of each type. Often in educational facilities and group learning centers, the responsibility for firing is taken over by the instructor or technical assistant, leaving the student with little opportunity to understand or "feel" the process. Because of possible dangers and consequent liabilities, firing often is done with little or no student involvement. The select few who are driven to develop the firing skills and techniques generally start late in their junior or senior years, or when they become apprentices at studios in interactive but controlled situations. It is not until you experience control of the firing yourself that you really begin to understand the process entirely. It is a method of learning by doing.

Robin Hopper (RH). In my case, I was fortunate to learn firing processes at art school. There was a big gas kiln in a small room with little space down each side to maneuver to operate gas valves or control air vents and the chimney damper. My teacher had become petrified of firing the kiln after a few burner blowbacks that singed his eyebrows. Since I was the only male in the class, I was informed that if I wanted reduction fired results (I hardly knew what they were but they sounded intriguing!), I would have to fire the kiln. (Way back then, females didn't do such dirty studio work!) I guess I was expendable, but it was the best thing that could have happened to me at that stage of my education. So I read about it, talked to a couple of potters and went ahead, learning as I went, entrusted with firing all of the student work for three years. Randy studied at a school where the firing was done by someone else. Although he had been receiving high national acclaim for his work in major competitions, he was entirely ignorant about kilns and firing.

RB. I was lost after I got out of school. I decided that I would have to take on the challenge and learn to fire my own kiln. I was teaching at a small school, but saved my money and purchased 250 firebricks. Everything I read in books about clay assured me that I would be able to make a kiln and burner with little effort. I stacked bricks in the form of a cube, put a shelf in the bottom, 4" from the floor of the kiln, and reversed a vacuum cleaner engine so it would blow. I even spliced the gas line from the house full force, stuck it into a 2" pipe, hooked up the vacuum blower to the pipe, turned the gas on full, turned the blower on full and proceeded into the house to find a light. I got the matches, started to light the kiln and "Bang!" The roof of the kiln knocked a hole in the carport, I landed against my neighbor's house with no hair on my head, but most importantly, I gained a completely new understanding and healthy respect for air and gas! This was the beginning of my exploration into the variables of kilns and their firing. There were so many mechanical things I didn't understand about firing clay. With ceramics, all steps in the process are equally important — construction of the clay, glazing the ware, and how it is fired.

RH. A manually operated, commercial gas-fired kiln is probably the easiest place to learn the principles of combustion firing and kiln design. This type of kiln usually comes with a manual that explains the procedures. Once you learn the basic principles of firing, you easily can adapt them to fit any type of combustion firing. As you build confidence in your abilities and understanding of the firing process, you will develop your own methodology. No two people will fire the same kiln in exactly the same way, and the sensitivity to external contributors to the firing, such as weather, winds and humidity, always are interpreted differently. No single way of firing is right or wrong — it is a matter of what works best for you to develop the qualities you are looking for in the final object.

RB. If you are building your own kiln, a simple cube-shaped or cylindrical raku kiln with one burner is a good place to start learning about fire, air and combustion. You can purchase burners or make a simple burner from iron plumbing fittings. The burner needs a

Marilyn Richeda, USA, "Fox Head," hand rolled terra cotta slabs with doweled legs, head and tail, fired cone 04 in oxidation, 10" x 9" x 4", 2002.

Photo: Joseph Giunta

primary air intake to allow air and gas to combine and for combustion to take place at the end of the burner. The gas line will have a shut-off valve to control the amount of gas going through the burner. Gas is introduced by a tube with a brass cap that has been centrally drilled with a fine hole or orifice to allow a specific amount of gas to combine with the air and for ignition to take place. Burners can be forced air, where a blower blows air from behind the gas orifice to control combustion, or they can be natural draft, where the air is drawn through the primary air vents by the pressure of the gas. The ratio of gas to air controls the oxidation or reduction flame. Cutting back the air or increasing the gas will cause a reducing flame to develop. Oxidizing flames are short, fast and bluish, whereas reduction flames are long, slow and yellow or orange in color.

Here are a few frequently asked questions about firing.

Susan Le Poidevin, Canada, "Gulls on Kinghorn Town Hall," sawdust fired, low-fire slips and glazes, 5" x 4" x 8", 2000.

Jimmy Clark, USA, "Landscape," sawdust fired with resist slips and sulfates, stripped, sanded and sealed, 9" x 12", 2001.

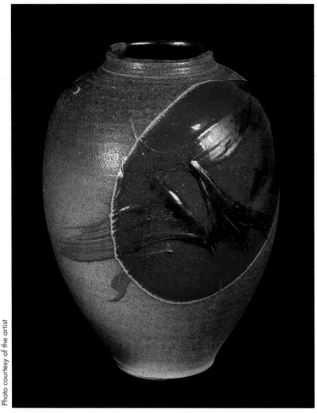

Gordon Hutchens, Canada, "Vase," stoneware, thick slip brushwork under copper red/green glaze, wood fire flashing on bare clay, anagama fired, cone 10, 9" x 6".

Louise Pentz, Canada, "Vase," smoked ware, 12" x 9", 2003.

What about a high-pressure gas line as opposed to one that's low pressure? Does the size of the orifice change based on the pressure? Yes, the orifice size changes with high or low pressure. Talk to your gas supplier to find out the recommended orifice size for the fuel you are going to be using.

Does propane gas differ from natural gas? Yes, propane carries three times the heat of natural gas.

Where does gas pressure come from? It comes from a regulator (high or low pressure) from the main gas source.

You will need to understand all of this to safely fire a small raku kiln at the studio. Once you have developed an understanding of firing a raku kiln, you are on your way to understanding basic firing principles for any type of kiln. The larger the kiln, the greater heat requirement and more burners it will need.

High-temperature, gas-fired kilns can be updraft, downdraft or crossdraft, depending on the path the flame takes through the kiln. In an updraft kiln, the burners are directly below the firing chamber, and the fire goes vertically through the kiln, with excess heat and gases going through a vent at the top of the kiln. The temperature in updraft kilns is often uneven within the chamber — sometimes extra hot at the bottom or at the top. Updraft kilns often are difficult to control in reduction firing, but they usually are cheaper to construct because they don't have chimneys. In a downdraft kiln, the burners normally are on both sides, or front and back. The flame movement is controlled by interior deflecting or bag walls and a chimney flue placed at the bottom of the kiln, which forces the flame down through the ware before escaping up the chimney. A crossdraft kiln has burners on one side, with bag walls deflecting the flame up, then down through the ware to a chimney flue on the opposite side of the kiln.

Oxidation and reduction are controlled by the primary air on the burners, the secondary air around the burner ports and a damper on the chimney. A damper is a sliding door in the flue that controls the amount of

Photo: John Bonath

Barbara Hoffman, USA, "Ewer," porcelain, cone 10 gas reduction fired, Shino glazed, dried with mesh Styrofoam wrapped around, changed further with reduction atmosphere and carbon trapping cone 010, 5" x 3-½" x 6-½", 2002.

back pressure that occurs in the kiln. With more back pressure, less oxygen goes through the kiln, producing a reducing atmosphere where colors and surfaces of glazes are changed, sometimes drastically. Learning to control a gas firing kiln requires an understanding not only of the kiln, burners and damper, but also of the weather conditions during the firing process. Barometric pressure, prevailing winds and humidity all affect the progress and outcome of a firing.

There are several books available on kiln design and construction (see the Bibliography). If you are planning to build a kiln, do as much research as possible to get it right. Downdraft and crossdraft kilns need a chimney to take off exhaust gases and assist in building heat in the firing chamber. How big does your chimney need to be? How tall should your chimney be in relation to your kiln? Depending on the size of the chamber and the British thermal units of gas supplied through each

Photo: Pierre Fortin

Pauline Pelletier, Canada, "Vase," cast porcelain, sawdust sagger fired, cone 04, gold leaf, reconstructed, fired with soluble materials, potassium chromate, iron chloride, copper oxide, 36cm x 40cm, 2003.

213

burner, the flue and chimney require a minimum 6" x 6" opening for a small kiln up to 25 cubic feet of chamber, 8" x 8" for up to 60 cubic feet, and up to 12" x 12" for kilns larger than 100 cubic feet. For very large kilns, a still-larger chimney will be needed. A good rule of thumb is that the height of the chimney is three times the height of the kiln interior.

What is the best kiln you can build for your money? Should it be made of hard brick, soft brick or fiber, or should you make your own casting materials and cast your own? All of these variables exist, and you must decide what is best for you. Any kiln is a major investment, and you need to consider the project thoroughly to make sure that whatever you purchase or build has the potential and flexibility to do what you ask of it. What you ask of it depends on your knowledge of the possibilities inherent in the ceramic medium and the results you visualize.

RH. If the studio property and local bylaws allow it, I recommend building a combustion-fueled kiln because the options for a wider range of work are much greater. Electric kilns are convenient, but they usually are fired only in oxidation. With gas firing, you can fire in oxidation or reduction. Gas, either natural or propane, is probably the most convenient and least messy fuel. If you opt for the sweaty romance of wood firing, be prepared to deal with concerns of high maintenance costs, wood availability, storage space, firing assistance and increased pollution.

What you choose as your major mode of expression in this medium controls the parameters you need to use in deciding what firing method and kiln type are most relevant for you. If you only have one kiln, make sure it will do everything you need. If you are only planning to do pit firing, sagger firing or primitive firing, you only need a small pile of bricks and some sheets of metal. If you are doing highly controlled crystalline glazes, you really need a good electric kiln with sophisticated computerized controls. As goes the vision and concept of the work, so goes the decision of the appropriate firing process. The more you know about the firing process in general, the more you can adapt to fit any situation and the more options you have for self-expression in this complex medium.

In the early stages of getting to know your kiln, it is

Photo by the artist

Michael Sheba, Canada, "Bowl," hand-built, wheel-thrown foot ring, impressed, combed, and stamped textures and marks, airbrushed glazes and underglazes, tape resist, multi-fired raku with inlaid low-fire enamels, 9" x 3-¼".

worth keeping accurate records of how you fire — how long, the weather conditions, what glazes were where and how tightly or loosely the kiln was packed. Many people keep detailed and accurate records and graphs for future reference. You can't always trust memory. To check the overall variations in the firing chamber during the first few firings, place packs of cones in several places — top to bottom, front to back and side to side. This will show you hot and cool spots in the chamber. Record this very useful information, since many glazes have preferences for minute variations in temperature and atmosphere.

Most experienced potters agree that it usually takes about five firings and copious note-keeping to understand any kiln. Larger kilns likely will take longer to learn. Even though they might be built to identical specifications, no two kilns will fire exactly the same time after time. If you want reliable results, you need a solid understanding of the idiosyncrasies of your particular kiln. Like people, they have personalities. Some are easy to get along with, and others aren't. The better you understand them, the better they will behave for you.

Photo by the artist

Dick Lehman, USA, "Flattened Bottle," thrown, flattened and altered porcelain, sagger fired to cone 08, vegetation inside sagger turned to activated charcoal released a film of carbon that was absorbed by porous bisque-fired pot, 11" tall, 2002.

Photo by the artist

Richard T. Notkin, USA, "The Gift" detail, a view of some of the 1,106 individual earthenware tiles that comprise the ceramic mural, 1999.

Object Placement

Knowing how to fire a kiln isn't the only important aspect of coaxing work through a firing to get the best results. How the objects are placed in the kiln also can have a profound effect on the final result. This is another aspect where note-keeping will be helpful. Some people keep meticulous notes of all firings throughout their lives; others rely on memory and often wish they had recorded processes and results of firings. This is particularly true of glazes they use only occasionally. Some glazes need a good degree of space around them, at least ½" from the nearest object, to perform optimally; others can almost be touching. It would be impossible to say which glazes are particularly fussy and which aren't (although copper reds, Chüns and crystalline glazes would be close to the top of the fussy list), as there are too many variables to consider, but it is certainly something of which to be aware.

One of the great joys of making pots or ceramic objects lies in the opening of the kiln and hopefully finding that all of the effort you expended and all the understanding of the processes of making, surfacing and firing have combined to fulfill your expectations or visions. It often takes months or years of frustrating (but character-building) experience to get to this point. When it happens, the satisfaction is extreme. Then you try something else!

Exploration and experimentation in all the potential that different firing processes offer — raku through earthenware, mid-fire and high-fire stoneware and porcelain, oxidation and reduction — give an enormous range of possibilities. For the adventurous ceramist, there are always new things to learn and different ways to explore old themes. In this medium, you need never be at a loss for different directions to take. This spirit of personal search into the unknown is what keeps many ceramic artists energized about their work and the buying public and collectors excited about this medium.

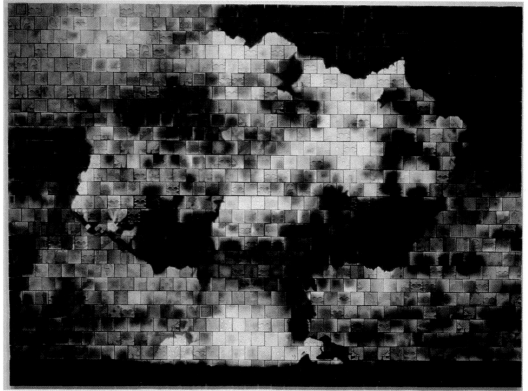

Richard T. Notkin, USA, "The Gift," earthenware tiles individually fired in sawdust filled saggers to achieve various shades of white, gray and black, tiles chosen and arranged to match the photograph of the mushroom cloud image, 80-½" x 112" x 3", 1999.

Photo by the artist

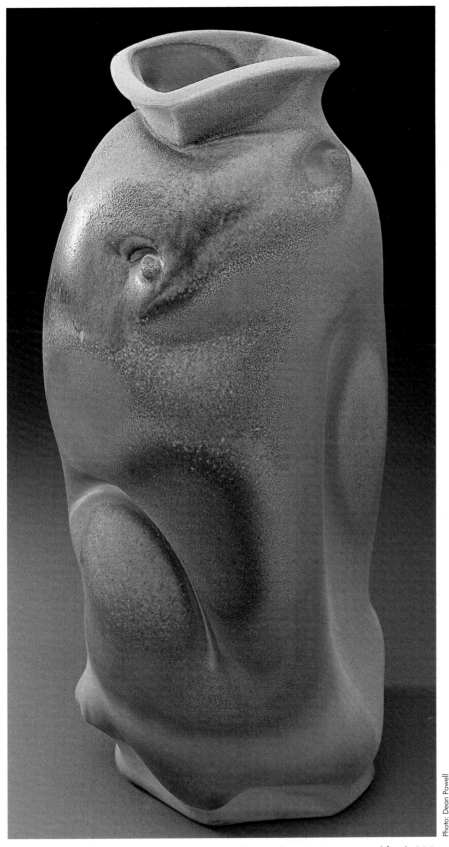

Photo: Dean Powell

Chris Gustin, USA, "Vase," thrown and hand-built porcelain, anagama wood fired, 21"
x 10-½" x 9-½", 2002.

Walter Keeler, UK, "Tea Pot" detail, stoneware, salt glazed. Private collection. Photo: Judi Dyelle.

CHAPTER 18

Marks of Vapor and Fume

The interactive action of firing combustion-fueled kilns is probably the most intimate of firing procedures. Knowing how the fuel you are working with gives its best results, together with knowing what is going on inside the kiln at all times, is more necessary and more acute in this type of firing than any other. How the elevation or the weather affects the firing also is critical to the final results. It is in the repeated firing of gas- or oil-fueled kilns where you learn this intimate understanding of the firing process. When to speed up, when to slow down, when to reduce, how much and for how long all are vital to the final result. With very experienced ceramists, firing kilns is as much about intuition and perception as it is about technology. These, combined with the alchemy of glaze and color development, are aspects of the ceramic medium that give combustion firing its essential mystery.

Salt/Soda Firing

Starting in the 12th or 13th centuries A.D. in Germany, potters developed vapor glazing processes by introducing salt into the kiln as it was nearing top temperatures for the vitrification of the ware. Nobody knows exactly when or why a potter first threw salt into a kiln and observed the results as sodium chloride dissociation took place and the sodium combined with the silica in the clay, producing a textured sodium/silicate glaze. Like most things in this alchemistic business, it probably was an accidental discovery that then was capitalized on.

Salt starts to vaporize in the kiln as early as bisque firing temperatures, but it usually is partially absorbed

Dick Lehman, USA, "Bottles," porcelain, thrown and altered, Shino-style glaze, wood fired, 7" and 9" tall, 2001.

Photo by the artist

218

Vince Palacios, USA, "Homage to Artist Cup," porcelain, slip, glaze with soda ash wash, 7" x 4".

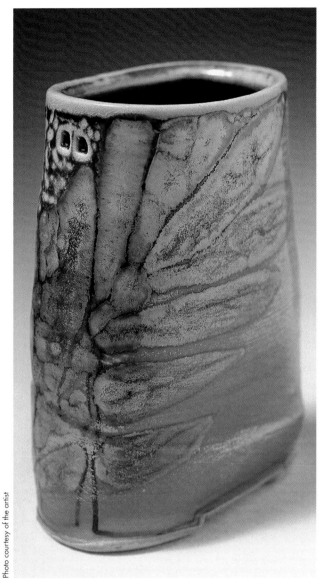

Cathi Jefferson, Canada, "Leaf Oval Vase," wheel thrown with base and altered, salt/soda fired, 4" x 3" x 2".

into the porous bisque, taking soluble colorants with it and creating a wide range of possible surface effects that become an important part of the low-fire salt and sagger firing vocabulary. At these low temperatures, from cone 012 to cone 04, the body remains porous and absorbs much vapor from both salt and other sodium compounds, such as sodium carbonate and sodium bicarbonate, and from soluble colorants in salt, sulfate or chloride form, such as copper sulfate, cobalt sulfate, nickel sulfate, iron chloride and potassium permanganate. Combustible materials, such as charcoal, wood, pine cones, fruit skins and seaweed, as well as salt crystals, surrounding an

object in a closed sagger firing will burn and smoke. This causes localized low-temperature reduction to take place, creating carbon impregnation into the body and altering coloration. Sagger fired objects usually have to be treated with a liquid wax coating to fully bring out the colors of the salts impregnated in the surface.

In high-temperature firings, salt and other sodium compounds start to completely break down to form a silica-seeking vapor between cone 4 and cone 6, but they become most responsive at about cone 9 to cone 11. When you determine the temperature you want to fire to, the firing usually proceeds in an oxidizing state until about cone 8 or 9. If you want a body reduction to darken iron-bearing clays, that usually is done between cone 08 and cone 1. As the temperature rises toward the vitrification point of the ware, feed salt into the kiln in repeated small batches until there is a sufficient buildup of glaze on the surface. This can be determined by placing a series of clay rings inside the kiln and drawing them out on a long metal rod between saltings. When the coating on the draw trials is satisfactory, the kiln usually is closed down and left to cool for 24 to 48 hours, depending on the kiln construction and heat retention.

Kilns for salt and soda firings usually are built of hard brick that is more resistant to the corrosive actions of salt vapors than soft or insulating brick. A regular coating of kiln wash over the whole interior of the kiln, including bag walls, salting ports, salt channels, flue exit and burner ports, will prolong the life of the kiln greatly. A suitable kiln wash for this purpose would be 50 percent kaolin and 50 percent alumina hydrate, both of which repel the actions of the salt and maximize on the amount of salt being used to get a satisfactory buildup on the ware. The salting ports are placed so the salt deposits are dropped into a channel directly in front of the burners. Salt is sodium chloride. In the firing, the sodium vapors flow through the kiln and the ware like a river of mist, attaching themselves to the silica content of the clay and/or slips on the surface of the clay. The chloride part of the salt goes up the chimney as chlorine gas and becomes a pollutant capable of denuding surrounding vegetation. Ceramists should take stringent health precautions when firing salt kilns by wearing suitable respiratory safety masks and eye protection.

Since the early 1970s, much research has been done to find less-polluting sodium compounds, the most promising of which have proven to be sodium carbonate (soda ash), sodium bicarbonate (baking soda) and sodium borate (borax). These don't seem to work in quite the same way as salt, and most ceramists mix a combination of sodium compounds with other materials, like wood ash, seaweed, rice, pearl barley or sawdust, to dispense into the kiln. Sometimes the salt charge is put into a length of angle iron and carefully put through the salt port, where it is turned to drop the charge in front of the burners. Sometimes the salt combinations are put into packages weighing about a pound (400 to 500 grams) and pushed through the salt ports with a metal rod. Some ceramists prefer to dampen the salt, others don't. Others make a brine solution from salt and water or soda ash and water at the concentration of approximately 1 pound of sodium compound to 1½ gallons of water. They spray this mixture into the kiln at the appropriate stage and check results on the draw trials.

A fairly open placement of pieces through the kiln allows for greater salt buildup on the exposed surfaces. Salt vapors don't glaze the interiors of taller or narrow pieces, so they will need to be pre-glazed. Traditional interior liner glazes for salt-glazed wares often have been of high iron content that produces rich results with the sodium. Since the salt vapors flow like a river, the side of the objects facing the flow usually will have heavier deposits than the sides facing the interior of the kiln. Pots or kiln posts can be positioned to deflect the flow for other flame and vapor variations to occur.

The reaction to salt vapors allows a wide range of surfacing processes to be done before the salting takes place. Slips and engobes can be made that encourage or discourage the buildup of salt. Calcium carbonate, alumina hydrate and wollastonite (calcium silicate) can be mixed into slips to alter and matte the surface of the salt. Magnesium carbonate can be added to cause the slip to crawl or reticulate, giving very interesting textures. Silica sand, granite sand, granite chips, crushed feldspar or burnout materials, such as coffee grounds, rice, pearl barley or other organic materials, all can make interesting textures that respond well to salt and soda firing. The most complete visual overview of high-temperature salt and soda firing I have seen is in Gordon Hutchens' two-video program available at http://www. PotteryVideos.com.

Wood Firing

From a technical viewpoint, what happens in a salt/soda firing is very similar to what occurs in a wood-fueled firing. In a salt/soda firing, the silica content of the clay attracts the sodium vapors to create a sodium-silicate glaze. In a wood firing, the calcium-based wood ash combines with the silica in the clay to form a calcium-silicate glaze. Clays are roughly 50 percent silica and 50 percent alumina. The alumina produces the stability, and, in regular glazes, creates the bonding mechanism between body and glaze. Salt firings often are combined with wood as the fuel source, and the surface of the pieces becomes glazed with a combination of sodium and calcium silicates.

Wood ash, or more correctly, ash from organic vegetation, has been used as an ingredient for the development of glazes for at least 2,000 years. Glazes utilizing wood ash are rooted firmly in the ceramic traditions of the Orient and have been described in many publications dealing with Oriental glazes. Organic ashes come from the burnt remains of trees, bushes, grasses and even vegetables. Since their cellular structure

Photo: Tom Mills

Suze Lindsay, USA, "Footed Bud Vase," stoneware, hand-built and thrown elements, assembled, paddled feet, brushed on porcelain slip, paper resist motif with copper glaze applied over top, paper removed, accented with black stain brushwork, salt fired cone 10, 8-½" x 5" x 1", 2003.

gets its mineral sustenance from the soil, it is logical to assume that the residue of ash from the burnt matter also contains those minerals. Different plants absorb different amounts of minerals; even ashes from the same type of plant taken from different sites or at different times of the year will vary considerably in their chemical content. With these variables in mind, organic ash is likely to contain mineral oxides in following amounts:

- Silica   30% to 70%
- Alumina   10% to 30%
- Calcium   up to 30%
- Potassium   up to 15%
- Phosphorous   up to 13%
- Magnesium   up to 10%
- Iron   up to 5%

There almost certainly would be trace elements of other mineral oxides present, depending on the source of the vegetation. These mineral oxides are all materials fundamental to glazes. All organic ashes will turn to glass at a temperature between cone 6 and cone 10.

If there is an overabundance of either sodium vapor or wood ash in the kiln, combined with rising temperatures, the alumina will be unable to absorb the excessive fluxing power, and sluggish to melting to fluid surfaces will result. If the fluid glazes are contained in low open bowl or plate forms, gravity will cause the glass to pool deeply in the interiors. On external surfaces, the calcium silicate glass formed from melting wood ash, combined with silica, may vary from hard, crusty deposits to a lick of gloss and color, to a fluid melt, depending on the heat and the length of time the kiln is held at its highest temperatures.

Kilns for wood firings can be anything from small studio versions to the huge community kilns of China, Japan and Korea that can be up to 100 feet long and hold several months' work by families of potters. Small, efficiently designed kilns can be fired by one person in the same 10- to 14-hour time frame that a regular gas firing might take. Larger kilns may take a trained crew several days to fire. In parts of Japan, the work might be in the kiln firing for up to a month. The longer the firing takes, the greater likelihood of heavy deposits of ash. As with salt and soda firings, learning about the

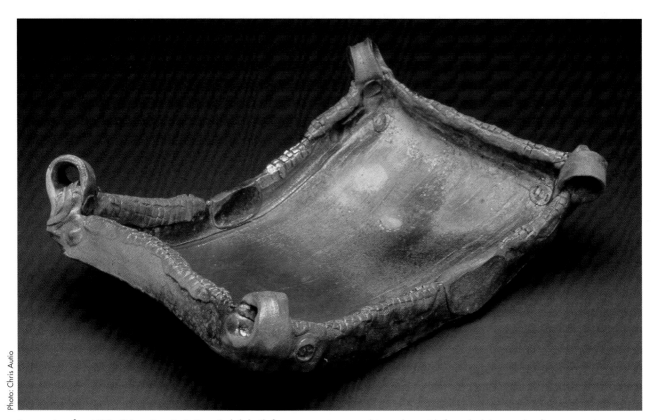

Photo: Chris Autio

Jayson Lawfer, USA, "Hanging Fruit Tray," slab-built form, texture pressed into clay with found object, color from wood ash, no glaze or slip, anagama fired porcelain, 2003.

movement of flame through the kiln and the control or influence of that movement by object placement and spacing are crucial for the best results.

A combination of baffles and objects that shield other objects from the direct impingement of the flame and ash flow create the opportunity for "painting with fire." Some artists who specialize in wood-fired work prefer the lightest touch or licking of flame and ash deposit, while others particularly are drawn to the heavier encrustations that result from the firing process. Stoneware objects placed in or close to the firebox or grate may develop surfaces related to volcanic lava, while porcelains placed in areas with low ash deposits may develop surfaces like fine skin with beautiful pink blushes. The tonal range of colors from wood-firing tend to be in the subtle and subdued range of earth colors, blacks, browns, yellows, silvers, red-browns and pinks, depending on the clay body that is used.

Wood-firing kilns naturally have a kiln atmosphere that fluctuates between oxidation and reduction. When the firebox is freshly charged with wood, the kiln normally goes into reduction. When the wood is burning fiercely, it is usually in oxidation. Further atmosphere control can be achieved with one or more dampers. Reduction also can be maintained as the kiln cools to achieve yet different results.

There are many varieties of wood-firing kilns — groundhog, anagama, noborigama, dragon, beehive, catenary, bottleneck, train — all of which are fired differently and have their own special qualities. There isn't enough space here to describe all the variations in kiln or firing procedures, but there are several books that give this information. Any artist who is intrigued with wood firing would be advised to read about others' experiences and then gain personal experience by becoming part of a firing crew. This book is about surfacing options, and one of the many is to fire with wood. There are many wood-firing kilns in operation, and their owners often are looking for helpers. It is hard, hot and sweaty work, and firings often will take days to complete.

Wood firing, in conjunction with many of the other mark-making processes discussed throughout this book, opens a whole world of possibilities. Cut and fluted surfaces, those covered with traditional slipware

Photo: Brian Oglesbee

Peter Voulkos, USA, "Sculpture," stoneware, wood fired, 13″ x 25″ x 22″, 1998. Gift of the artist, Schein-Joseph International Museum of Ceramic Art, Alfred University, 2000.

Photo courtesy of the artist

Pamela Nagley Stevenson, Canada, "Reliquary for Purity of Heart," wood-fired porcelain, 32cm x 47cm.

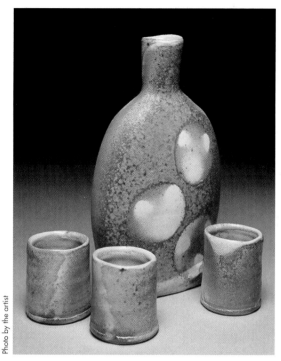

Photo by the artist

Mark Peters, USA, "Whiskey Flask with Three Shots," wood-fired stoneware, side fired with the three shots stacked on it, 8" x 5-½" x 3-½", 2001.

Photo: Janet Dwyer

Deb Taylor, Canada, "Martini Glass," hand-built porcelain, clear glaze on inside, no glaze on exterior, flashing and ash deposits, four day Noborigama firing, 7" x 10", 2003.

Photo: Will Ruggles

Will Ruggles and Douglass Rankin, USA, "Paddled Bottle," wheel thrown and squeezed on the wheel, altered, coil feet added, white stoneware with kaolin slip, metal slip, and glaze decoration, wood fired cone 9 to 10 with salt and soda, 5" high, 2002.

Photo: Didier Veysset

Patty Wouters, Belgium, "Two Vases," porcelain clay thrown and altered, terra sigillata with iron sulfate and combustibles, sagger fired in gas kiln, height 35cm and 30cm, diameter 9cm.

Photo courtesy of the artist

Randy J. Johnson, USA, "Covered Form with Bird," stoneware, wood fired.

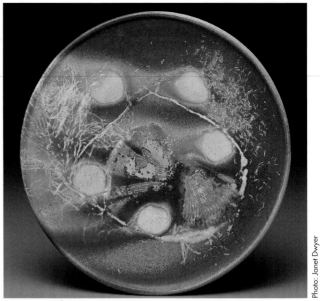

Photo: Janet Dwyer

Pat Webber, Canada, "Comet Series," platter, wood fired, horsetail and clamshell marks, matte crystals developed in the halo of the shell and wadding areas.

decoration and those made with colored clays all can develop extra mysteries from their interactions with wood ash. Perhaps the simplest form of ash glaze, other than the natural deposits of ash that occur in a wood-fired kiln, is created by spraying pots with wood ash, or by painting pots with glue, then rolling them in sieved ash, shaking off the excess and firing them to between cone 6 and 10 in either oxidation or reduction. At this temperature, the ash will melt easily, and the result, to the nonpurist, is almost indistinguishable from pottery fired in a wood-firing kiln. I remember visiting a well-known pottery in Japan renowned for its wood-fired pots and seeing a woman swathed in indigo cloth spraying wood ash in a fairly thick coating on the pots. The pots, I subsequently found out, were going to be fired in an electric kiln! To the untrained eye, the ash-coated, electric-fired object can look remarkably similar to the wood-fired one, and many decorative processes can be used that would likely be obliterated by a full-fledged wood firing. Painting decoration with glue or slip and lightly sprinkling with salt and/or wood ash while wet can further extend the possibilities. Small amounts of salt can have a major effect on the surface. Small amounts of wood ash or salt are unlikely to affect the kiln elements.

Flashing and Fuming

Controlled localized flashing and fuming open

other options. Flashing occurs when some materials at higher temperatures become volatile in the kiln and leave a coloration change on the body adjacent to the glaze. This causes interesting (or annoying, depending on personal taste) effects in the color and surface of glazes. It is noticed in various ways. Volatile materials, such as sodium, lead and boron, and to a lesser extent barium, strontium, zinc, and potassium, may produce shiny glazed areas, occurring like a haze in unglazed areas of the ceramic object. The hazy surface often is an attractive toasty color on stoneware and a pinkish blush on porcelain. It can be used for special decorative effect, such as wax resist brushwork direct to the body. The glaze coating is resisted by the wax, and after the wax is burned off in firing, a flashing or haze often will occur within the brushwork, working its way in from the glazed surface. Very subtle coloration can be achieved in this way with fairly reliable control, even in electric firing.

Some colorants — chromium, copper and to a lesser extent manganese and cobalt — also are volatile and can distribute themselves onto other glazed pieces in the same kiln firing. In the case of chromium, even the kiln walls can be impregnated. The oxide can volatilize out in another firing, turning white, tin-opacified glazes pink. These serendipitous occurrences can be encouraged, as they have been for hundreds of years. The Chinese potters of the Sung Dynasty often painted the inside of

Photo: Janet Dwyer

Walter Keeler, UK, "Tea Pot," stoneware, salt glazed. Private collection.

saggers with copper to volatilize onto the pots, giving pink, red and blue flashing to the opalescent glazes known as Chün or Jün.

Fuming is the name given to the action of volatile oxides and colorants that may color the surface of both clays and glazes in various ways. Fuming might be looked at as a fault if it is not what you want, or it can be an asset if it can be harnessed to work creatively and used to positive effect. Some of what is true of flashing is relevant here, too. Some colorants will fume or volatilize, affecting the work itself, as well as neighbors in the kiln. Chromium and copper are particularly good at this. Organic materials that are calcium-based, such as bones or shells, may create fuming around themselves between cones 6 and 10. The calcium of bones and shells dissociates in heating and mixes with the silica of the clay body, creating a calcium-silicate that can look like localized salt glaze or wood ash firing.

Fuming also is done by putting certain materials, such as stannous chloride, barium chloride and bismuth subnitrate, into the kiln during cooling at around 750°C to 500°C. This may create opalescent or iridescent surfaces on the glaze. The method of introducing the fuming agent in the kiln is similar to that done with salt firing. A long-handled spoon, usually made of beaten and shaped wrought iron, holds the fuming agent and is introduced through a spy hole or fuming port. The agent can either be tipped out onto a kiln shelf or held in the spoon until it stops smoking and is burned up. Small newspaper packages containing fuming material can also be used.

The combinations of fuels, kilns and firing variations give a limitless range of possibilities for experimentation. The more you play with these variables, the more you increase your depth of understanding of the whole ceramic process and of the options you can explore. The possibilities of resurfacing previously fired objects and multiple firing processes are described in the next two chapters.

Robin Hopper, Canada, "Hummingbird Series Plate" detail, sandblasted through, luster glaze with cut plastic sheet resist images. Photo: Judi Dyelle.

CHAPTER 19

Marks of Fired Surface Removal

Even after the final firing, surfacing or resurfacing options still exist through a few methods of surface removal. These can be anywhere from light and subtle hints, like a fine mist, to heavy and obvious statements, like a tornado or hurricane. Removal processes can slightly soften the tactile and visual qualities of a surface or blast it away entirely.

Sandblasting, Grit-Blasting and Air-Erasing

Sandblasting, grit-blasting or air-erasing all are done with spray gun-like tools that spray a stream of abrasive sand or grit under pressure. The abrasive material eats through the surface of the object being blasted, leaving anything from a dulled surface to one that can be riddled with textured holes.

All the masking should be in place before sanding. To create images by sandblasting, objects usually are masked with masking or other tape to resist the abrasion. Unless a major amount of cutting is being done, masking tape is quite resilient; its slightly spongy surface bounces as the abrasive sand hits it. Duct tape also can be used. Larger images can be cut from heavy plastic or rubber sheet and temporarily glued to the surface of the object with rubber cement.

The work usually is done in an enclosed booth with holes cut in the front to hold long, heavy-duty rubber gloves for manipulating the work under the abrasive spray. The sandblasting booth should have a good, built-in extractor fan to remove dust and minimize the amount of dust in the atmosphere. It also needs interior lighting and a large window to view the process.

The gun is attached to an air hose connected to an air compressor. A second hose leads to a hopper that contains the abrasive material. As the trigger is pulled, the compressed air sucks the sand up the tube to produce the abrasive spray. A booth usually is good

Paasche air-eraser.

228

Angelo di Petta, Canada, "Untitled," press molded and slipcast, fired cone 04, sandblasted, 10-¼" x 8-½" x 3-¼", 2003.

Photo courtesy of the artist

Harvey Sadow, USA, "Untitled," multiple raku firings, sandblasted, airbrushed, 9" x 13" x 13".

for working on smaller objects up to 15". If the pieces to be sandblasted are too large to be manipulated in an enclosed booth, the blasting can be done in the open air, or the pieces often can be taken to a monument works that makes gravestone markers. Check with local monument companies as to cost and any specific requirements. Industrial sandblasting is used to cut letters into granite or other extremely hard and dense surfaces. The process is usually very fast; masking out the piece to protect what you don't want to blast is what takes the time.

Sandblasting usually is done on either bisque-fired or glazed surfaces to remove surface coatings. Doing it on unfired greenware may cause the piece to crack, because the pressure of the sanding gun may eat through the fragile clay very quickly.

An air-eraser basically is a miniature spray gun or airbrush with a hopper for erasing compound mounted above the hardened steel or tungsten spray tip. It is held like a pen and pointed at the surface approximately 3" or 4" away. The air-eraser is a tool for doing fine, well-controlled work. A pressure release button controls the force of spray. The erasing compounds usually are made from fine zircon or alumina sand that is sprayed under pressure at the surface of the object. A ¼ horsepower compressor is fine for small work suitable for the air-eraser.

Sandblasting and air-erasing can create very interesting surfaces that look as though they could have been etched with acid. Used very lightly, the sandblasted surface can look as though a fine mist covers the blasted areas, while heavy blasting can eat completely through a considerable thickness of clay or bisque.

Paul Dresang's porcelain vessel on page 232 is unglazed and comes out orange in color from the residual salt firing. He carefully masks areas that complement the line work in the piece and uses a sandblaster to obtain the gradations into the white of the porcelain body. The treatment gives his pieces a soft and sensuous quality.

Acid Etching

Acid etching is a process used in the ceramic

Photo courtesy of the artist

Jim Connell, USA, "Red Sandblasted – Carved Lidded Jar," stoneware, 15" x 15" x 15".

industry to cut patterns into high-value dinnerware, giving a delicate, embossed design that often is covered with liquid bright gold for its final treatment. Over the glazed areas, the gold will be glossy; over the etched areas, it will be matte.

In industrial use, the resist-decorated pieces are dipped into vats of either hydrochloric acid (muriatic acid) or hydrofluoric acid. In a studio situation, the process can be achieved by first coating the surface of the object in wax, scratching/drawing designs through the wax to the glaze, and either dipping the piece in a bath of hydrofluoric acid or putting it into a lead-lined cupboard amid fumes of hydrofluoric acid. The degree of etching can be tested with a toothpick or small wooden point.

When the etching is the desired depth, the hydrofluoric acid is washed off, and the wax is removed with turpentine oil.

Safety precautions of rubber gloves, safety glasses and a mask suitable for toxic fumes should be worn at all times while working with acids.

Drill Engraving

Drill engraving is done with flexible, shaft-small drills, such as those manufactured by Dremel Inc. and Foredom Inc.

A wide variety of abrasive tips can be fitted into the chuck. For working on bisque-fired clay, silicon carbide tips and cutting wheels work well, but for the harder surface of glazed ware, tungsten-tipped drill bits or grinding tips are needed.

The tool is held like a fat pen, and the drawing is done directly into the surface. The lines can be covered with resinate lusters to create drawings in gold

Judi Dyelle, Canada, "Black Lidded Box," porcelain, sandblasted tape resist design.

and silver (palladium or platinum). Any excess luster should carefully be removed before firing. Drill-engraved drawings into previously glazed and fired surfaces can have color rubbed into the drawing and be refired at the regular glaze temperature and atmosphere to seal the engraving in the glaze.

For artists who enjoy doing line drawing or gesture drawing, this decorative process offers great possibilities. Subtle shading can develop in the depth variations when glazes are applied over the engraving, much as they do over fine fluting or incising with a needle tool.

Always use a dust mask and safety glasses when working with any grinding tools. It often is useful to have an electric fan to blow dust away from the work in progress.

Paul Dresang, USA, "Untitled," porcelain, thrown, wood fired, masked and sandblasted.

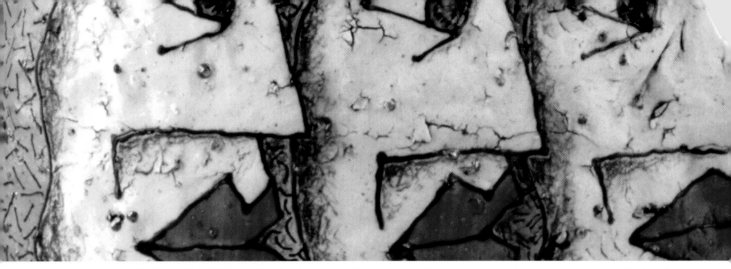

Rimas VisGirda, USA, "Flicka, Ricka & Dicka," detail, sculpture, coil built, porcelain with granite bits — Fabriky Porcelany Walbrzych, slip trail, underglaze pencil, overglaze, lusters, 14″ x 8″ x 6″, 2003. Photo by the artist.

CHAPTER 20

Marks of Multiple Firing

The ceramic surface can be altered at any time, even after you might think it's completed and even after hundreds or thousands of years, through the many post-glaze firing options or cold finishing processes available to the artist. The problem sometimes is in knowing where to stop. There is always another option or method to expand the range of possibilities. Some of these processes are better suited to painterly, sculptural or contemplative work than for objects of a functional nature. Whatever gives the result the artist visualizes is fair game for exploration. Post-glaze firing (usually third and subsequent firings) allows a great variety of further surface development by the use of on-glaze processes such as china painting, overglaze enamels, lusters, decals,

Photo courtesy of the artist

Kirsten Abrahamson, Canada, "Observation of a Year," paper clay, underglaze, glaze, gold leaf, metal, 48cm x 51cm x 15cm, 2002.

233

and photographic applications. Usable processes more identified with the ceramic industry than the studio artist are also discussed here.

Although I am familiar with and have worked with all of these processes sporadically, I have asked Rimas VisGirda, a ceramic artist who works extensively with post-glaze firing processes, to write the remainder of this chapter.

VisGirda's familiarity with the processes far exceeds my own, and his work follows this introduction. At the end of the chapter, there is an informative piece on working with gold leaf by Steve Irvine of Canada, as well as some more specific safety warnings and recipes for Islamic luster pigments and resinate bases.

Safety Warning

All work with enamels and lusters, including firing, should be done in a well-ventilated area. Working with overglaze enamels and lusters may cause health hazards. Solvents, such as mineral spirits, lacquer thinner, toulene, turpentine, etc., can be encountered. Oil-based inks (china paints/overglazes) and lusters contain solvents and exotic oils such as pine oil, oil of lavender and oil of cloves, among others. People with delicate skin or respiratory problems should take proper precautions that could include protective gloves, aprons, and respirators. If used, respirators should be capable of filtering vapors. Children should not work with any of these materials. Adults should be aware of their personal limits and sensitivities and take appropriate precautions.

Photo: Robert Nelson

Barbara Schwartz, USA, "The Journey," porcelain, multifired, painted lusters, 12", 1999.

Barbara Schwartz, USA, "Vessel," wheel thrown and altered, applied coils of porcelain clay, cone 10 reduction, Shino glaze, multifired, metallic luster, cone 018, 12" x 5" x 2", 2003.

Photo: Linda Cordell

Christyl Boger, USA, "Chymical Object," ceramic, terra sigillata, low-fire glazes, commercial decals and gold luster, 17" x 14" x 14", 2001.

Historically, one of the greatest influences to Western ceramic art has been Chinese porcelain, which was produced as early as the 9th century A.D. Its importance to modern ceramics was formed in the 14th century with the massive importation of Chinese decorated ware and the West's efforts to copy and reproduce both the material (porcelain) and the decoration. The decoration particularly was desirable because it was unfamiliar and foreign to the Renaissance trained eye. The discovery of very low-melting fluxes and a wider range of refractory colorants and stains, coupled with a formula for European porcelain, led to an entire field of decoration in the West — techniques that require one or more additional firings specifically for the decoration after the initial glaze firing.

Enamels

Enamels are known by a number of different names, depending on which book or catalog you pick up: on-glaze enamel, on-glaze color, on-glaze, O/G, overglaze enamel, overglaze color, overglaze, O/E and china paint.

Enamel is defined as a soft, low-melting glass used for decorating ceramic, metal or glass objects. Specifically in ceramics, enamels are ceramic colors applied over a fired glaze and fused in a second firing. In the most general sense, enamel is composed of silica (flint) for the body or glass segment; boric and lead oxides for a flux or fluxes; and metallic oxides for color. The firing temperature of enamel depends on the glaze it will be fused onto and requires a firing approximately 300°C lower than the maturing temperature of the underlying glaze. All enamels, independent of their application, have a firing range of 700°C to 900°C (Orton cone 019-010). The terms "porcelain enamel" and "vitreous enamel" imply a ceramic association, but they are misnomers, because they are enamels on sheet or cast iron, such as enameled metal pots, old street signs, cast iron bathtubs and the like.

The earliest examples of enamel decoration are found on metal — a gold ring from a 13th century B.C. Mycenean tomb in Cypress, cloisonné from 5th century B.C. Greece, and champlevé from 1st century B.C. Britain. The names champlevé and cloisonné refer to particular techniques of separating and fusing enamel onto metal, typically gold, fine silver and copper.

Enamel on ceramics made its first appearance in 13th century China as red or green decoration on porcelain, usually to accent underglaze blue designs. The 15th century Ming Dynasty produced a wider range of colors and introduced polychrome (multicolor) decoration. The Cheng Hua period (1465-1487) is known for the tou-ts'ai style of polychrome designs with underglaze blue outlines. A bolder technique, also attributed to the Ming Dynasty, is medium-temperature enamels applied and fired onto high-fired but unglazed pieces with "cloisons," depressed areas on the surface, to separate the colors.

The debut of enamel decoration in Europe also can be partly attributed to Arabian lusterware. In 15th century Italy, a new decorative technique, majolica, was developed in an attempt to copy Hispano-Moresque lusterware. Majolica is a polychrome decoration applied to tin-glazed, unfired terra cotta. The name majolica derives from the island of Majorca, through which the lusterware was imported from Spain. Majolica was exported throughout Europe from Faenza, the center for its production. The Northern Europeans, in an effort to copy majolica, developed enamel painting on fired, white, tin-glazed terra cotta. In reference to Faenza, the new technique in turn became known as faience in France and fayence in Germany.

The popularity of the bright, colorful ware led to extensive experimentation, and by 1660 in Germany a full palette of enamel colors existed for faience decoration.

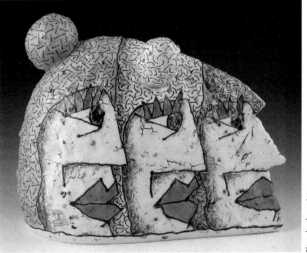

Photo by the artist

Rimas VisGirda, USA, "Flicka, Ricka & Dicka," sculpture, coil built, porcelain with granite bits —Fabriky Porcelany Walbrzych, slip trail, underglaze pencil, overglazes, lusters, 14″ x 8″ x 6″, 2003.

The development of the extensive enamel color palette in Europe quickly found its way to the Orient, leading to the further development of polychrome decoration on Chinese and Japanese porcelain.

The 17th century saw a decline in trade with China and an increase in Japanese trade, especially for enamel-decorated wares. The growth of Japanese trade during the Edo period, to the end of the 17th century, resulted in ware being developed primarily for export. Imari export ware is characterized by a lavish and attractive decoration with an emphasis on red and gilding with a purplish underglaze, although black, blue, green, purple and yellow examples have also been found. The designs are derivative of textile patterns, copies of Chinese decorations and scenes from daily life. The export ware is characterized by its asymmetrical designs, which were unusual to Europeans and gained great popularity. The Imari period export porcelains also are known as Nishikide ware. A domestic ware for local use, Kutani, is known for its rich enamel decoration. Nabeshima ware, not well known in the West, was reserved primarily for Japanese royalty. The popularity of imported motifs, coupled with an expanded enamel color palette, resulted in heavy production of polychrome Oriental motifs on tin-glazed earthenware, faience, throughout Northern Europe, particularly by the Dutch. Faience retained its popularity throughout most of the 18th century.

"Potiche Jar", Ming Dynasty, China, late 16th/early 17th century, porcelain, wucai, 16.5cm high. Gift of Syd Hoare. Courtesy of the Art Gallery of Greater Victoria, Canada.

"Hispano Moresque Bowl," luster bowl, bird motif, Spain, 17th century A.D., earthenware with painted and reduced luster over a cream glaze. Gift of J.J. Maro. Courtesy of the Art Gallery of Greater Victoria, Victoria, B.C., Canada.

"Delftware Dish – Blue Dash Charger," Holland, 1700 to 1725, painted in blue, green, yellow, orange, and manganese on white ground, Adam and Eve and the Serpent, flanked by sponged trees, blue dashes on narrow border. From the collection of J.E. Horvath with Financial Assistance from B.C. Lotteries and Mrs. Margaret B. McElney. Courtesy of the Art Gallery of Greater Victoria, Victoria, B.C., Canada.

The search for a porcelain formula in Europe resulted in the discovery of soft paste (clay and powdered glass frit) porcelain late in the 16th century. Factories in Rouen, St. Cloud and Sevres, among others, produced soft paste through the 17th and into the 18th century. The search for true porcelain finally reached success in Germany, and Meissen produced its first polychrome hard paste porcelain in 1710 to 1715, with designs copied from the Japanese. Limoges and Sevres switched to hard paste during the 1770s and also copied Japanese Edo/Imari motifs. The discovery, desirability and dominance of hard paste (true) porcelain contributed to the decline of faience production throughout Europe during the late 18th and into the 19th centuries.

Oriental motifs remained popular, as well as designs based on the current European art styles. Some of the original Orient-inspired designs, primarily in blue underglaze, still are being produced today in a few

Photo: Janet Dwyer

Imari square lidded bottle, Japan, Edo period, late 17th/early 18th century, Imari ware, porcelain with underglaze blue and overglaze enamels, 21cm high. Gift in memory of Johannes G. Nordal. Courtesy of the Art Gallery of Greater Victoria, Victoria, B.C., Canada.

Photo: Janet Dwyer

"Kutani Plate," large plate, stoneware with overglaze enamels, Japan, Edo period, early 19th century. Gift of James and Joanna Davidson. Courtesy of the Art Gallery of Greater Victoria, Victoria, B.C., Canada.

Photo: Janet Dwyer

"Nabeshima Plate," porcelain with overglaze enamels, Nabeshima ware, Japan, circa 1803, dish has vegetable pattern that is identical to famous 18th century Nabeshima design. Fred and Isabel Pollard Collection. Courtesy of the Art Gallery of Greater Victoria, Victoria, B.C., Canada.

Photo: Brian Oglesbee

Cindy Sherman, USA, "Madame de Pompadour (nee Poisson)," 21 piece tea/breakfast service, porcelain, glazed, teapot 20.3cm x 19cm x 12cm, 1990. Museum purchase, Corsaw Collection, Schein-Joseph International Museum of Ceramic Art, Alfred University, 2000.

old, established factories, such as Meissen and Royal Copenhagen.

Decorated pottery became accessible to the masses with the advent of underglaze transfer printing techniques developed in the mid-18th century. Invention of true decal transfers in the mid-19th century further competed with hand-decorated ware. The Industrial Revolution, along with mass production methods, such as molds and jiggering, furthered the accessibility of decorated ware for the masses and added to the decline of hand decoration.

In 1871, England's first "studio" was founded for amateurs to paint on porcelain. This became an approved pastime for Victorian ladies in England as well as the United States and came to be known as china painting. It remained a popular activity through the turn of the century, and remnants of the hobby can be found today in the accessibility of plain porcelain ware suitable for enamel decorating through companies such as

"Pair of Covered Ewers," hard paste porcelain, overglaze enamels, Meissen, circa 1730 A.D., Germany. Courtesy of the Gardiner Museum of Ceramic Art, Toronto.

Photo: Pierre Gauvin

Léopold L. Foulem, Canada, "Imari-Style Teapot in Mounts," slab, low-fire, decals, gold luster and found objects, 25.3cm x 26cm x 17.2cm.

Rynne. China paints in powder form, along with various oils, are available to the public through major ceramic suppliers. Supplies also can be located in ceramic "pour and paint" hobby shops or vendors that cater to hobby oriented, part-time or amateur enthusiasts.

The West Coast of the United States has had the most influence in nontraditional studio values. The laid-back lifestyle and proximity to Asian, primarily Japanese, influences allowed the ceramic artists of the 1950s and '60s to diverge from the more formal established ceramic values that governed pottery. The push in the direction of sculpture and experimentation with hobby shop-oriented materials and techniques led to the introduction of enamels, decals, lusters, low-fire glazes and molds into the contemporary ceramic artist's studio.

Several primary innovators from the Pacific North Coast were Robert Arneson, Robert Hudson, Richard Shaw and Howard Kottler. Their work stands as a milestone to the state of decorated ceramics in the individual studio.

Enamel Process

Enamels can be brushed, sprayed, sponged, printed, dusted and applied directly to a glazed surface in almost any conceivable manner. Enamel designs also can be printed on special papers for direct transfer or water-slide decals, addressed later in this chapter. Industrially, enamels are prepared by fritting — firing powdered raw materials in a crucible until they become liquid. They then are released into a container of cold water, causing the hot liquid glass to fracture. This is then ground to a very fine consistency. An extensive range of reasonably priced colors is commercially available.

It is possible for potters to make their own enamels, but the resulting material might require a slower and longer firing due to the coarseness of the particles; it would be difficult to match the quality of the industrial product without a frit furnace and a grinding capability. The vast palette and uniformity of commercially available enamels also adds to the convenience of purchasing rather than trying to make your own.

Traditionally, powdered enamels are mixed with an oil medium. The type of oil depends on the desired drying time, brushing consistency and the artist's preference. Linseed oil, fat oil of turpentine, lavender oil and mineral oil all can be used, but mineral oil should be used only when the drying time needs to be extended indefinitely. Commercially available oil is graded as light, medium and heavy. A heavier oil is available as "squeegee" oil for silkscreen printing. Enamel powder and oil are mixed using a palette knife or flat-faced pestle on ground glass until smooth and creamy. Enamel or oil can be added as the grinding progresses to reach the desired consistency. Few artists mix their own, as oil- and water-based enamels are available in mixed, moist, ready-to-use form.

Enamels usually are applied on glazed porcelain or glazed whiteware. The white ground brings out the brilliance of the enamel, much like watercolor on white paper. The glaze provides a smooth, slick surface that enhances the brilliance and richness of the fired product. Transparent enamels are referred to as china paints, and the more opaque enamels are referred to as overglaze enamels. The prototypical painting technique starts by spreading light tonalities and developing the image by adding darker colors and accents. Highlights are achieved by "wiping out" some of the color. The work typically is fired many times, with color added after each firing until the final image is achieved. Colors normally are allowed to dry before firing, as a quick rise in temperature could volatilize the wet oil and cause it to disrupt the enamel. Enamels often are formulated with different bases to accommodate the melting temperature of the metallic

Photo: Susan H. Smith

Linda Stanier, Canada, "La Entrada," multifired ceramic, stains, underglazes and low-temperature texture glazes, 23" x 16" x 4".

Courtesy Garth Clark Gallery.

Kurt Weiser, USA, "Masquerade," covered jar(s), porcelain, china painting, 13" x 14", 1999.

oxide or stain; it is not recommended to combine enamels because the combination can have unpredictable results. Test mixtures before committing to a piece of work.

Applying one transparent color over another can achieve rich and varied tonalities and beautiful complexities of color, but the work should be fired between colors. The china painted vessels by Kurt Weiser are contemporary examples of traditional china painting. At the other end of the spectrum, Kirk Mangus uses a guttural impasto style that embodies a cross between Impressionism and Abstract Expressionism. In his "Dirty Plate" series, Robert Arneson used a painterly technique perhaps influenced by his colleague, painter Wayne Thiebaud.

Opaque enamels can be sprayed through spray guns or airbrushes, or they can be applied by brush or through stencils. For spray applications, the enamel should be mixed with lighter, more fluid mediums. The exact consistency depends on the requirements of the spray gun or airbrush and the preference of the artist. The mixture should be strained through a fine sieve to prevent clogging. Stenciling and brushing require heavier mediums, but again the working consistency ultimately depends on the artist's preference. In the 1930s, Hall China sprayed a line of teapots and kitchenware with cadmium-based overglaze enamels to achieve certain desired orange and red colors, which were elusive in high fire. European factories also used the process to produce solid-color coffee services. Ron Nagle, a West Coast ceramic sculptor, uses multiple layers of airbrushed enamels to achieve the rich surfaces on his sculptural cups. Jolanta Kvasyte, a Lithuanian ceramic artist, brushes opaque enamels to color and embellish her sensual, humorous, porcelain figurines.

Enamel decoration gained and retained popularity due to the wide range of available colors. Rich complexities and tonalities of color also are easy to accomplish, adding to their appeal. The enamel firing is between 700°C and 900°C.; enamels are fired at approximately 300°C lower than the base glaze, which allows the glaze to "soften" without flowing and makes the surface receptive for the fluxed enamel. The glaze

Photo: Rimas VisGirda

Kirk Mangus, USA, "Untitled," vase, stoneware, coil built, overglaze enamels (impasto), 5-½" x 8-½" x 5", 1985.

Photo: Rimas VisGirda

Hall China Co., "Donut Jug," orange-red pitcher, "Airflow," orange-red teapot, porcelain, cast, overglaze enamels, pitcher 8" x 9" x 4", teapot 7" x 10" x 5-½", late 1930-1940. Private collection.

firing for earthenware typically is 1,000°C to 1,150°C; for porcelain or stoneware it is 1,250°C to 1,350°C. The exact second firing temperature depends on the hardness of the base glaze.

Enamels, lusters, and decals purchased at hobby shops generally state the firing range as Orton cone 019-018 (approximately 680° to 720°C). The manufacturer assumes the hobby enthusiast is using Orton cone 06-05 (1,000° to 1,050°C) glazes.

Consequently, ceramists working on stoneware or porcelain need to adjust the firing temperature higher according to the fluxing temperature of their underlying glaze. It always is best to run tests, because some of the enamels become elusive at the higher temperature ranges required for stoneware and porcelain glazed pieces.

Enamels also can be mixed with water vs. oil, which makes cleanup much easier. Sugar water can be used to make the enamel more manageable; the sugar or syrup

Photo: Judi Dyelle

Ron Nagle, USA, "Untitled," white earthenware cup, colored overglazes, 1989. Gift of Aaron Milrad in memory of Bella and Joseph Milrad. Courtesy of the Gardiner Museum of Ceramic Art, Toronto.

Photo: Rimas VisGirda

Jolanta Kvasyte, Lithuania, "Untitled," figurine, stoneware, porcelain, hand-built, overglaze enamels, 5" x 5" x 4", 2003.

acts as a binder to hold the enamel much like the oil in the traditional techniques. A saturated sugar solution will add to the durability of the decoration as the sugar recrystalizes and becomes hard when dry. The addition of various gums or antifreeze can add to the smoothness and brushability of the mixture. The American Art Clay Company offers a range of eight water-based and oil-based moist enamels under the trade name Versa Color.

A disadvantage of enamel decoration is the need for extra firings, which require energy. Noxious odors associated with exotic oils and petrochemical solvents, both in working and firing, can be a health hazard. Poor resistance to abrasion and wear due to softness and a low melting point detract from the durability of enameled ware. Lead and cadmium exposure also can be a health hazard, although fritted lead and encapsulated cadmium, along with proper firing procedures and temperature controls, minimizes the dangers.

The disadvantages, however, could all be outweighed by the enormous palette, brilliance and beauty compared to high-fire or in-glaze decorating techniques.

Ceramic Decals

John Sadler of Liverpool, England, is credited with inventing ceramic transfer printing in 1755. He saw children placing printed material onto ceramic shards and rubbing the back of the print. As the ink technology was relatively crude, inks of the era were not especially fast drying, and the rubbing transferred the image to the broken crockery. Sadler's "invention" was to ink etched or engraved copper plates with overglaze enamels. These could then be printed onto tissue paper and transferred by rubbing to a ceramic surface and fired.

Robert Hancock, also English, extended Sadler's invention to blue underglaze in the 1760s. This formed the basis of transfer printing for the following 100 years. The 18th century was a tremendous time of experimentation and discovery that extended well into the 19th century. The Industrial Revolution took hold in England and led to the development of mass production techniques in manufacturing as well as decorating the ware. Many novel variations of the basic transfer technique were developed, including assembly line systems where the image from an inked plate was picked up by a flexible balloon and then pressed onto a plate, lid or some other uneven surface. The transfer

Rimas VisGirda, USA, "Untitled," tumblers, white stoneware, thrown, in-glaze, 3" x 3" x 3" (left) and on-glaze decals, 3" x 2-½" x 2-½", 2002 (right).

technology mostly was used with underglazes, resulting in monochromatic scenes. Black, red or brown, as well as other less-common colors, can be found, but blue gained and retained the most popularity. Polychrome decorations occasionally were produced, but these were usually underglaze transfer prints with enamel washes over the glazed fired image.

Ceramic decals as we know them today appeared around 1850. A ceramic decal is an image printed with oil-based ceramic inks onto paper coated with a water-soluble film such as glue, cellophane or starch. The "ceramic inks" can be overglaze enamels for on-glaze decoration, ceramic stains for in-glaze decoration or underglazes. After printing the colors, a cover coat of clear-burning shellac or lacquer is applied over the image to hold the ink in place.

Two common methods of application have evolved over the years: water slide and direct transfer. Both methods involve exposing the print to water, hence the necessity for oil-based ceramic inks and non-water-soluble lacquers for cover coats.

Water slide is the method most commonly used today, both in factories and private studios. Open stock decals, available in hobby shops and through mail-order catalogs,

are the water-slide type. They are printed right side up and must be transferred to a glazed or slick nonporous surface. Layering decals can lead to interesting designs but requires a firing between each decal application.

Direct-transfer decals are printed on tissue or another type of thin, flexible paper. A varnish or other tacky non-water-soluble material is applied to the ware. The decal is placed face down on the varnished area and rubbed until the entire image is attached to the surface. The paper is soaked off the back, and the image remains attached to the ware. Direct-transfer decals must be printed backwards, as the image is reversed when it is applied. Underglaze decals, by necessity, are of the direct-transfer type; the bisque ware is porous and will not hold a water-slide decal. The underglaze-decal decorated bisque ware must be refired to burn off the varnish or cover coat before the pieces can be glazed.

For on-glaze, overglaze enamel decals, the ware is fired to approximately 300°C below the maturing temperature of the underlying glaze. The resulting decoration will attach itself and lay on top of the glaze, hence the term "on-glaze" decoration. For in-glaze ceramic stain decals, the ware should be fired to the maturing fluxing point of the underlying glaze. Typically, in-glaze decals are

Rimas VisGirda's 6′ x 8′ decal screening work space.

found in cobalt blue, but any color can be used as long as it can endure the fluxing temperature of the base glaze. As the glaze liquefies, the stain will be absorbed into the body of the glaze and reside in the glaze itself, hence the term "in-glaze" decoration.

The decal ware must be fired in a clean atmosphere. In a top-loading electric kiln, the lid should be left ajar, and some lower kiln vents should be left open to draw in fresh air until the varnish and/or cover coat is burned off and the smoking has subsided. In a fuel kiln, an oxidizing atmosphere is sufficient, because fresh air is introduced as a function of the firing. A venting system for electric kilns is convenient to keep a flow of fresh air going through the kiln, eliminating the need for lid or vent adjustments during the firing. A clean atmosphere during the initial stages of the firing is necessary, because a reducing atmosphere will cause soot and organic combustion residue from the cover coat to remain in place. The residue can affect the glaze by causing a ghost or stain to appear around the design.

Decals can be printed by silkscreen or lithography. The difference from normal (paper and ink) printing is the use of the special decal papers, ceramic materials as inks and a cover coat over the finished print. Silkscreen printing generally is more convenient for individuals and suppliers who deal with small runs. The screening process requires a minimum of equipment and technical involvement.

Lithography, as used industrially, requires specialized equipment, such as complex, large presses beyond the means of the individual ceramic studio. Few art school print departments even have industrial presses, and they limit the student's lithographic experience to using stones and hand-operated presses.

Silkscreen printing, on the other hand, requires minimal and easily accessible tools and materials. A screen is a wooden frame that has a fabric stretched over the open portion, much like a canvas stretched for a painting. The fabric mesh size controls the amount of ink allowed to pass through the fabric. Areas of the fabric that are blocked stop the ink from passing through, and areas that are left open allow the passage of ink. The typical ways of placing an image on the screen are by direct block out, direct emulsions and films.

Direct block out, as the name implies, is a liquid material applied directly onto the fabric, normally with a

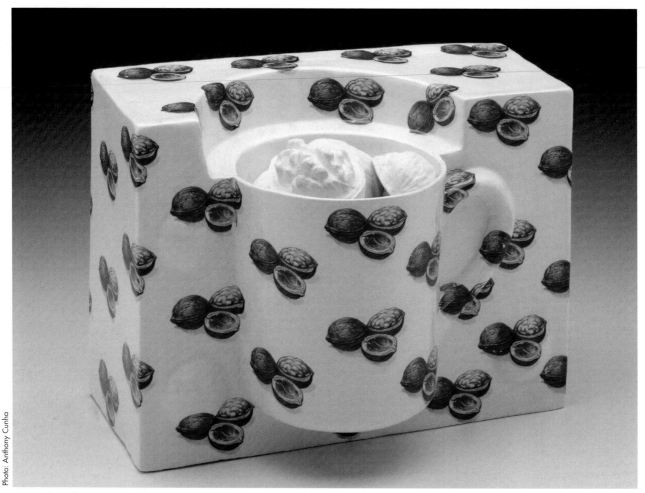

Photo: Anthony Cunha

Howard Kottler, USA, "Walnut Cup," whiteware, 4-¾" x 6-¾". Courtesy of the Howard Kottler Estate. Image provided by Garth Clark Gallery, New York.

brush, over the areas to be blocked. The unblocked, open areas become the image to be printed. Petroleum-based block out is used for water-based inks, and, conversely, water-based block out is used for oil-based inks. Hand-cut paper stencils can also be easily attached to the fabric. The stencil can be placed under the fabric, and the first ink pull will attach it to the screen.

Direct emulsions are applied to the screen fabric in liquid form and allowed to dry. The image is created by placing an opaque master image, usually on acetate, on the emulsified screen, then exposing it to light. The emulsion exposed to the light becomes partially insoluble, and the protected image portion of the emulsion remains soft and soluble, so it can be washed out with a spray of water. Once the screen is dry, it can be used with either water-based or oil-based inks. A special remover is necessary to remove the emulsion and reclaim the screen.

Films are a coating on an acetate backing. They are available as photo-sensitive and nonphoto-sensitive types. Nonphoto-sensitive films are cut with a sharp blade, and the image areas are removed while on the acetate. The coating is attached to the fabric with a solvent, and the acetate is peeled off, leaving the image ready to be printed. Photo-sensitive films are exposed off the fabric, then attached to the fabric. The acetate is peeled off, and the image is washed out as with direct emulsions.

For printing, the screen is placed on a piece of decal paper, and a squeegee is used to drag ink across the screen, pushing the ink through the open areas and onto the paper. The screen is lifted, the printed paper is removed, and a new decal paper is put in its place. When the prints are dry, the cover coat can be applied by screening, spraying, rolling or brushing over the printed image. Screening is the conventional method of applying

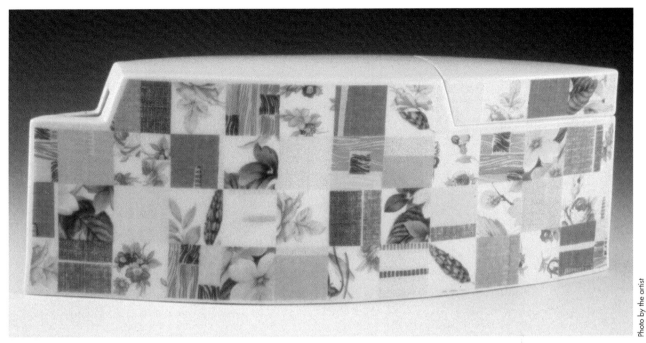

Billie Jean Theide, USA, "Butte Czech – 3," porcelain, cast, Czech porcelain factory decals, 5" x 10" x 2-¾", 1997.

the cover coat. It provides even coverage and can be economical if the screen is designed with a window to cover just the print itself, thereby minimizing waste.

It is possible to print directly onto a ceramic surface if the surface is flat. Printing on a curved surface in only one direction also is possible with practice and precise coordination. Some beverage cans and bottles are printed in this manner by computerized robotic machines.

Lithography normally is used for printing mass-produced, open stock, on-glaze decals. The technology offers the advantage of speed, finer detail and more exacting registration. The fine detail and precise registration permits easy production of photographically separated four-color prints. The smaller dot pattern, compared with silkscreen printing, allows for more exact copies of multicolor originals, such as paintings and other colored artwork. Lithography results in a very thin ink film, which for most purposes is adequate. The resulting decal usually is fired onto a white ground that doesn't require much color to develop richness and depth. Additionally, the translucency of a thin coat of overglaze enamel, as it combines with a gloss underlying glaze, is what gives the resulting fired image its brilliance.

Silkscreening allows for a thicker ink layer, which may be necessary for some applications, such as decals for glass, decals for dark glazes, in-glaze decals or underglaze

Howard Kottler, USA, "Pastoral Wood," porcelain, 10-¼" diameter, 1968. Courtesy of the Howard Kottler Estate. Image provided by Garth Clark Gallery, New York.

decals. For glass applications, a thick layer of overglaze enamel is necessary for its opacity. Glass is transparent, and a thin layer will be translucent and appear washed out or faded. The same or even greater opacity is necessary if a light-colored image is applied to a dark glaze; a

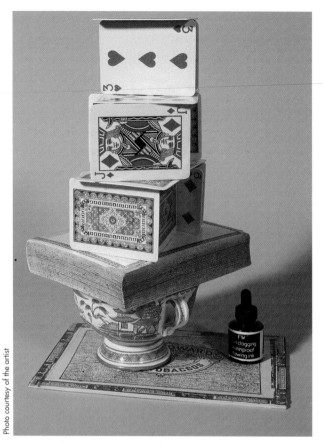

Photo courtesy of the artist

Richard Shaw, USA, "House of Fear," sculpture, porcelain, decals, overglazes, 2002.

Photo courtesy of the artist

Victor Spinski, USA, sculpture, stoneware with overglaze enamels and decals.

translucent coating would tend to disappear on a dark ground. In-glaze and underglaze decals also require more pigment to retain their intensity of color as they interact with the fluxed glaze. A decal with low color saturation would tend to dissolve into the liquefied glaze and fade in color or disappear entirely if very thin.

The mesh of the screen fabric, the thickness of the emulsion or film and the shape of the squeegee edge also are factors that control the thickness of the ink deposit. Larger, more open fabric mesh allows a thicker deposit. Direct emulsion can be made thicker by applying multiple coats, allowing each coat to dry before the next. A rounded squeegee will deposit a thicker ink coating than a standard square, sharp-edged model.

Thicker ink coatings also can be achieved by multiple printing onto the same paper, but this generally requires exacting registration. Thicker ink coatings most easily can be achieved by printing a varnish or other tacky material onto decal paper and dusting the print with dry overglaze enamel powder. The powder will stick to the tacky material, and the excess can be brushed off and reclaimed.

Artists easily can produce decals in the studio. All it takes is a little screen printing experience or a good basic text on the process. Stretched screens are readily available at art supply stores or graphic design supply houses, and they come in a variety of sizes. Larger supply houses easily can make up screens to custom specifications. Many different kinds of fabrics are available, including polyester, nylon and stainless steel. Fabrics also come in various colors for specialized uses. A starting point would be to use white polyester 300-mesh for printing and 100-mesh for the cover coat. Polyester comes in two types of fabric: monofilament and polyfilament. Monofilament should be used with direct emulsions and polyfilament with films. Overglaze enamel inks can be purchased moist, ready-to-use, from ceramic supply houses. Artists also can make their own inks by buying squeegee oil and mixing it with enamel powder for on-glaze decals, and with powder stain for in-glaze decals.

Few artists design decals and then use them as the sole decoration in their work. That idea generally is limited to larger factories that produce a distinct line of ware and design a decal to accompany the production. Smaller factories will sidestep the design process and adopt open stock decals for their forms.

Artists like Howard Kottler and Billie Theide use open-stock decals, but they alter them to illustrate their

Paul Scott, UK, "Cumbrian Blue(s): A Millennium Willow for Sellafield or Plutonium is Forever (Well 24 Millenia Anyway)," plate 7/10, readymade porcelain, in-glaze decal collage, gold luster, 1-½" x 12-½" x 12-½", 2000.

personal vision. Some artists appropriate imagery to be made into decals. Richard Shaw uses playing cards, cigar box labels, book bindings and the like to illustrate and clarify his porcelain assemblages. Victor Spinski appropriates cardboard box labels, as well as labels from products such as cola cans and beer bottles, for his trompe l'oeil sculptures. Paul Scott scans old Currier & Ives type etchings and manipulates the images in subtle ways as a social commentary. Scott's images are printed as in-glaze decals and fired onto commercially available porcelain.

Katherine Ross has developed a technology for sepia-tone in-glaze decals that she fires onto tiles for her commentary on personal hygiene. She has found that iron oxide is an ingredient in Apple and Hewlett Packard black and white laser printer inks. She scans an image and prints it directly onto decal paper. The laser print must be cover coated just like any water-slide decal. The decal is then applied to the ceramic surface and fired to approximately 300°C below the fluxing temperature of the underlying glaze, at which point the glaze should become tacky, but not liquid. The dye portion of the ink burns away, leaving a film of iron oxide on the glaze surface. If the firing is too low, the glaze does not get tacky enough, and the iron oxide will brush off the surface. If the firing is too high, the

iron oxide will sink into the glaze and tend to distort, as well as weaken in intensity. Some experimentation may be necessary to find the right firing temperature where the base glaze gets tacky enough to just capture the iron oxide, preserving the integrity of the printed image.

Another area of experimentation, primarily in England, is with decals printed with water-based materials, thereby avoiding contact with the fumes and toxins of petrochemical solvents, cleaners and oil-based inks commonly associated with printmaking. Mixing overglaze enamels with acrylic media, making the ink impervious to water when dry, is the easy part of the solution. The difficult part is finding a water-based cover coat that will burn off cleanly without leaving a shadow or ghost around the image.

Lusters

Lusters in ceramics are metallic surfaces or coatings on a glaze. Lusters should not be confused with luster glazes, which have a lustrous appearance after the glaze fire. Lusters can be classified into three categories: transmutation, reduction and resin. All three types require a second firing after the initial glaze firing.

Lusters made their first appearance as gold decoration on glass in 8th century pre-Islamic Egypt. The technology quickly spread to Mesopotamia and was adapted to earthenware pottery. Innovations during the 9th and 10th centuries produced colors ranging from ruby and brown to chartreuse and lemon, often appearing simultaneously on the same piece. By the end of the 10th century, Islamic religious forces standardized the decorations to monochromatic brown or yellow. Luster technology accompanied the Islamic expansion and found its way to Spain where it became known as Hispano-Moresque. Spanish lusterware was produced extensively in the 13th to 17th centuries. During the 16th century, the ware was a popular and desirable export to Italy, which led to the invention of majolica decoration and indirectly to overglaze enamels.

Transmutation lusters are known as Persian, Arabian or Hispano-Moresque, depending on their associated historic period or geographic location. The basic technology relies on the migratory nature of copper oxides and the ability of strong reduction to reduce the copper oxide to copper metal. A design is painted on a fired, typically alkaline glazed piece using a slip loaded with copper oxide or carbonate. The slip decorated

Rimas VisGirda, USA, "Viva Las Vegas," platter, vitreous china, cast, slip trail, decals, lusters, 1" x 12" x 12", 1997.

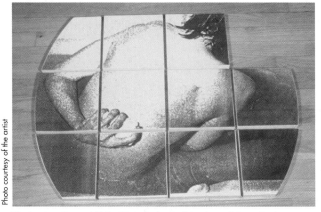

Katherine Ross, USA, "Prophylaxis/Hygiene," installation detail, porcelain, slab, digital in-glaze decal, 1999.

piece then is refired to approximately 700°C in a heavy reduction atmosphere. The copper oxide travels from the slip to the glaze; the heavy reduction strips away the oxygen and turns the transferred copper oxide into colloidal copper metal on the glaze surface. The firing must be high enough to soften the glaze and make it receptive to trapping the copper oxide as it leaves the slip. Care must be taken not to fire too high, or the slip will fuse to the molten glaze and ruin the surface.

Traditionally, the designs were arabesque due to Islamic influence and aesthetic. Hispano-Moresque lusterware, also known as Arabian, combined underglaze blue decoration with copper luster. The ware produced during the 14th century was particularly beautiful and technically well accomplished. The slip used was fluid and allowed for intricate designs. Ochre also was present in the clays, and the iron assisted with the reduction. Sometimes silver was added to the slip, resulting in a golden luster, even though gold was never used. In later years the clay portion of the slip was eliminated; the typical new formula consisted of three parts copper, usually carbonate; seven parts ochre; and an adhesive. Wine or vinegar was the adhesive in old formulas. Today, gum would be a more efficient and effective substitute.

A further form of transmutation luster was developed in France in the last quarter of the 19th century by Clement Massier. It was brought to North America by Jacques Sicard, one of Massier's assistants, on a short-term contract for the Weller Pottery in Ohio to satisfy the demand for Art Nouveau imagery. The process is to glaze an earthenware piece with an alkaline glaze colored with copper and fire to about cone 04 (1,040°C). The resulting turquoise glazed piece is then painted with a brushed wax resist pattern. This is followed with a thin, all-over coating of either liquid bright gold or a gummy silver nitrate solution. When dry, it is fired to cone 018 and put into heavy reduction for between 15 and 30 minutes. This causes the copper in the glaze to turn red and, in conjunction with the gold or silver, give a wide range of lustrous colors.

Reduction lusters are a simplified variant of the transmutation type. In their case a design is painted with copper oxide onto an unfired alkaline glaze. The piece is fired normally, and the result is a green design. When the piece is refired in a heavy reduction atmosphere, the top copper oxide layer is reduced to colloidal copper and cuprous (red copper) oxide, resulting in a reddish metallic copper luster on the glaze. For reduction lusters, it may be possible to eliminate the second firing by reducing the kiln at the appropriate temperature during the cooling cycle.

Resin lusters are an industrial product and are purchased in liquid form. The basic ingredients consist of a resin for local reduction, a light oil as a fluid vehicle and metallic salts for color. The solution is applied on a fired glaze surface. When dry, the piece is refired to approximately 600°C to 700°C. The firing temperature, as in overglaze enamels, depends on the hardness of the underlying glaze. The firing temperature for lusters

Photo: Rimas VisGirda

"Reproduction Tile," Hispano-Moresque style/technique, commissioned for presentation to International Academy of Ceramics conference attendees, terra cotta, blue underglaze, transmutation lusters, 8-½" x 8-½" x ½", circa 1984 Spain. Private collection.

tends to be approximately 30°C lower than that for overglaze enamels. During the initial stages of the firing, the oil burns off. At 500°C to 600°C, the carbon in the resin reduces the salt to its metallic form, and the firing continues until the glaze becomes tacky and receptive to holding the metal.

Bismuth nitrate is a strong flux; bismuth nitrate with zinc acetate, lead acetate and alumina produces clear iridescent lusters. Coupled with chrome alum, it produces yellows. Combinations of nickel nitrate, cobalt sulfate,

manganese sulfate, iron chloride and uranium nitrate, among others, can produce a large variety of hues. Glenn C. Nelson, in "Ceramics, A Potter's Handbook," recommends "Literature Abstracts of Ceramic Glazes" by J.H. Koenig and W. H. Earhart as a reference for more complete investigation.

Platinum and palladium are used to produce opaque, silver-colored lusters called liquid bright platinum and liquid bright palladium, which are actual platinum and palladium coatings, or platings, on the glaze surface. Gold

Photo: Judi Dyelle

"Deruta," lusterware charger, earthenware, Italy 1521.
Courtesy of the Gardiner Museum of Ceramic Art, Toronto.

is used to produce liquid bright gold, a gold plating on the glaze, which is available from 10 karat to 24 karat content. In combination with other ingredients, gold can be found as green gold, bronze gold and burnish gold. Burnish gold fires matte and can be burnished to a satin finish; green gold and bronze gold are colored as their names imply. Gold also is used to produce various reds, purples, pinks and black. Palladium, platinum, gold and the colors derived from them are the most expensive; the price depends on the actual metal content and the current market price for that metal.

A typical luster is composed of three to five parts resin, one part metallic salt and seven to 10 parts light oil. The resin, typically gum dammar, is heated until liquid, and the metallic salt is added and dissolved. The oil, usually oil of lavender, is added slowly, and the resulting solution is filtered, or cooled and decanted. Few ceramic artists have the chemistry background, the laboratory or the patience to make their own lusters. An exception to the rule is Greg Daly, an Australian ceramic artist who has spent many years making and using lusters. His luster mixture is essentially the same as above, with the exception of pine resin instead of gum dammar. He uses gold chloride, bismuth nitrate, zinc nitrate and cobalt nitrate singly and in various combinations to achieve his color palette.

Lusters can be sprayed, sponged, stamped, brushed and applied in as many ways as the imagination allows. Spraying can be wasteful, unless an efficient recovery system for overspray can be implemented. Sponging and stamping may need a thicker mixture than comes commercially. Lusters can be thickened by pouring some onto a glazed tile and allowing the solvents to evaporate until the desired viscosity is achieved. A rubber brayer or printmaker's roller can be used to roll an even coating onto a tile to be picked up by a sponge or stamp. Conversely, if a luster gets too thick, it can be thinned with a commercially available product known as "essence." Palladium, platinum and gold should be thinned only with special gold essence; colored lusters should be thinned with luster essence. The essence should be added one drop at a time because it is easy to overthin a luster. Luster essence and gold essence normally can be purchased from the same supplier as the lusters.

All colored lusters have a tendency to coagulate over time and by contamination. Once a luster has coagulated, it is not possible to reconstitute it or thin it to a usable condition. Extra care should be taken with contamination of the reds. They tend to be the most sensitive and the first to coagulate; they also are the most expensive of the colors. It may be wiser to purchase a number of smaller bottles, using one at a time, rather than a large bottle that can go bad all at once. Lusters also can be susceptible to changes in temperature and humidity and have been known to coagulate while in their original unopened jars. Lusters may be refrigerated if purchased in larger quantities, used infrequently or stored over long periods of time.

Brushing is the most common method of application. Good quality camel hair brushes work well, and the largest size suitable for a particular job should be used. Proper brush technique is important and comes with practice. The brush should be well saturated, but not dripping. The stroke should be smooth without dragging. Dragging is an indicator of too little luster on the brush. The lustered area should have a wet appearance without puddling, and the wet area should be continuous. Purplish areas after firing, particularly with liquid bright gold, are caused by too thin an application. Too thick an application usually results in dull or cloudy areas and sometimes blistering and flaking. It may be best to luster some practice pieces, because application problems only

Wilhelm Kage, USA, "Plate," porcelain, glazed, silver, 4.5cm x 29.2cm. Manufactured by Gustavsberg Factory.
Gift of William Pitney, Schein-Joseph International Museum of Ceramic Art, Alfred University, 2000.

Photo: Janet Dwyer

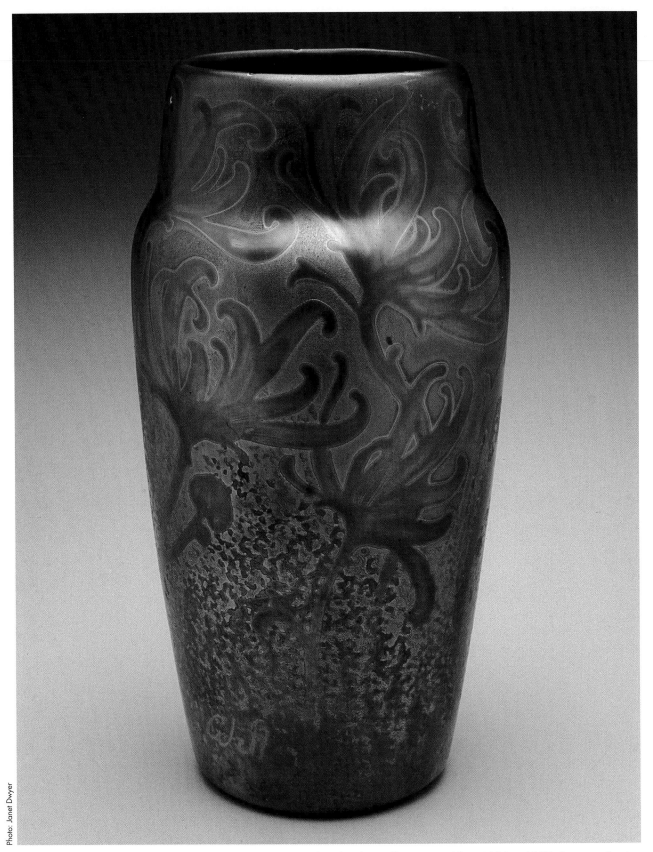

Jacques Sicard, France/USA, resist decorated lusterware produced at the Weller Pottery, Ohio, 1902 to 1907. Private collection.

"Meissen Teapot," Germany, 1730, hard paste porcelain, gold luster. Courtesy of the Gardiner Museum of Ceramic Art, Toronto.

are apparent after the firing.

The utmost care should be taken to ensure the cleanliness of the pieces as well as the work area. If lustered over, fingerprints, especially on gloss glazes, will appear in the finish after the firing. Pieces can be cleaned with denatured alcohol or any good degreasing agent. A lint-free cloth or paper towel should be used for the cleaning. Care should be taken to ensure that the cleaned piece is completely dry and all the alcohol and water have evaporated or been wiped dry. Moisture causes white spots in the fired luster. Coughing, sneezing, talking and cigarette smoke can impart moisture on the piece, thereby causing imperfections. Dust in or on the wet luster will fire out as darker blemishes. Avoid using brushes that have been used with water-based materials; water trapped in the ferrule can work its way out while brushing the luster. Brushes previously used with oil-based materials also should be avoided, because petrochemical solvents or oils left in the ferrule may not be compatible with the luster. Alcohol is not recommended for cleaning brushes, because water might be trapped in the ferrule and spoil the luster. Brushes should be cleaned with commercially available brush cleaner. If lustering is to be a significant part of your process, set aside a separate brush for use with each color.

Lusters must be fired in a well-ventilated kiln. The kiln should remain partially open until all of the smoke and odor have subsided. Overfiring or insufficient ventilation during firing may cause blistering, flaking or cloudy and dull lusters. Poor adhesion usually is the result of underfiring, but it also may be due to poor ventilation or contaminated ware.

Lusters take on the nature of the surface onto which they are fired. They will appear shiny on a gloss glaze and dull on a matte glaze. Lusters also can be applied over unglazed surfaces and will take on the nature of the surface. A colored luster will fire transparent and imbue only its color, allowing the nature and texture of the surface to retain its character. The liquid bright metals — gold, platinum, palladium and copper — and black fire opaque and tend to obscure the nature of the surface, allowing only the texture to show.

Lusters usually are found in combination with other decorative devices such as underglazes, overglaze

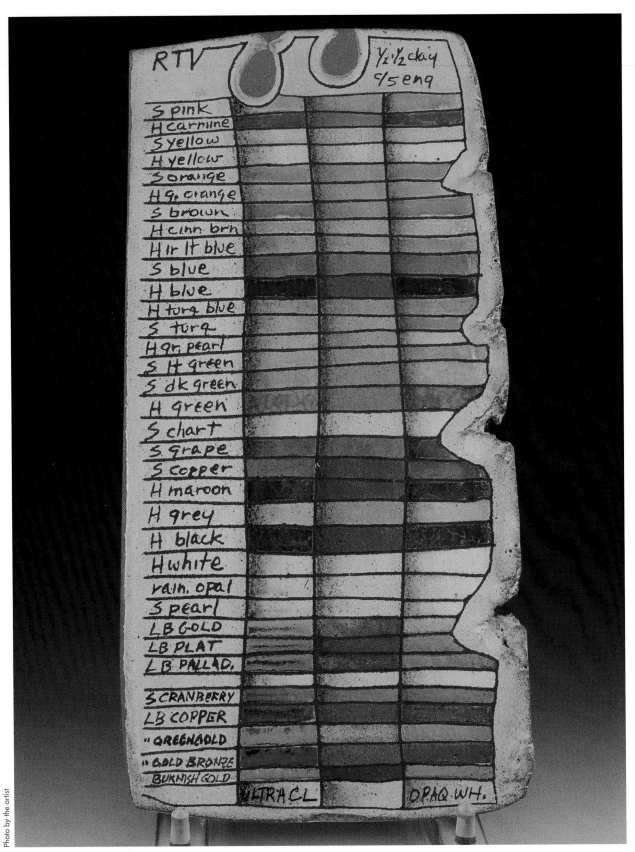

Rimas VisGirda, USA, "Luster Color — Test Tile," left column clear glaze, middle column vitreous (white) engobe – no glaze, right column white glaze, stoneware, slab, vitreous engobe/wax inlay, selected glaze, underglaze pencil, lusters, 12" x 5" x 1", 1970.

Greg Daly, Australia, "Luster Bowl," gold, silver leaf, and enamel.

enamels and decals. They rarely are used as an effect by themselves. A few exceptions are Hall China's Golden Glo kitchenware line, Philip Cornelius' all-gold lustered thin ware porcelain teapots, Christopher Dworin's swirling lusters and Tom Rippon's porcelain sculptures.

Cold Finishes

Although not fired, cold finishes are surface effects that are accomplished after the final firing. They include painting, gold and other leaf applications, decoupage and polishing. Sandblasting or grit-blasting, carborundum cutting and acid etching are addressed in Chapter 19.

The earliest examples of cold finishing date from the 1st century in Greece, where egg tempera was used for painting large vases and amphorae in colors not normally associated with ceramic objects of that time.

If you wish to have colors or surface textures outside the normal range of ceramic colorants, you can utilize various forms of paint or inks from acrylic to oils or glued-on metallic leaf applications. This also allows for more control of exactly where specific colors are placed. A few examples and artists who use them are included here.

Paint: Christine Federighi

After firing, Christine Federighi's pieces are sealed with a solid color painted "ground," usually black spray paint.

Oil paint is drybrushed over the surface and is used in a painterly way, layering one tone of color over another for a deeper and varied color quality. The oil paint is allowed to dry, usually two weeks, and then is sealed with a clear satin polyurethane.

The process is similar to painted bronzes of Remington's era. The oil paint has a depth and

Photo courtesy of the artist

Kinichi Shigeno, Canada, "Devil Gold ½" cast stoneware, high-fire and low-fire glazes, lusters (polychrome), 54cm x 29cm x 13cm, 1995.

complexity when layered that gives the pieces a sense of mystery, drawing the viewer into the work.

Golf Leaf: Bennett Bean

Bennett Bean's work occasionally contains some painted elements, but the most prominent effect is the gold leaf. Gold leaf is an ancient technique for gilding items.

An adhesive is applied to the areas to be gilded and allowed to get tacky. Extremely thin gold foil then is placed on the adhesive and burnished into place. The foil can be treated with any number of tools for effects ranging from high gloss to satin to wire brushed and distressed. The leaf is actual gold, so the gilded area exhibits that special quality that only gold itself can convey.

Decoupage: Doug Jeck

Doug Jeck's work tends to play at the borders of macabre. He makes a head out of ceramic, takes photographs of a person's head from innumerable angles, and applies the photos at their appropriate places onto the ceramic head. He probably has to make color copies of the photographs for the image to be flexible enough to go around certain curves that would be difficult for actual photos because of their stiffness.

The crafting of the decoupage is relatively crude, adding to the bizarre quality of the piece. The head might be described as a rough three-dimensional David Hockney-like photo collage.

Polishing: Michael Moore

Michael Moore's work is fired to 1,060°C. Once cold, the forms are sanded by hand using coarse to medium sandpaper, followed by fine grades of aluminum oxide sandpaper. The piece is freed of dust, and a sealant

Photo courtesy of the artist

Greg Daly, Australia, "Vase," pigment reduced luster, 14" high.

normally used to coat unglazed terra cotta floor tiles is applied to the polished surface in two coats. The sealant is called golvpolish, and it is produced in the Netherlands.

Chapter 20 guest author Rimas VisGirda is a senior ceramic artist and educator working in Illinois. His work specializes in the dynamic use of post firing processes of surface enrichment, the subject of a book on which he currently is working. His work is in major collections around the world.

Photo by the artist

Rimas VisGirda, USA, "Woman with Red Scarf," sculpture, stoneware, coil built, vitreous engobes/wax inlay, selected glaze, underglaze pencil, overglazes, lusters, 24" x 18" x 6", 1990s.

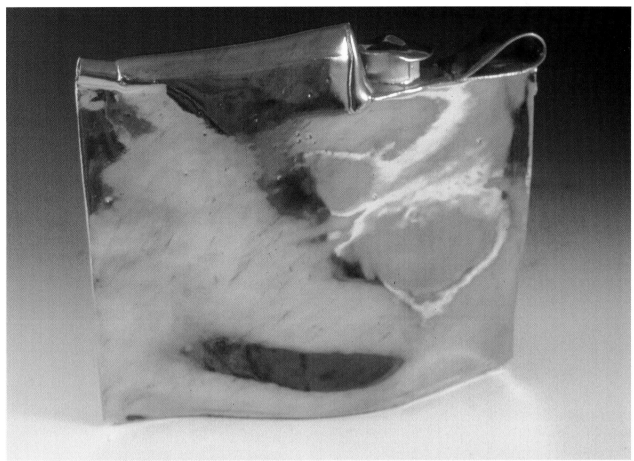

Philip Cornelius, USA, "Gold Stone," porcelain, slab built (thin ware), gold luster, 9" x 10" x 3", 2002.

Put Safety First

All work with enamels and lusters, including firing, should be done in a well-ventilated area. Do not let children work with these materials. Recommended safety gear includes protective gloves, aprons and glasses. See Page 234 for additional safety information.

DECALS: Pigments may contain heavy metals such as lead and cadmium. Ensure compliance with applicable FDA and state regulations when used on ware that will come into direct contact with food. Wash hands after application of decal. To comply with the Lip and Rim Standard, please test the finished product or have at least 20mm between the top of the rim and the decal. Keep out of reach of children unless properly supervised. This product (Cookson Mathey open stock decals) conforms to ASTM standard D-4236. *Warning note from Cookson Mathey.*

ENAMELS: Conforms to ASTM D-4236. Not for spray applications. Exposure may cause anemia, nervous system changes, kidney damage, or harm to developing fetus. Contains soluble lead silicate frit, cadmium, and pine oil. Skin irritant. Avoid prolonged contact with skin. If skin contact occurs, wash with soap and water for five minutes. Eye irritant. Keep away from eyes, if eye contact occurs, rinse immediately with water. Remove contact lenses, then flush with tap water for 15 minutes. If symptoms persist, see a physician. When using, do not eat, drink, or smoke. Wear apron and impermeable gloves. Wash hands immediately after use. Avoid using if pregnant or considering pregnancy. Keep out of reach of children. For further health information, call a poison control center. MSDS sheets are available from suppliers and manufacturers. *Warning note from AMACO (Versa Color).*

LUSTERS: Danger: Flammable. Harmful or fatal if swallowed. Vapor may be irritating to eyes, skin and mucous membranes. Contains lead, organic solvents, turpentine and other terpenes. If swallowed call physician. Keep container closed. Use with adequate ventilation. Keep away from heat, sparks and open flame. Keep out of the reach of children. *Warning note from Hanovia.*

Photo: John Brennan

Christopher Dworin, USA, "Luster Bowl," porcelain, gold luster over copper red glaze, 16" diameter.

Arabic, Islamic or Reduction Luster

Below are 10 recipes for Islamic luster pigment to go over low-fired prefired glazes, terra sigillatas or possibly even slips and clay bodies. The clay or ocher content of these pigments facilitates brushing and helps the luster develop under a protective coat. It will be washed off after firing to show the luster. Mix the ingredients with vinegar to a creamy brushable paste, brush the mixture on the glazed object, allow it to dry, fire to cone 018 (approximately 750°C) and reduce heavily for 15 to 30 minutes. For electric kilns, you can do a sugar reduction with sugar wrapped in small newspaper cones (small enough to get through the spy hole without burning yourself) or even restaurant style packages of sugar. Repeat when the smoking has stopped for 30 minutes. Cool and remove the ware from the kiln. When cold, wash the surface to remove the residue of the pigment. All being well, a thin film of metallic luster will have been deposited on the glazed or other ceramic surface, varying from gold to pink and ruby. The recipes below are intended for tests and are in grams. When you are satisfied with the results, you easily can increase the ratios of materials for larger batches. Gum may be added to help adhesion.

You can test these glazes on regular white glazed bathroom tiles or glazed earthenware pieces, or try

Islamic Luster Pigment Recipe

Material	1	2	3	4	5	6	7	8	9	10
Red art clay or red ochre	20	20	20	20	20	20	20	20	20	10
Silver nitrate	5	10	15	20	--	--	--	--	10	10
Copper carbonate	--	--	--	--	5	10	15	20	10	10

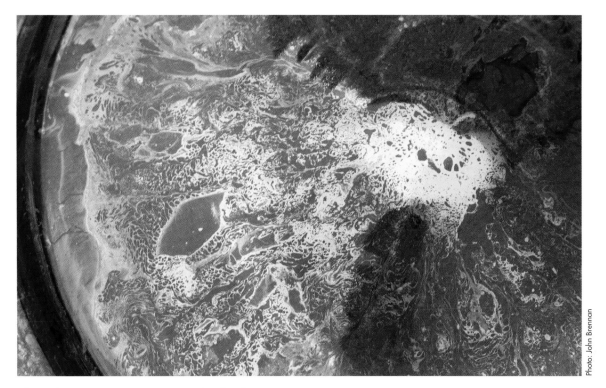

Christopher Dworin, USA, "Luster Bowl " detail.

them over fired terra sigillata or other surfaces. They may or may not work over high-fired bodies or glazes. Try it and see!

Resinate Lusters

Resinate lusteras are ceramic coatings that give an iridescent or lustrous surface over the glaze. They essentially are a mixture of resin or rosin, sometimes referred to as colophony, mixed with bismuth and essential oils, such as oil of lavender and/or oil of cloves, then heated to form tacky, varnish-like liquids.

Resinate Base Recipe

Resin	20
Bismuth nitrate	5
Lavender oil (hot)	30

Resinate lusters need constant stirring until they are thoroughly mixed. When warm, a resinate luster should be sieved through a silkscreen or fine tea strainer. When warm or cold, further thinning to an easily brushable consisetency of hte material can be done with methyl hydrate, turpentine or acetone. Methyl hydrate (wood alcohol), turpentine or acetone also can be used as solvents to clean up any mistakes before firing. These solvents also can be splashed or sprayed on the unfired luster to develop marbled or splotched effects.

To control color development, much testing should be done, varying the volume of colorant in relation to the resinate base and also in cross-blending colorants together. Metallic colorants are added to the mix in amounts up to 5 percent. The following will give colors:

- Titanium — blue
- Chromium — yellow-green
- Iron — brown
- Platinum — silver
- Copper — red
- Gold —pink

Once the mix is made, add colorants and apply it with a brush or sponge. When dry, fire to the appropriate temperature. Resinate lusters are fired in an electric kiln or oxidizing atmosphere. The burning resin and oils create a local reduction, causing colorants to change to their reduced state. The usual temperature range is from cone 018 to cone 016 (720°C to 750°C or 1,320°C to 1,350°F).

There is little literature about resinate lusters for studio potters. Try "Ceramic Colors and Pottery Decoration" by Kenneth Shaw, published in 1969 by Frederick A. Praeger of New York, and "Ceramic Glazes" by Cullen W. Parmelee for more information.

GOLD LEAFING METHODS

By Steve Irvine ©

Gold leafing, or mechanical surface gilding, is a technique of bonding thin sheets of pure or nearly pure gold to a surface. The leaf itself is an interesting material to work with and may redefine your concepts of the word "thin." Each sheet is only 0.0001 millimeter thick — or put another way, a stack of 10,000 sheets of gold leaf would have the thickness of a dime!

Gold leaf is sold by the book containing 25 leaves. The standard size for a gold leaf is 3-$\frac{3}{8}$" x 3-$\frac{3}{8}$". A book will cover about 1-$\frac{1}{2}$ square feet. There are two types of books sold: transfer and loose. Transfer books have the leaf attached to a piece of white tissue, making it easier to handle if it is windy or if precise overlapping of the leaves is needed. Loose books have each leaf separated from the others by a page of saffron-colored tissue paper. I prefer the loose books. The kind I use is 23 karat and is made by a company in Florence called Giusto Manetti, which has been in the gold leaf business since the early 1800s.

Mechanical surface gilding involves the use of a special adhesive called gold size. Gold size is a viscous liquid made of 50 percent nonvolatile ingredients like phenolic resin, ester gum, tung oil and linseed oil, plus 50 percent volatile ingredients like turpentine. There are two types of gold size: the standard type, which is ready for gilding after 10 to 12 hours, and the quick dry, which is ready for gilding after one to three hours, depending on temperature and humidity. I prefer the quick dry. An even coat of gold size is brushed onto the surface and allowed to begin drying.

The key to successful gold leafing is knowing exactly when the size has dried to the correct tack (degree of stickiness) and is ready for the leaf. To test tack readiness, touch the surface with your knuckle and listen for a slight "tick" sound as you pull it away from the surface. The size should be dry enough that it no longer is in a liquid state, but still sticky to the touch. The key to getting a rich gold surface is to apply the leaf when the size has just the right amount of tack. If it is applied too soon, the size will force its way into the leaf and give it a mushy look. If it is applied too late, the leaf will not adhere properly. With a bit of experience, you'll get a feel for the timing. It usually takes at least an hour for quick dry size to reach tack readiness. It will adhere best to glazes and surfaces that have a very slight texture or tooth, like a matte glaze. The surface must be free of dust and grease.

The application of the gold leaf should be done in a calm atmosphere (both the room and yourself!). The slightest draft in the room, even your own breath, will send the fragile leaf flying. Traditionally, the leaf is transferred out of the book and onto the surface with a gilding brush. This is a soft, broad brush made of camel's hair or sable. Stroke the brush through your hair a few times to give it a static charge, and then hold the brush over the gold leaf. The leaf will jump up to the brush because of the static charge, and it can then be lifted to the prepared surface and smoothed into place with the brush. A good quality artist brush can substitute for the more expensive gilding brushes. I prefer to lift and move the gold leaf with two pairs of tweezers and then use a brush to smooth it on the surface.

A day or two after the gold has been applied, the size will be thoroughly dry and the gold can be gently burnished with a cotton ball or piece of plush velvet. This will bring out the true luster and brilliance of the gold. Because the gold leaf is so thin, its color is affected to some extent by the color of the background surface. I usually apply at least two layers of gold to get a deep, rich color. The second layer is applied a day after the first.

Other metallic leafs are available, such as silver and variegated compositions. Silver leaf will tarnish, so aluminum leaf often is used when a silvery look is needed. Aluminum does not have the warm look of sterling, but it is inexpensive and won't tarnish.

Gold leaf supplies can be found in well-stocked art supply stores, but you are more likely to find them at sign painter supply businesses, because sign painters use gold leaf on a regular basis. Prices vary, but a book of loose gold leaf typically costs about $30. Gold leaf is very durable – its main commercial uses are for outdoor signs and truck lettering — but I would not recommend it for pottery that will be used in an oven or dishwasher, since these environments may affect the bond of the gold size. Gold leaf is especially effective on outer surfaces of jars, vases, teapots and such; it has a rich depth to its appearance that is different from gold luster, which is painted on and refired. Give it a try!

Steve Irvine is a ceramist with more than 30 years studio and teaching experience from Ontario, Canada. His diverse ceramic vessels are in major collections worldwide.

Sally Bowen Prange, USA, "Wrecked Vessel," wheel thrown with added slabs and incision, barnacle slip, matte glaze, shiny glaze, lusters, electric fired, 12-½" x 7" x 8", 1987. Collection of N.C. Pottery Museum.

Photo: Richard Faughn

Photo: Ken Mayer

Joanne M. Copp, Canada, "Clapotis," ducate gold leaf 23.6 karat, 27cm x 20cm wide.

Richard Hirsch, USA, "Altar Bowl No. 22," 19" x 21" x 11", 2002.

Photo: Geoff Tesch

Photo: Karen Benidict

Gary Merkel, Canada, "Frui 'tea-pot'," slipcast, coil, slab then assembled, underglaze background and brush work, rubber resist design, gold line, clear glaze, 18" x 16" x 6".

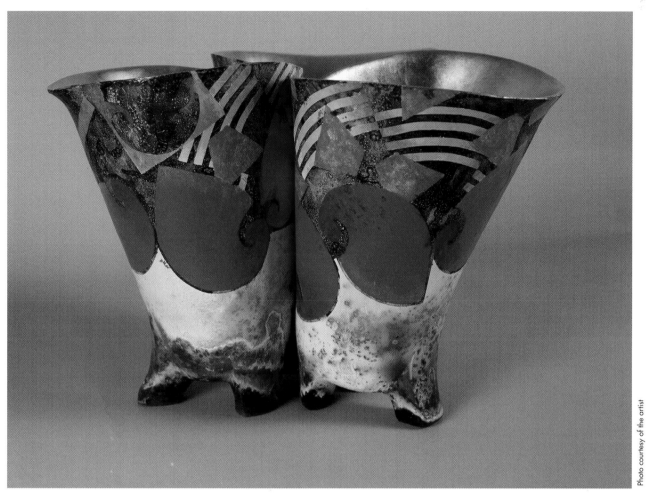

Bennett Bean, USA, "Dancing Lily," pit fired, gilded, painted earthenware, 16" x 11", 2003.

Karen Thuesen Massaro, USA, "Twin Roll," assembled porcelain slipcast elements, underglaze, glaze, china paint, surface graphics applied with brush, multifired, 5-½" x 16" x 21", 2002.

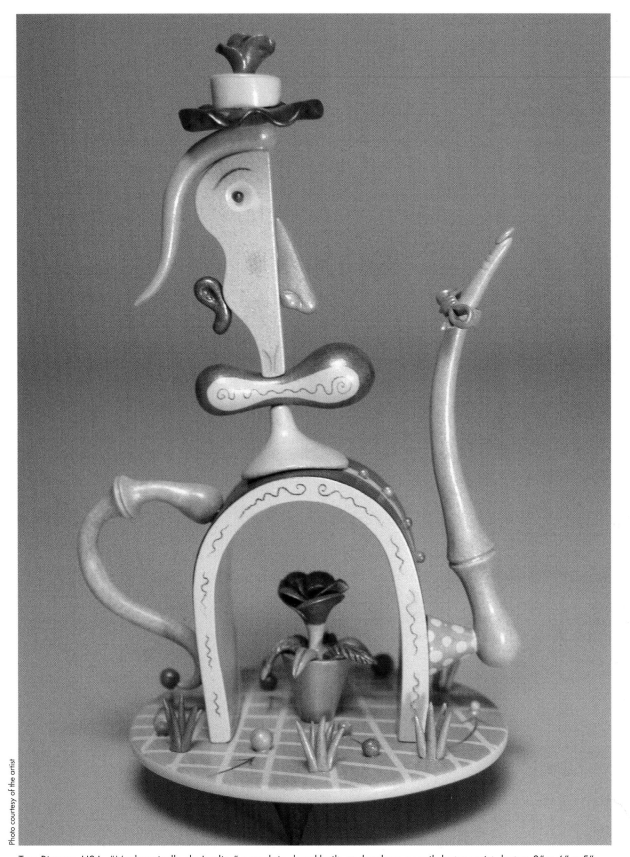

Tom Rippon, USA, "Mademoiselle du Jardin," porcelain, hand-built, underglaze pencil, luster resist, luster, 8" x 6" x 5".

George Bowes, USA, "Nurture," porcelain, underglazes, glazes, on-glazes, cone 5, 1-½" x 9", 1998.

Christine Federighi, USA, "River Wrap Down," ceramic, hand-built, black base, drybrush oil paint, 71" x 8" x 7", 2002.

Doug Jeck, USA, "Virtual Father," ceramic, mixed media, decoupage, 10-½" x 5-½", 1999. Courtesy Garth Clark Gallery.

273

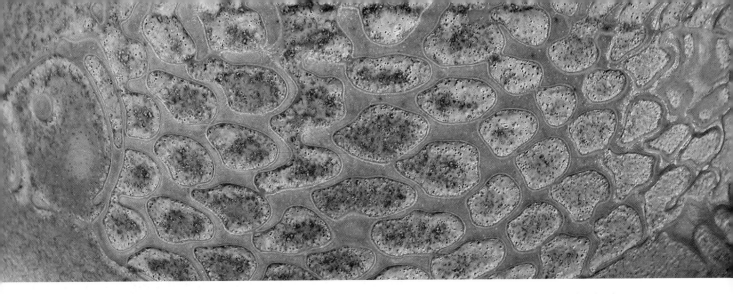

Robin Hopper, "Porcelain Deep Bowl," trailed slip, glazed, then rubbed down with Scotch pad, fired at Cone 10 reduction. Photo: Judi Dyelle.

CHAPTER 21

Marks of the Maker

The usual way artists develop their work is to find some form of inspiration, concept, vision or idea and proceed through several working stages to realize or resolve the idea in its final, concrete art form. Ideas might come in a sudden blinding flash or, more likely, develop over time from several different sources that might be totally unrelated or mutually interdependent. Sometimes they are slow in coming; occasionally they come in rapid succession. Sometimes they need to be jump-started through playing with the process itself. As you will have noticed in the previous chapters, when ideas are formulated, there is an incredibly wide range of possibilities available to their interpretation before arriving at a final ceramic artwork, possibly as many as all other visual arts combined. Although the form of an object is set after firing, the surface can be further developed and totally altered even hundreds of years after a piece is made. The potential of the ceramic medium is almost infinite.

Some artists are extremely analytical in how they work, building their ideas from great depths of soul-searching and rationalization, sometimes with intricate drawings, color notes, layering concepts and firing procedures. Others work in a more organic, intuitive way, reacting to the various stages of the process as they happen. It usually is easy to realize what type of ceramist you might be. Some are preoccupied with the tactile process of making; some are predominantly fire people; some are drawn to the chemistry and technology of the medium; and some are artistically sound, but they may be technically inept, not realizing that the technical aspects of the medium can easily be understood or kept to a minimum. A few get excited by the complex mass of possibilities and experiment freely across all variations of the medium, much like a well-trained musician who can play anything from jazz to classics and feel comfortable in more than one genre.

Some methods of turning a vision into a reality may be relatively simple to achieve, even in one firing. Various methods of wood firing are examples of this (see Chapter 19), where the placement of the object in the kiln and arrangement of pots, baffles and deflectors force the flame to take predescribed paths through the ware, painting the surfaces with fume and ash deposit. Here, the experience of the maker, in conjunction with object placement and the knowledge and control of the kiln, gives the kiln the primary say on the final result. Much is in the lap of the gods. Other more complex surfaces may require multiple enrichment methods and multiple firings as shown in Chapter 21. Since ceramics is a technical art form, ideas must: be interpreted in terms of the technical ability to make the form; deal with the surface development and the decorative processes to be used, and, if layered, in what order; and decide how it is to be fired and how many and what type of firings are necessary to achieve the initial vision. There is much to consider in the development of truly original work.

Over my own ceramic career of close to half a century, several themes have recurred and resolved themselves in different ways, using many variations of the ceramic medium to explore and interpret new ideas. These primarily have revolved around four themes: human cultures and their ceramic history; the landscape; geology; and the garden. This chapter analyzes a few ways the path from concept to reality has been followed. What did I want to say, and how did I want to say it? What did I need to know to make it happen? I trace the development of some of

my own works with the integration of form, development of imagery and processes of final surface enrichment. This is done with a series of photo montages leading from the inspiration source to the reality of completion and what happens in between. I have selected six objects that represent six different series of work from the last 30 years. I hope they help to portray the road followed from vision to object.

Although I have worked in most variations of this medium for nearly 50 years, my preference is to work in cone 10 porcelain. It can be fired in either reduction or oxidation to make the most of the color potential the firing method makes possible. All the work shown here

Landscape Series: Slab/Thrown Porcelain Bottle

The form of this bottle could have been inspired by the shape of a rubber hot water bottle. It wasn't, but it could have been. I wanted to develop a two-sided shape I could use like a "canvas" for painting a landscape with glazes and dry ceramic minerals. Once I determined the shape and image and decided to use making methods of part thrown and part slab, I did glaze and color testing to develop the range for the subject. I chose a similar base glaze plus several variations in colorants to lessen the likelihood of running glazes on a vertical form, when heat, time and gravity combine to make glazes flow downward. Since several glazes overlapped, I applied them thinly for the same reason. High alumina glazes containing about 50 percent feldspar, 25 percent

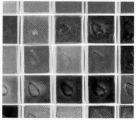

kaolin and 25 percent alkaline earth material, such as dolomite, calcium, talc, strontium or barium, usually are stable on a vertical surface. The application methods I used on the bisque-fired bottle were a combination of pouring, dipping, trailing, brushing and glaze intaglio,

where I would scrape away parts of one glaze and fill in with another. I dry-mixed granular rutile, ilmenite and powdered wood ash, then placed the mixture in a pepper shaker to shake over wet, freshly applied glaze. It was fired in a gas kiln in reduction at cone 10.

is in variations of porcelain, but if I worked with other clays at other temperatures, the process of "vision-to-object" would remain constant, regardless of changes in technology. I am the type of ceramist who likes to know what might be coming out of a kiln before it goes in. I am not against "happy accidents" and will gladly accept serendipitous occurrences.

With initial art training in painting and printmaking, where layering methods are the norm, I use layering processes in most of my work. I seldom use a simple process; more often it's multiples. The serendipity, when it happens, is usually from the way that layering transforms in the firing process, building unexpected colorations and subtleties.

The longer you watch the process and analyze results, the better informed you can be in how to plan and coax the maximum out of the medium and realize the initial vision. After a time, you'll become able to preplan accidents by being aware of what probably caused them to happen and capitalizing on that knowledge.

Footed Vase: Mocha Diffusions on Porcelain

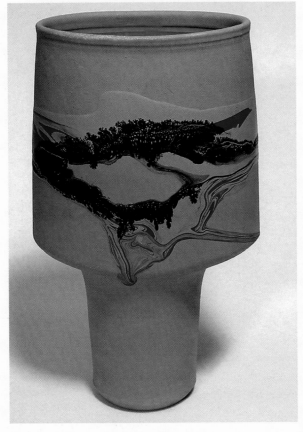

The shape of some Chinese bronze bells from the Shang Dynasty (1300 to 1030 B.C.) has intrigued me since I first saw them many years ago in a traveling exhibit of discovered buried treasures. The ceramic form I developed for my work is made from two wheel-thrown pieces. I threw one right way up and oval (the top part), and the other upside down (the bottom part).

I joined the parts at roughly the halfway point and finished with a carpenter's Surform plane and a copious amount of sponging to remove drag marks. When the form was leather-hard, I applied a coating of liquid colored slip, followed by a mocha tea (30 percent copper carbonate and 70 percent manganese dioxide colorant mixed with apple cider vinegar) dripped onto the wet slip. Clays and clay slips are predominantly alkaline, and the acidic mix of colorant and vinegar creates a reaction referred to as mocha diffusions. Historically, this decorative process was done on earthenware and covered with a transparent honey-colored glaze. When dry, I bisque fired

the piece, glazed the inside, then refired it in a gas kiln reduction at cone 10 to achieve a surface evocative of a piece of dendritic limestone rock, one of many geological patterns that has interested me because of its relationship to ceramic historical objects.

Faceted Three-Color Porcelain Agateware: Wide Feather Basket Bowl

These pieces also reflect a long-term interest in geology and the similarity of pattern found in some early Tang Dynasty Chinese (7th to 10th centuries A.D.) earthenware, where patterned clays are developed through layering, cutting, rolling and joining processes (see Chapter 11).

The concept of the Wide Feather Basket Bowl developed from a previous knowledge of working with all of the historical variables of colored clay use and of doing a considerable amount of agateware, usually faceted or fluted to reveal the interesting patterns hidden in the swirling and spiral clay strata.

A chance happening while on a country walk suggested the image. I was walking around a local lagoon, the wind was blowing ripples across the open water, and there were tree branch reflections in the ripples, giving an agitated appearance. I immediately wondered how I might achieve such an image in clay, and the nearest thing that I could think of was fluted agateware, but I didn't want the whole object to be agatized, just the wide, flat outer rim of the plate or bowl. So I decided to

make it in two parts.

The final form of the bowl is similar to the shapes of some decorated baskets and woven spruce root hats of the indigenous Haida nation of the Canadian Pacific Northwest. The patterns of the fluted agateware often suggest the patterns found on feathers, hence the name "Wide Feather Basket Bowl."

The central porcelain bowl has no color in the clay. I threw it relatively thickly and left it to stiffen to leather-hard. Then I

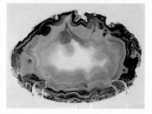

used colored clays to make a thrown cylindrical collar with no base that was the width of the bowl. This was inverted on the lower part, carefully joined, and, with the wheel going very slowly, pulled out almost horizontally. When it had stiffened, I trimmed

the piece on a chuck made to fit the inside of the bowl. After trimming, when the colored clay section also had stiffened, I fluted it with wire-ended tools.

When the piece was bone dry, I sanded off all the rough edges and bisque fired it. I glazed only in the center and fired in oxidation to cone 8. After firing, wet and dry silicon carbide paper was used to carefully sand the whole of the unglazed areas until they were as smooth as an eggshell.

Chado Series: Kama Form Lidded Jar

The form of this piece is taken from the traditional forms of bronze or cast iron Japanese kettles, or *kama*, used for boiling water in the Japanese tea ceremony Cha-No-Yu.

The raised decoration is trailed on using a slip made of the same clay as the form, liquefied with water and a small amount (about 1 percent) of sodium silicate.

After the bisque firing, I glazed the interior with a smooth, serviceable glaze. For the exterior glazed surface I wanted to achieve the look of ancient patinated bronze. I used the same basic clay, powdered and fluxed with barium and lithium carbonates, to develop a dryish, alkaline, matte glaze that would respond well to the colorants of copper and rutile, developing soft broken turquoise and sandy colors. I fired the piece in oxidation to cone 8.

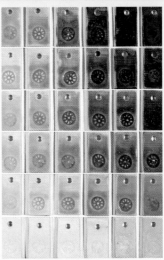

Southwest Series: Trifoot Plate

Many historical cultures and ethnic pottery use the triad of black, red and white pigmentation, which often is symbolic as well as purely decorative.

Prime examples of the use of these colors are found in much pottery made by many of the indigenous people of the American Southwest.

This large plate has a recess in the center and a wide, flat rim for painting in simple, sweeping, calligraphic brush movements. Its trimmed foot is wire cut to form a tripod.

When bone dry, I sprayed the plate with a light ball clay terra sigillata to which I had added 10 percent tin oxide to create a brighter white. I then polished the piece with soft cloth — part of an old sweatshirt — until smooth and glossy.

I painted on the calligraphic brushwork and let it dry, then high fired it to cone 10. When it came from the kiln, I trailed and brushed it with a lead-based chrome red glaze.

This glaze is not suitable for functional objects designed for storing acidic foods or liquids, but it is perfectly fine for a decorative piece. It is the only way this vibrancy of red can be achieved using ceramic materials.

I did the glaze firing to cone 06. During the firing, chromium also had a chemical reaction with the tin in the sigillata and developed a hazing and smoky halo around the areas where the scarlet glaze occurred. After firing, I sanded the piece with wet and dry silicon carbide paper to a smooth, satiny surface.

Clematis Series: Basket Form

This basket form was adapted from the shape of the ancient Chinese Shang Dynasty bronze cauldron — an interplay of an altered oval thrown form and repeating curved thrown handles.

I developed glazes to approximate the colors of Clematis Nellie Moser, a flowering vine in the garden.

After bisque firing, I glazed the piece all over with a high alumina, creamy white, satin-matte glaze, followed by large brush strokes in the same basic glaze with 3 percent copper carbonate added.

When applied thinly, the nature of copper in reduction is to fume and create a watercolor-like reaction with surrounding white glazes, usually giving a variety of grays, pinks, and mauves.

I mixed another glaze from the same base with a combination or 1 percent chromium dioxide and 1 percent cobalt carbonate added to give the pale teal-green.

I did the brushwork using a fine watercolor brush and black stain mixed with a little gum and water, then the glaze trailing with a glossy white glaze containing 10 percent tin.

In the reduction firing at cone 10, the trailed glaze pulled the copper from below and gave a further series of reds, grays and purplish hues. Since the black stain contained cobalt, when the glossy white glaze was trailed over in small dots, it turned to a soft, pale blue.

I don't try to paint realistic floral images, but I try to achieve the feeling or impression of the plant and the subtlety of its coloration.

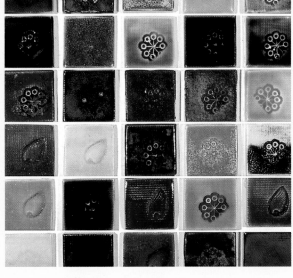

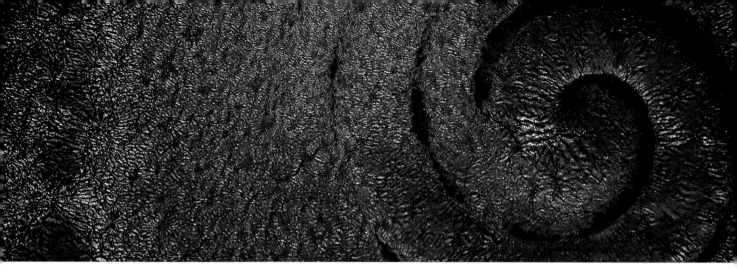

Judi Dyelle, Canada, detail of "Contemplation Bowl," Kamloops series 2003. Photo: Judi Dyelle.

CHAPTER 22

Marks of Excellence

The key to achieving excellence in any art, but particularly ceramics, lies in the strength of vision of the maker and the technical ability to carry it through from concept to reality. The final part of this book looks at a portfolio of work by different artists for whom the ceramic surface is both a challenge and an inspiration. The artists were chosen for their special abilities in different variations of process to try to convey some idea of the breadth of possibilities that the ceramic medium offers. It takes a great deal of tenacity to work through the many technical problems that are inherent in this medium. However, when you give enough attention and

understanding to these important aspects, the doors of limitless potential and variation open wide. Each variation of surface enrichment adds to the vocabulary of the artist and increases the ability to create poetry from mundane materials.

Because I am a maker of vessels rather than sculpture, the photo selections for this portfolio and throughout this book reflect my personal bias towards the vessel format.

Other than this introduction, there is no text. The works speak for themselves, requiring no explanation or justification.

Photo courtesy of the artist

Jimmy Clark, USA, "Two Sides," bowl broken in two pieces, sawdust fired with sulfates, reassembled, 10" x 12", 2001.

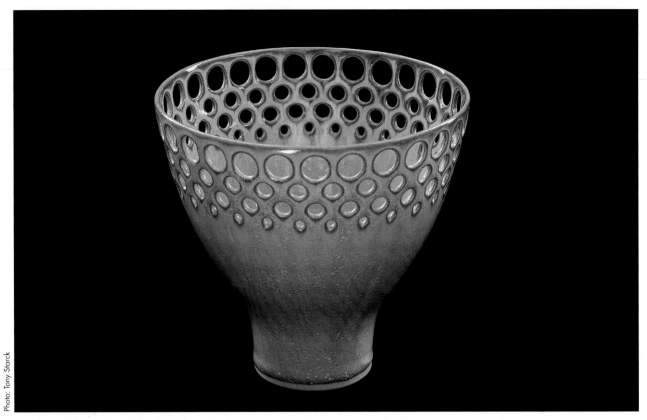

Photo: Tony Starck

Judi Dyelle, Canada, "Pierced Bowl," porcelain, microcrystalline glaze, gas fired cone 10.

Photo courtesy of the artist

Elaine Coleman, USA, "Carved Bowl," incised porcelain frog/leaf cut top bowl, blue celadon glaze, 7" x 11", 2003.

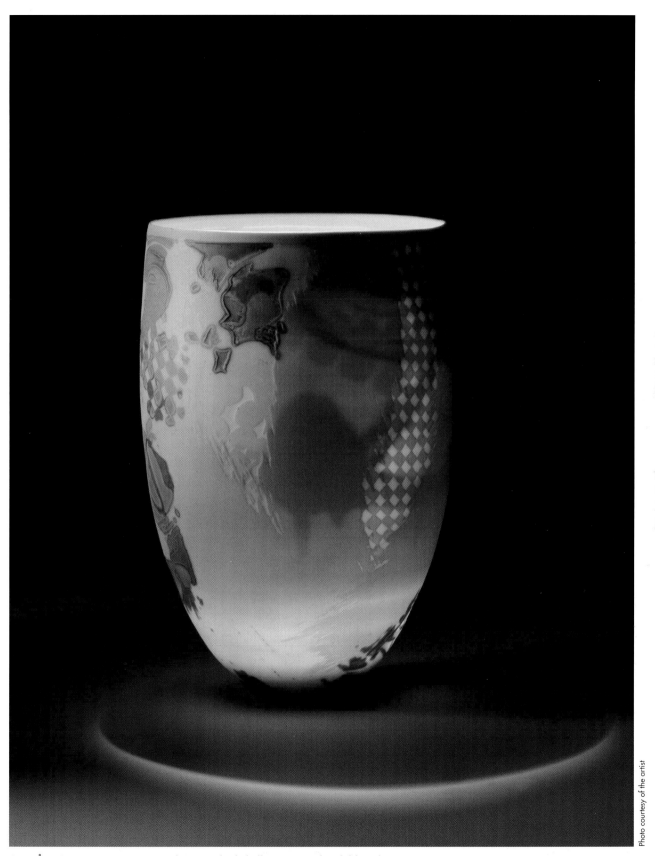

Arne Åse, Norway, "Vase," porcelain, washed shellac resist with soluble colorants.

Photo: Al Surratt

Steven Hill, USA, "Covered Jar," thrown and altered, ribbed slip application, sprayed multiple glazes, single-fired stoneware, 9'' x 8'' x 8'', 2003.

Curtis Benzle, USA, "Repast," vitreous porcelain, slab construction, imagery obtained using nerikomi technique or slip painting, sagger fired, 7'' x 7'' x 4'', 2003.

Malcolm Davis, USA, "Shino Tea Pot," stoneware with Shino glaze, fired in heavy reduction at cone 10.

Linda Arbuckle, USA, "Spring Forward," ewer, majolica on terra cotta.

Photo by the artist

Jeff Oestreich, USA, "Beaked Pitcher," thrown and cut, wax resist decoration, soda fired, 10'' x 10'' x 4'', 2002.

Photo: Michael Dismatsek

Carol Rossman, Canada, "Vessel — Illusion Series," underglazes with slight sheen painted on specific areas, then layers of matte glazes airbrushed onto entire piece, oxide mixes applied to specific areas, 8-¼'' x 8-½''.

Bennett Bean, USA, "Quartet On Base," pit fired, gilded, painted earthenware, 36'' x 21'' x 15-½'', 2002.

Karen Dahl, Canada, "Continuing Journey," white earthenware, slipcast, hand-built, airbrushed, multifired underglazes, glazes, and lusters, 8'' x 14'' x 10'', 2001.

Photo: Pierre Gauvin

Léopold Foulem, Canada, "Lustrous Black Flower Vase with Bouquet of Yellow Roses," thrown, low-fire glazes, decals, gold luster, 31cm x 23.5cm.

Photo: Bob Matheson

Photo courtesy of the artist

Walter Dexter, Canada, "Falling Light," stoneware, oxidation cone 6, multiple firings, lithium glazes at cone 05, 20'' x 12'' x 4''.

Tom Coleman, USA, "Lidded Jar," porcelain, oxide and brush decorated, 12'' x 13'', 2003.

Photo by the artist

Thomas Hoadley, USA, "Nerikomi Bowl," colored porcelain, unglazed, electric fired cone 6, gold leaf, 6-¼'' x 8-¼'' x 6-½'', 2003.

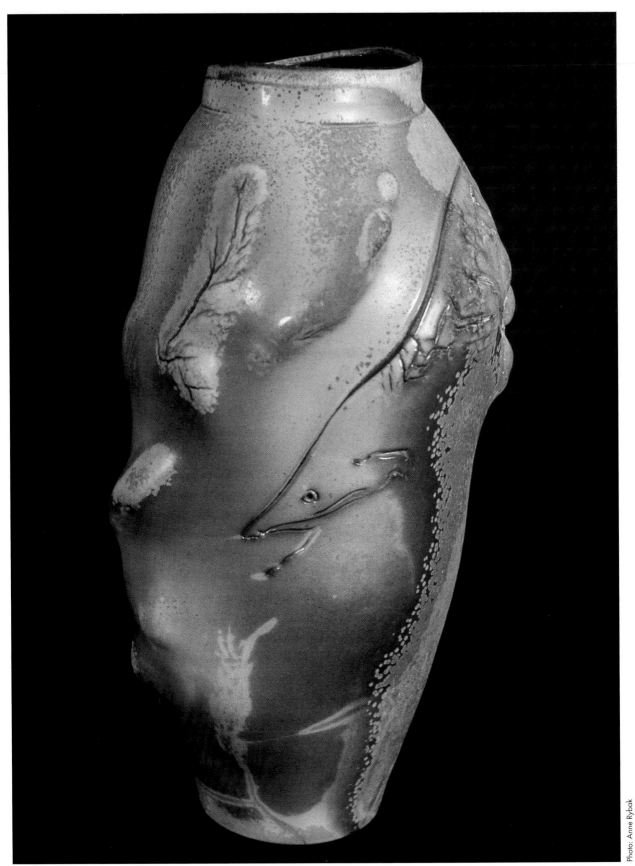

Frank Boyden, USA, "Smoky Fish Vase," wood-fired porcelain.

Photo: Anne Rybak

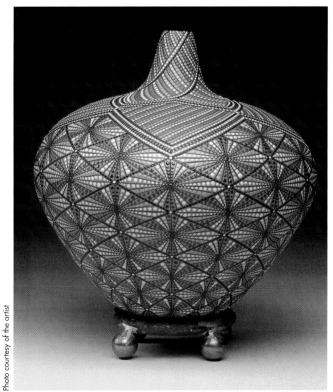

Ricky Maldonado, USA, "Turban Vessel," 13'' x 11''.

Karen Newgard, USA, "Teapot with Gold."

Lana Wilson, USA, "Buddha Vase," white stoneware, black slip painted on and sponged off, fired cone 6, Red Art formula put on and sponged off, refired to cone 06 or 04, 9'' x 8'' x 6'', 2003.

Ron Myers, USA, "Lidded Jar," red earthenware, white slip, colored engobes, transparent glaze, fired to cone 04, 16'' x 11'', 2000.

Sergi Isopov, "Freeze," 20'' x 18'' x 13'', 1999. Courtesy of the Ferrin Gallery, Lennox, Mass., USA.

Photo courtesy of the artist

Georgette Zirbes, USA, "Manoa III Conversations No. 12," 16'' x 14'' x 8-½'', 2002.

Photo: Brian Oglesbee

David Shaner, USA, "Cirque," stoneware, glazed, 5'' x 18-½'', 1993. David and Ann Shaner Collection, gift of David and Ann Shaner, Schein-Joseph International Museum of Ceramic Art, Alfred University, 1993.

Kasia Piech, Canada, "Tricycle," oxidation cone 04, mixed media, 36'' x 24'' x 36'', 2002.

Photo by the artist

Sam Chung, USA, "Tea Pot," slab construction, soda fired porcelain, sprayed glaze, cone 10, 7'' x 6'' x 4'', 2003.

Photo: Neil Patterson

Sandi Pierantozzi, USA, "Big Hips Vase," earthenware, slab built, 7'' x 8'' x 4'', 2003.

Bibliography

Chapter 1

Edwards, Betty, "Drawing on the Artist Within, A Guide to Innovation, Invention, Imagination and Creativity," Simon and Schuster, New York, 1986.

Edwards, Betty, "Drawing on the Right Side of the Brain, A Course in Enhancing Creativity and Artistic Confidence," Revised Edition, Jeremy P. Tarcher Inc., Los Angeles, 1989.

Franck, Frederick, "Art As a Way, A Return to the Spiritual Roots," Crossroad Publishing, New York, 1981.

Franck, Frederick, "The Awakened Eye, A Companion Volume to The Zen of Seeing, Seeing/Drawing as Meditation," Vintage Books, Division of Random House, New York, 1979.

Franck, Frederick, "The Zen of Seeing, Seeing/Drawing as Meditation," Vintage Books, Division of Random House, New York, 1973.

Nicolaides, Kimon, "The Natural Way to Draw, A Working Plan for Art Study," Houghton Mifflin Company, Boston, 1941.

Patterson, Robert, "Abstract Concepts of Drawing, A Guide to the Study and Appreciation of Drawing," Thomson Seyffer Graphics Ltd., Canada, 1981

Rawson, Philip, "The Art of Drawing, An Instructional Guide," Prentice-Hall, Inc., Englewood Cliffs, N.J., 1984

Chapter 2

Adachi, Fumie, "Japanese Design Motifs, 4,260 Illustrations of Japanese Crests," Compiled by the Matsuya Piece-Goods Store, Dover Publications Inc., New York, 1972.

Appleton, Leroy H., "American Indian Design and Decoration," Dover Publications Inc., New York, 1971.

Aria, Barbara, and Gon, Russell Eng, "The Spirit of the Chinese Character, Gifts from the Heart," Chronicle Books, San Francisco, 1992.

Bentley, W.A., and Humphreys, W.J., "Snow Crystals," Dover Publications Inc., New York, 1962.

Cooper, J.C., "An Illustrated Encyclopaedia of Traditional Symbols," Thames and Hudson Ltd., London, 1978.

Eberhard, Wolfram, "A Dictionary of Chinese Symbols, Hidden Symbols in Chinese Life and Thought," Routledge, New York and London, 1986.

Enciso, Jorge, "Design Motifs of Ancient Mexico," Dover Publications, New York, 1953.

Fazzioli, Edoardo, "Chinese Calligraphy, From Pictograph to Ideogram: The History of 214 Essential Chinese/Japanese Characters," Abbeville Press Publishers, New York, 1986.

Fundaburk, Emma Lila, and Foreman, Mary Douglass Fundaburk, "Sun Circles and Human Hands, The Southeastern Indians Art and Industries," The University of Alabama Press, Tuscaloosa, Ala., and London, 2001.

Garai, Jana, "The Book of Symbols," Lorrimer Publishing, London, 1973.

Gimbutas, Marija, "The Civilization of the Goddess, The World of Old Europe," Harper San Francisco, Division of Harper Collins Publishers, 1991.

Gimbutas, Marija, "The Goddesses and Gods of Old Europe, 6500-3500 B.C., Myths and Cult Images," University of California Press, Berkeley, Calif., and Los Angeles, 1982.

Gimbutas, Marija, "The Language of the Goddess," Harper and Row Publishers, San Francisco, 1989.

Hall, James, "Dictionary of Subjects and Symbols in Art," John Murray Publishers, Ltd., London, 1979.

Huxley, Francis, "The Way of the Sacred," Doubleday and Company, Inc., Garden City, N.Y., 1974.

Koch, Rudolf, "The Book of Signs," Dover Publications Inc., New York, 1930.

Lehner, Ernst, "Symbols Signs and Signets, A Pictorial Treasury With Over 1,350 Illustrations," Dover Publications Inc., New York, 1950.

Reader, John, "Man On Earth," Penguin Books, Ltd., England, 1988.

Schuster, Carl and Carpenter, Edmund, "Patterns That Connect, Social Symbolism in Ancient & Tribal Art," Harry N. Abrams, Inc., Publishers, New York, 1996.

Sill, Gertrude Grace, "A Handbook of Symbols in Christian Art," Collier Books, Macmillan Publishing Company, New York, 1975.

Stokes, William Michael and Stokes, William Lee, "Messages on Stone, Selections of Native Western Rock Art," Starstone Publishing Co., 1980.

Young, M. Jane, "Signs from the Ancestors, Zuni Cultural Symbolism and Perceptions of Rock Art," University of New Mexico Press, Albuquerque, N.M., 1988.

Chapter 3

Allen, Jeanne, "Designer's Guide to Japanese Patterns, Volume 2," Chronicle Books, San Francisco, 1988.

Allen, Jeanne, "Designer's Guide to Japanese Patterns, Volume 3," Chronicle Books, San Francisco, 1989.

Bager, Bertel, "Nature as Designer, A Botanical Art Study," Frederick Warne and Company, London, 1967.

Blossfeldt, Karl, "Art Forms in Nature," Universe Books, Inc., New York, 1967.

Critchlow, Keith, "Islamic Patterns, An Analytical and Cosmological Approach," Schocken Books, New York, 1976.

Dolmetsch, Heinrich, "The Treasury of Ornament Pattern in the Decorative Arts," Portland House, New York, 1989.

Dresser, Christopher, "The Language of Ornament Style in the Decorative Arts," Portland House, New York, 1988.

Feininger, Andreas, "Roots of Art, The Sketchbook of a Photographer," The Viking Press, New York, 1975.

Guyler, Vivian Varney, "Design in Nature," Art Resource Publication, Division of Davis Publications Inc., Worchester, Mass., 1970.

Halen, Widar, "Christopher Dresser, A Pioneer of Modern Design," Phaidon Press Ltd., London, 1993.

Hibi, Sadao, "Japanese Detail: Architecture," Chronicle Books, San Francisco, 1989.

Jones, Owen, "The Grammar of Chinese Ornament," Portland House, New York, 1987.

Jones, Owen, "The Grammar of Ornament," Portland House, New York, 1986.

Justema, William, "The Pleasures of Pattern," Reinhold Book Corp., New York, 1968.

Kranz, Stewart, and Fisher, Robert, "The Design Continuum, An Approach to Understanding Visual Forms," Reinhold Publishing Corp., New York, 1966.

Kunst und Naturform, "Form in Art and Nature, Art et Nature," Universe Books Inc., New York, 1967.

Miles, Walter, "Designs for Craftsmen," Doubleday and Co. Inc., Garden City, N.Y., 1962.

Storr-Britz, Hildegard, "Ornaments and Surfaces on Ceramics," Kunst +Handwerk/Verlagsanstalt Handwerk GmbH Dortmund, Germany, 1977.

Washburn, Dorothy K., and Crowe, Donald W., "Symmetries of Culture, Theory and Practice of Plane Pattern Analysis," University of Washington Press, Seattle and London, 1988.

Zelanski, Paul, and Fisher, Mary Pat, "The Art of Seeing," Prentice-Hall, Inc., Englewood Cliffs, N.J., 1988.

Chapter 4

Birren, Faber, "Color Perception in Art," Schiffer Publishing Ltd., West Chester, Pa., 1986.

Birren, Faber, "Principles of Color, A Review of Past Traditions and Modern Theories of Color Harmony," Van Nostrand Reinhold Company, New York, 1969.

Birren, Faber, "Principles of Color, A Review of Past Traditions and Modern Theories of Color Harmony," Schiffer Publishing Ltd., West Chester, Pa., 1987.

Birren, Faber, "The Symbolism of Color," Citadel Press, Secaucus, N.J., 1988.

"Color," Marshall Editions Limited, London, 1983.

Guptill, Arthur L., "Color Manual for Artists," Van Nostrand Reinhold Company, New York, 1962.

Itten, Johannes, "The Art of Color, The Subjective Experience and Objective Rationale of Color," Van Nostrand Reinhold Company, New York, 1973.

Itten, Johannes, "The Elements of Color, A Treatise on the Color System of Johannes Itten Based on his Book The Art of Color," Van Nostrand Reinhold, New York, 1970.

Kuehni, Rolf G., "Color: Essence and Logic," Van Nostrand Reinhold Co., New York, 1983.

Rawson, Philip, "Design," Prentice-Hall, Inc., Englewood Cliffs, N.J., 1987.

"The Human Body, The Eye: Window to the World," Torstar Books, New York, Toronto, 1984.

General Ceramics

Fournier, Robert, "Illustrated Dictionary of Pottery Decoration," Prentice-Hall Press, New York, 1986.

Hamer, Frank, "The Potter's Dictionary of Materials and Techniques," Pitman Publishing, London, Watson-Guptill Publications, New York, 1975.

Hopper, Robin, "The Ceramic Spectrum, A Simplified Approach to Glaze and Color Development," Second Edition, Krause Publications, Iola, Wis.

Nils, Lou, "The Art of Firing," Gentle Breeze Publishing, A+C Black, 1998.

Norton, F. H., "Ceramics for the Artist Potter," Addison-Wesley Publishing Company, Inc., Reading, Mass., 1956.

Olsen, Frederick, "The Kiln Book," Krause Publications, Iola, Wis., 2001.

Ostermann, Matthias, "The Ceramic Surface," A & C Black, London, University of Pennsylvania Press, Philadelphia, Pa., 2002.

Parmelee, Cullen W., "Ceramic Glazes," Second Edition Revised by E. D. Lynch and A. L. Friedberg, Industrial Publications, Inc., Chicago.

Peters, Lynn, "Surface Decoration for Low Fire Ceramics," Lark Books, Asheville, N.C., 1999.

Reents-Budet, Dorie, "Painting the Maya Universe: Royal Ceramics of the Classic Period," Duke University Press, London, 1994.

Rhodes, Daniel, "Clay and Glazes for the Potter," Revised and Expanded by Robin Hopper, Third Edition, Krause Publications, Iola, Wis., 2000.

Savage, George, and Newman, Harold, "An Illustrated Dictionary of Ceramics," Van Nostrand Reinhold Company, New York, 1976.

Scott, Paul, "Painted Clay, Graphic Arts and the Ceramic Surface," A & C Black, London, 2001.

Shaw, Kenneth, "Ceramic Colors and Pottery Decoration," Frederick A. Praeger, Publishers, New York, Washington, 1969.

Turner, Anderson, "Glazes: Materials, Recipes and Techniques, A Collection of Articles from Ceramics Monthly," Published by the American Ceramic Society, Westerville, Ohio, 2004.

Resources

Supplies, Tools, Equipment

Aardvark Clay and Supplies
1400 E. Pomona St.
Santa Ana, CA 92705
(714) 541-4157

Aftosa
1034 Ohio Ave.
Richmond, CA 94804
(510) 233-0334

Amaco/Brent/Genesis
4717 W. 16th St.
Indianapolis, IN 46222
(800) 374-1600
http://www.amaco.com

Artist Brushes – Keith Lebanzon
13195 SW Glenn Ct.
Beaverton, OR 97008
(503) 643-4548

Axner Co., Inc.
490 Kane Ct.
Oviedo, FL 32765
(800) 843-7057

AWT World Trade, Inc.
4321 N Knox Ave.
Chicago, IL 60641
http://www.awt-gpi.com

Bailey Pottery Equipment Corp.
P.O. Box 1577
Kingston, NY 12402
(845) 339-3721

Bison Studios
1409 South Commerce St.
Las Vegas, NV 89102
(702) 388-2085

Bluebird Manufacturing, Inc.
P.O. Box 2307
Fort Collins, CO 80522-2307
(970) 484-3243

Continental Clay Co.
1101 Stinson Blvd. NE
Minneapolis, MN 55413
http://www.continentalclay.com

Creative Industries
1946 John Towers Ave.
El Cajon, CA 92020
(619) 449-1834

Cress Manufacturing Co., Inc.
4736 Corvair Dr.
Carson City, NV 89706
(775) 884-2777

Dolan Tools
P.O. Box 15161
Scottsdale, AZ 85267-5161
(800) 624-3127

Euclid Kilns and Euclid Elements
1120 Speers Rd.
Oakville, Ontario, L6L 2X4 Canada
(905) 849-5540

Geil Kilns
7201 Clay Ave.
Gardena, CA 92648
(800) 887-4345

Great Lakes Clay and Supply Co.
120 S. Lincoln Ave.
Carpentersville, IL 60152
(847) 551-1070

Highwater Clays
P.O. Box 18284
Asheville, NC 28814
(828) 252-6033

Laguna Clay Co.
14400 Lomitas Ave.
City of Industry, CA 91746
(800) 452-4862 ext. 223

Mason Color Works, Inc.
P.O. Box 76
East Liverpool, OH 43920-5076
(330) 385-4488

Mayco Colors
1004 Delta Ave.
Tipton, IA 52772
(614) 876-1171

Michael Sherrill Mudtools
923 Edney Inn Rd.
Hendersonville, NC 28792
(828) 625-1852

Mile Hi Ceramics, Inc.
77 Lipan St.
Denver, CO 80223
(303) 825-4570

Miles Ceramic Color
2112 South Grand Ave.
Santa Ana, CA 92705
(714) 556-1329

National Artcraft Co.
7996 Darrow Rd.
Twinsburg, OH 44087
http://www.nationalartcraft.com

Olympic Enterprises, Inc.
P.O. Box 321
Campbell, OH 44405
http://www.olympicdecals.com

Olympic Kilns
P.O. Box 1347
Flowery Branch, GA 30542
(770) 967-4009

Peter Pugger Mfg.
12501 Orr Springs Rd.
Ukiah, CA 95482
(707) 463-1333

Royal and Langnickel Brush Co.
6707 Broadway Ave.
Merrillville, IN 46410
(219) 660-4170

Shimpo Ceramics
1701 Glenlake Ave.
Itasca, IL 60143
(630) 924-7138

Skutt Ceramic Products
6441 SE Johnson Creek Blvd.
Portland, OR 97206
(503) 774-6000

Soldner Clay Mixers Muddy Elbow Mfg.
310 W. 4th St.
Newton, KS 67114
(316) 283-9219

Spectrum Glazes, Inc.
No. 32-40 Hanlan Rd.
Woodbridge, Ontario, L4L 3P6 Canada
(905) 851-8310

Standard Ceramic Supply
P.O. Box 4435
Pittsburgh, PA 15205
(412) 276-6333

Standard Ceramic Supply Co.
9 Sansbury St.
Carnegie, PA 15106
http://www.standardceramic.com/clay

Stewart's of California, Inc.
16055 Heron Ave.
La Mirada, CA 90638

Thomas Stuart Wheels
1220 S. Jason St.
Denver, CO 80223
(303) 832-2128

Thompson Enamel
650 Colfax Ave.
Bellevue, KY 41073

U.S. Pigment Corp.
135 N. Manchester Ln.
Bloomingdale, IL 60108
(630) 893-9217

Ward Burner Systems
P.O. Box 1086
Dandridge, TN 37725
(865) 397-2914

Educational Videos

Tara Publications, Canada
Produced Robin Hopper's DVD series
    "Making Marks: Ceramic
        Surface Decoration"
e-mail: info@potteryvideos.com
http://www.potteryvideos.com

Books and Magazines

Ceramic Arts Library
79 E. 3rd St.
Corning, NY 14830-3101
(607) 962-6042

Ceramic Review Publishing
25 Foubert's Place
London, W1F 7QF
United Kingdom
44-207-439-3377

"Ceramics Monthly"
P.O. Box 6136
Westerville, OH 43086-6136
(614) 794-5893

"Ceramics: Art and Perception"
120 Glenmore Rd.
Paddington, NSW 2021
Australia
61-2-9361-5286

"Clay Times Magazine"
P.O. Box 365
15481 2nd St.
Waterford, VA 20197
(540) 882-3576

"Kerameiki Techni: International
Ceramic Art Review"
P.O. Box 76009
Athens, Nea Smyrni 17110
Greece
30-1-93-25-551

"Neue Keramik"
Unter den Eichen 90
Berlin 12205
Germany
49-6229-960566

"Pottery Making Illustrated"
P.O. Box 6136
735 Ceramic Place
Westerville, OH 43086-6136
(614) 794-5893

Organizations

American Ceramic Society
P.O. Box 6136
735 Ceramic Place
Westerville, OH 43086-6136
(614) 794-5893

*Late Classic 600 to 900 C.E. Maya. While musicians play in the background and a ruler oversees, a dwarf
tastes the latest alcoholic brew. The text calls the event a drunken party. Rollout Photo © Justin Kerr.*

Index